Praise for *Head Game: Mental Health in Sports Media*

"*Head Game* represents the first book of its kind to tackle one of today's most pressing public health crises, one that has been forced into the shadows for far too long, through the lens of sport. Billings and Parrott explore the key media moments in this movement, the storytellers who shaped them, the institutional response from leagues and teams, and the first-hand accounts of elite athletes who have struggled to bring mental health awareness to the forefront—all of which has come to shape how we talk about mental health today. This timely, well-researched and expansive volume offers a powerful compilation of perspectives from prominent athletes like Olympians Michael Phelps and Gracie Gold, to the NFL's Brandon Bostick, to the NHL's Corey Hirsch. In combating the silence, stigma, stereotypes and prejudice that have often plagued discussions of mental health, *Head Game* tracks the modern movement for mental health advocacy within the world of sport and beyond. I highly recommend this book to anyone teaching courses in communication, sport and society, as students will undoubtedly find the material engaging and relatable, as well as to any reader interested in mental health portrayals in the media. I suspect everyone who reads *Head Game* will find a story within it that they can connect to."

—Leigh Moscowitz, Professor in the School of Journalism and Mass Communications, University of South Carolina

"For too long the discourse of 'mental toughness' has dominated sports culture, from the way we coach and train athletes to how athletes are covered in the media. Through interviews with elite/professional athletes who have publicly disclosed mental health issues, the sports journalists who cover their stories, and sports organizations' own efforts to address mental health, *Head Game* dissects how dangerous this discourse has been, and creates much-needed awareness on an issue that has been stigmatized in our culture. *Head Game* humanizes athletes, reminding readers that gold medals, championships, million-dollar salaries, corporate endorsements, or super star celebrity do not immunize athletes against mental health struggles. Sadly, what is at stake is a matter of life or death. *Head Game* is required reading for all athletes, coaches, journalists, sports fans, or anyone who cares about the mental health and well-being of athletes."

—Cheryl Cooky, Professor of American Studies and Women's, Gender, and Sexuality Studies, Purdue University

Head Game

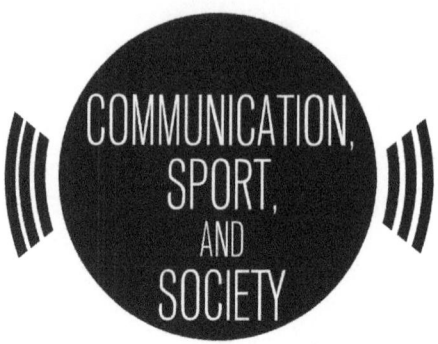

Lawrence A. Wenner, Andrew C. Billings, and Marie C. Hardin
General Editors

Vol. 9

The Communication, Sport, and Society series is part
of the Peter Lang Media and Communication list.
Every volume is peer reviewed and meets
the highest quality standards for content and production.

PETER LANG
New York • Berlin • Brussels • Lausanne • Oxford

Andrew C. Billings and Scott Parrott

Head Game

Mental Health in Sports Media

PETER LANG
New York • Berlin • Brussels • Lausanne • Oxford

Library of Congress Cataloging-in-Publication Control Number: 2022042004

Bibliographic information published by **Die Deutsche Nationalbibliothek**.
Die Deutsche Nationalbibliothek lists this publication in the "Deutsche Nationalbibliografie"; detailed bibliographic data are available on the Internet at http://dnb.d-nb.de/.

ISSN 2576-7232 (print)
ISSN 2640-8554 (online)
ISBN 978-1-4331-9109-1 (paperback)
ISBN 978-1-4331-9110-7 (ebook pdf)
ISBN 978-1-4331-9111-4 (epub)
DOI 10.3726/b18706

© 2023 Peter Lang Publishing, Inc., New York
80 Broad Street, 5th floor, New York, NY 10004
www.peterlang.com

All rights reserved.
Reprint or reproduction, even partially, in all forms such as microfilm, xerography, microfiche, microcard, and offset strictly prohibited.

Contents

Acknowledgments   vii

Head Game: An Introduction   1

1   Key Media Moment #1:
Michael Phelps   11

2   Key Media Moment #2:
Kevin Love   23

3   Key Media Moment #3:
Naomi Osaka   35

4   Key Media Moment #4:
Simone Biles   47

5   The Storytellers:
Marking a Moment   61

6	Organizational Synergy: Teamwork in Making Mental Health Work	79
7	Case Study: Michael Phelps, Olympic Swimmer	91
8	Case Study: Kearnan Myall, Premiership Rugby Union	103
9	Case Study: Brandon Bostick, National Football League	119
10	Case Study: Gracie Gold, Olympic Figure Skater	131
11	Case Study: Trey Moses, College and Professional Basketball	141
12	Case Study: Amanda Beard, Olympic Swimmer	151
13	Case Study: Corey Hirsch, NHL Goaltender	161
14	Case Study: Katie Uhlaender, Olympic Skeleton	173
15	Disclosing Mental Illness: Strategies & Considerations	181
	Notes on Authors	195
	Index	197

Acknowledgments

It's an age-old question in the academic world: should something be written solo, or in conjunction with another author? For us, the answer appeared quite simply: neither of us could have accomplished it alone. One of us had focused heavily on sports media; the other on health stigma in media. What happens when those cultures and issues collide? By working together, we hope we have revealed some answers.

We initially conceived of this project in 2019. It was pre-pandemic. Pre-Naomi Osaka. Pre-Simone Biles. Even then, our sense was that sports media was experiencing a mental health moment. We were right: the time for such a book was, indeed, prescient. We were also wrong: these subjects were being discussed in far more than a moment. When do enough moments accumulate to the point that the culture is irrevocably altered? We are not sure, but we are hoping that mental health in sports media has now reached such a "critical mass" level of distinction. There's no going back. Nor should athletes, teams, leagues, and larger sports entities wish to do so.

We must thank Niall Kennedy and his colleagues at Peter Lang Publishing for shepherding this book project. We also wish to thank Lawrence Wenner and Marie Hardin for their guidance and ultimate placement of this volume within the Communication, Sport, and Society series. We're honored to be a part of it. We are also grateful for the athletes, journalists, broadcasters, and industry leaders that were part of this interview-heavy process. You gave us the words; we just had to translate them. Finally, we thank our families, including a pair of extremely understanding wives who understood when the evening must be interrupted so we could conduct yet another Zoom interview.

We've been a part of many projects that we feel is important. This one joins the apex of those simply because of the magnitude of the need for mental health understanding in the United States and, indeed, the world. This is a conversation that needs to continue. It's been our privilege to advance it.

–Andrew C. Billings and Scott Parrott, May 2022

Head Game: An Introduction

"A single spark can start an inferno. Or it can flare harmlessly, like a firefly. The difference is oxygen, kindling, and luck."

–Hawley, 2022, p. 16

"Get your head in the game"

–*Hoosiers* (1986)

The head game.

In sport, the phrase summons images of extraordinary focus and mental jousting among competitors: a pitcher stepping off the mound and calling for the sign to disrupt a batter; a shooting guard leaving an arched palm hanging to remind her defender she just got schooled; a placekicker tuning out 100,000 screaming fans as the clock reads 0:01, then nodding for the snap.

Despite all the talk about physicality in sport, the weight rooms and work outs, Tommy Johns and twisted ankles, the world of athletic competition is one whose outcome is often decided by the mind. Athletes must be able to block out distraction, focus on the goal at hand, and out strategize the competition. In 1989, during his final Super Bowl-winning drive, San Francisco 49ers quarterback Joe Montana famously used valuable seconds in the huddle to gesture to the stands and calmly ask his teammates: "Look, isn't that John Candy?" THAT was the legend of a player known as "Joe Cool."

A few months later, professional golfer Scott Hoch was faced with a tap-in putt—less than two feet to win the U.S. Open—and missed. His nickname? Scott Choke.

The head game is key.

Still, that's not the reason we chose the title for this book. There is another head game taking place with much less fanfare within the sporting landscape, one whose outcome could mean winning or losing, success or failure, and sometimes, even, life or death. We are not exaggerating. Throughout the narratives in the fifteen chapters that follow, this book shares the stories of professional athletes who experienced mental illness while in the glare of the public spotlight. We named the book *Head Game* because these athletes—and others—navigated both positive and negative consequences when deciding whether to disclose their illness to teammates, coaches, family, friends, and ultimately the public via mass media. Using the term *game* does not trivialize the experiences of athletes and others who experience mental illness. Quite the contrary. Games describe periods, episodes, and times in which forces compete against one another toward an undetermined outcome. Such is the experience of mental health in sport, a conglomeration of ups and downs, along with struggles, successes, and questions concerning whom to trust and when, with the undetermined outcome being one's overall mental health.

Millions of Americans will experience mental illness at some point during their lives, yet societal stigma leads people to avoid pursuing help, telling loved ones, or openly discussing the subject of mental health. It is fair to argue that we are witnessing a sea change, though, led in part by professional athletes who are sharing their own experiences with depression, anxiety, and other conditions, and bucking stereotypes in which people with mental illness are condemned to unfulfilling lives. From quarterbacks to pitchers, power forwards to Olympic swimmers, athletes are increasingly using the mass media—including social media—to share their experiences with mental illness. Each athlete can now be a media producer. They have been given the megaphone and the ability to advance their narrative in a far less filtered manner than ever before.

So they have.

While their true expertise lay on the courts and the fields and the pitches, athletes are powerful persuaders of public opinion. Professional athletes' disclosures might be inspirational for fans (and even non-fans), nurturing heightened awareness of resources, treatment, and the commonality of mental illness. The importance of such dialogue cannot be understated, especially given the context of professional sport in which athletes are trained to be "tough" from a young age. In this book, professional athletes describe their own experiences with mental illness, including the challenges and opportunities they encountered in the locker room, field of play, and mass media. The athletes, who represent a spectrum of professional sports, describe their decisions to disclose and their recommendations for current—and future—generations of athletes.

Sport represents a cauldron for mental and emotional stress. Professional athletes work before thousands—at times millions—of people, their highs and lows exposed for the world to see and watch on replay time and again. They work lifetimes to reach "The Show," only to balance a fine line between success and failure. They shoulder the pressure of family, friends, alma maters, and hometowns in the quest to make it. They operate within a context in which Green Bay Packer quarterback Brett Favre was expected to play in a game one day after his father's death. They function in an ecosphere where a player like Boston Celtic Al Horford can be criticized in the media for wanting to be present for the birth of his child, as he was in 2016. *He should have induced the labor and chartered a private jet,* the critics said, *we pay him millions to make these kinds of sacrifices.*

And so they become legends via their steadfast dedication. They can become inspirations, larger-than-life personas perceived by jersey-clad 12-year-olds as superhuman, infallible, and indestructible. Their personal lives come under the media microscope with or without permission. They spend months away from family, living in hotel rooms and buses and clubhouses, trying to sidestep injury, fighting for playing time, and living in a culture that stigmatizes depression, anxiety, and other illnesses. Seeking mental help requires a consideration of dueling consequences: On one side, treatment could translate into health and well-being; on the other, disclosing mental illness could mean reduced playing time and being chastised by teammates, coaches, reporters and fans. American society stigmatizes mental illness. So, too, does sport. Think a fan won't bring up a personal struggle from a decade ago? Think again.

Consider Zack Greinke. In 2006, the major league pitcher took a break from spring training for the Kansas City Royals, generating attention from reporters. Ultimately it came to light that Greinke experienced depression and anxiety, illnesses that were threatening his love for the game. Greinke told reporters that the conditions never bothered him *on* the mound, adding that medication helped. Still, pundits and fans have dissected Greinke's mental health throughout his career with the Royals, Dodgers, and Astros. Others even went so far as to use the conditions as verbal weapons. The president of the San Diego Padres called Greinke "Rain Man," referencing a movie whose title character has autism. Yankees fans taunted Greinke as he warmed up in the 2019 American League playoffs, making fun of him for experiencing social anxiety.[1] Fans saw a chink in his armor and attacked. All is fair in love and war—and playoffs are war.

Or, consider the case of Kevin Love, All-Star power forward for the Cleveland Cavaliers. Love left the court before the final buzzer twice during the 2017 season, experiencing panic attacks so strong he thought he "might die." Beyond anxiety, Love also faced ridicule from high-profile teammates who described him as malingering. In March 2018, Love published an essay with *The Players' Tribune* in which he publicly shared his experiences with depression and anxiety. "Mental health is an invisible thing, but it touches all of us at some point or another," he wrote. "It's part of life." When he committed an on-court blunder in 2021, lackadaisically in-bounding the ball to have it easily stolen, media narratives were infused with Love's admission about mental health. *Be careful here*, even his advocates would note, seemingly treating him as though he might fall apart.

As stories in this book illustrate, an athlete's decision to disclose their experience with mental illness is sometimes forced by the mass media. Tennis phenom Naomi Osaka, a four-time Grand Slam winner, announced before the 2021 French Open that she would not participate in interviews with international media during the event. Citing mental health issues while writing on Instagram, she wrote that "I've often felt that people have no regard for athletes (sic) mental health and this rings very true whenever I see a press conference or partake in one." Athletes, she said, are often asked the same questions again and again, introducing (or reinforcing) doubt within the competitor, and the "whole situation is kicking a person while they're down."

While some professional athletes praised the 23-year-old, others criticized her decision, saying media interviews were part of a professional athlete's commitment. Fearing a mass exodus of players who felt similarly, French Open officials and organizers of the Grand Slam fined Osaka and threatened her with sanctions should she refuse to talk to the media. The Twitter account for Roland-Garros, where the tournament was being held, posted a photograph of other athletes

---

1 It's worth noting that Greinke will likely be enshrined in Cooperstown, professional baseball's Hall of Fame, after a career in which he won the American League Cy Young and played in numerous All Star games. Meanwhile, the Padres president resigned three months after insulting Greinke and leading the club on a double-digit losing streak. Back in the Bronx, police led the Yankees fan out of the game for which ticket costs broke MLB records. Greinke and the Astros won that game, ultimately advancing to the World Series.

completing press interviews with the statement, "They understood the assignment." The next day, Osaka withdrew from the event.

Indeed, mental health is a part of life touching everyone to varying degrees at varying times. Men and women who are paid millions of dollars and adored for playing the games they generally love are not immune. As the list of professional athletes who are openly discussing mental health grows, this is a concept we believe is increasingly becoming apparent for the general public.

The examples of Greinke, Love, and Osaka illustrate the myriad ways that professional athletes might disclose mental illness through the mass media. Greinke answered questions from inquiring journalists, Love wrote a first-person essay; Osaka explained her experience through social media. Other athletes offer a single disclosure with little clarification or desire to revisit it. Basketball star DeMar DeRozan tweeted a single lyric about depression from a rap song. UFC champion Ronda Rousey discussed suicidal thoughts on *Ellen*. Serena Williams posted an extended explanation of her postpartum depression on Instagram. Others are stories we never hear until after their passing: Eric Show, Tommy Hanson, Junior Seau. The list is long. Olympedia offers a list of Olympians who have died by suicide. A total of 170 names are posted. We also know the list is incomplete.

While the methods of coming out can be diverse, common themes also emerge as athletes describe their experiences with mental illness, questions concerning strength, stigmatizing attitudes within sport, and initial suspicions of psychologists, medication, and therapy. The athletes who do openly talk about their mental health are demonstrating strength by taking a risk. The implications, we are finding, can be incredibly important for society and other athletes. The more risks taken, the less risky it is perceived by others. Previous athlete disclosures function as a common thread in the case studies in this book. One athlete saw another athlete speak up and emerge seemingly better for doing so. Therefore, another athlete grabbed the baton. Academics now are left to synthesize and ascribe meaning to it.

The Sociology of Mental Health in Sport

A multitude of disciplines—with sociology arguably leading the way—have explored the relationship between mental health and overall performance. Varying degrees of findings have been revealed, yet with one consistent throughline: mental health matters...substantially. Sport can help—or harm—one's mental acuity depending on the role it plays in your life. Jewett et al. (2014) surveyed 853 adolescents, finding that involvement in a school-sponsored sport lowered depression and perceived stress, with those athletes self-reporting higher levels of mental health standards.

However, elite sport appears to introduce additional variables that can hinder wellness overall. Sociological insights reveal a culture of "appearing strong" at all costs, infused with hegemonic masculinity and external pressures that facilitate a stigmatizing environment. Atkinson (2019) advances ties between athletics and disordered eating, suicidal ideation, depression, and a plethora of other disorders. Souter et al. (2018) focused on male athletes, finding that they were "vulnerable to profession-specific stressors" (p. 8). To encapsulate the mindset often found in elite sports, athletes often concede that "you have to be mental" (Coyle et al., 2016, p. 10) to succeed.

Exacerbating such problems are a lack of psychiatric and psychotherapeutic care within sports organizations (Pichler & Claussen, 2020). Left to their own devices, athletes are fed—and then ultimately feel pressure to maintain—a mindset of invulnerability. As Larson et al. (2021) contend, "the relative failure to address mental health in sport over the years has been in part due to prevailing stigma and false conceptions that athletes have an indestructible psyche" (p. 2). Instead, athletes are informed that to excel, they must compartmentalize, failing to acknowledge the degree to which elements of their sporting and non-sporting public and private lives intertwine (Roderick et al., 2017).

Consequently, athletes receive messages that sport should be embraced as a mechanism for navigating mental health concerns rather than acknowledging that, particularly at sports' highest levels, injuries, and threats to one's overall career viability may amplify rather than mitigate these concerns (see Rice et al., 2016). The challenge then tacitly becomes to debunk stereotypes impeding an athlete's mental health by defining the mental aspect of the athletic experience by grappling "with the oft contested assertion that sport can be an effective elixir to manage mental illness" (Atkinson, 2019, p. 6).

Overall, it seems athletes face comparable mental illness rates as the general population. However, they face unique challenges and stigmatizing environments, including a pressure to perform in a short period of time, monetary strains, consequences of physical injury, and abusive related stakeholders (e.g., fans, coaches, teammates). Thus, examining elite athletes within the heightened media spotlight appears highly warranted. We adopt a strategy akin to Gibson and Gorczynski's (2019) work that connects media to mental illness via the philosophy of the spectacle while also concurring with the argument that "winning 'at any cost' is incompatible with a modern sport system that values the human behind the performer" (Larsen et al., 2021, p. 2).

Head Game: An Overview

While Charles Barkley might claim to be nobody's role model, people look up to athletes and listen to what they say. Athletes' conversations about mental health can help educate the public, improve attitudes toward people with mental illness, and inspire people who need help to seek it. Still, sport can be slow to change, so the de-stigmatization of mental illness will take time. We hope the information presented here can be a step toward the goal. We want the work to help athletes understand the commonality of mental illness, the potential benefits of treatment, and the consequences (both positive and negative) of coming out to family, friends, teammates, and coaches. Meanwhile, we hope the stories contained in these pages will help the public appreciate that mental illness affects everyone.

As we started to request interviews for this book, we learned there were generally two types of responses: fairly enthusiastic "yes's" and private and somewhat perfunctory "no's." Neither type of response should be judged negatively. Some athletes have started foundations and have become accustomed to the media spotlight—even finding advantages by embracing it. Others are still in the early stages of discovering their own mental health realities or have already navigated difficult terrain and do not wish to revisit what is often the darkest moments of their lives. Each response to our query, whether affirmative or negative, informed us of the sensitivity in which these topics must be covered. We hope we have done so with the proper tact and tone.

We discussed this project with a group of college students who generally were thrilled to see a book being advanced on these topics. It was so needed, they stressed, but also they asked: "do you think you should offer a trigger warning?" Yes, given the topics that are covered in this book, ranging from suicidal ideation to body dysmorphia to substance abuse, that seems appropriate. Consider yourself warned. There are some dark passages here.

There's a logic to what unfolds in this book. We open with four key "media moments" in Chapters 1–4 that seem to define the discussion we are currently having with mental health in sports. The first focuses on Michael Phelps, arguably at the pinnacle of all athletic achievement at the time that he entered a rehabilitation facility and then voluntarily opted to speak with the media about the elements that led to that moment. We follow with the more curated example of

Kevin Love, who revealed elements of a 2017 panic attack in a first-person narrative via *The Players' Tribune*, leading with the moniker that "everyone's going through something." In doing so, Love expanded the conversation to infer: we know others are out there, if only they'll speak about it.

The two other "media moments" we chronicle in detail come from women in light of the unparalleled circumstances the world found itself in during the year 2021. First, Naomi Osaka's media moment was predicated upon the media itself: opting not to participate in press conferences during the French Open led to controversy over the decision, which led to her withdrawal. "I've often felt that people have no regard for athletes' mental health and this rings true whenever I see a press conference or partake in one," Osaka offered via Instagram, equating it to "kicking a person while they're down." The fact that the resistance to Osaka's stance was strong—even with her agreeing to the fines that would be incurred—denotes the entrenched sports media machine that athletes seeking to invoke wellness much challenge when discussing mental health. Several months later, a different case emerged via Simone Biles, whom many preordained at the ascending unequivocal "world's best" until the realities of the disorienting disorder colloquially referred to as the "twisties" emerged in the opening days of the Tokyo Summer Olympics. The adoring public was seemingly offering the imperative: "Dance for me, Simone," to which she tacitly replied "I would, but I can't." "But we only ask for this every four years," came the response from the uninformed masses. Seriously, Simone Biles could not provide the fans with what they wanted—nay, demanded—in return for the adoration they had offered her in prior years.

Next, we look inside the sports media industry more directly: both inside it as well as its ancillary components. First, in Chapter 5 we interview four sports media journalists/personalities who have had roles in telling the stories of mental health within the sports world. Through the voices of former *New York Times* journalist Karen Crouse, legendary television broadcaster Bob Costas, *Time* magazine Senior Sports Correspondent Sean Gregory, and *USA Today*/CNN/ABC News/NPR reporter Christine Brennan, the chapter explores how athlete stories have changed, as well as explicating the role the media plays in responsibly rendering these stories.

Then, we adopt an institutional perspective to addressing the media in Chapter 6, synthesizing how sports media, leagues, and teams have approached the media moment related to talking about and advancing mental health initiatives. To do so, we utilized exemplars, with ESPN serving as the example from media, the National Basketball Association (NBA) serving as the example for league responses, and the National Football League's Indianapolis Colts as the example for team responses. A common vein of narrative is revealed within these organizational responses, as each seek to find the optimal manner in which mental health can be responsibly covered and usefully advanced in the world of sports.

Next is the core of the book, as Chapters 7–14 provide first-person voice to the athletes that have opted to speak in the media about issues related to mental health. The athletes we interviewed who are receiving full case study focus include:

- o Olympic swimmer Michael Phelps
- o Rugby Union footballer Kearnan Myall
- o NFL tight end Brandon Bostick
- o Olympic figure skater Gracie Gold
- o NCAA and now professional basketball player Trey Moses
- o Olympic swimmer Amanda Beard
- o NHL goaltender Corey Hirsch
- o Olympic skeleton athlete Katie Uhlaender

There are tons of ways these stories could be divided. Some are likely athletes you know; some are likely unfamiliar. Some are Olympians whose spotlight comes every four years; some enjoy a lesser but continual media gaze. Some are elite and never felt a mental health disclosure threatened their place in the sports world; others felt considerable pressure not to make any waves that could prematurely end their career. Permutations abound, including elements of biological sex and race as well. However, one common thread can be extracted: each opted to share their mental health status not only with their family and friends but also with the media writ large.

Other athletes have opted to tell their mental health stories in singular form, sometimes in something as simple as an isolated tweet. Those stories still should be embraced, as it is not every athlete's responsibility to "own" this issue by making it a continual thread in which their narrative unfolds. Nevertheless, the case studies from the interviews in this book are also particularly insightful from the perspective of telling one's tales, gauging the response, and ultimately coming back to embrace the issue in even more replete dimensions.

Finally, we conclude in Chapter 15 with recommendations for athletes who are affected by mental illness. We outline strategies for maintaining mental health while competing. We relay recommendations from professional athletes concerning disclosure. Through the stories shared here, we hope to communicate helpful information athletes might not have encountered in little league or youth ball or camp, the challenges of a largely hidden part of sport: the head game.

References

Atkinson, M. (Ed.). (2019). *Sport, mental illness, and sociology*. Emerald Press.

Coyle, M., Gorczynski, P., & Gibson, K. (2016). 'You have to be mental to jump off a board any way': Elite divers' conceptualizations and perceptions of mental health. *Psychology of Sport & Exercise, 29*, 10–18.

Gibson, K., & Gorczynski, P. (2019). Mass mediation of mental illness in sport. In M. Atkinson (Ed.), *Sport, mental illness, and sociology* (pp. 143–160). Emerald Press.

Hawley, N. (2022). *Anthem*. Grand Central Publishing.

Jewett, R., Sabiston, C. M., Brunet, J., O'Loughlin, E. K., Scarapicchia, T., & O'Loughlin, J. (2014). School sport participation during adolescence and mental health in early adulthood. *Journal of Adolescent Health, 55*(5), 640–644.

Larsen, C. H., Moesch, K., Durand-Bush, N., & Henriksen, K. (Eds.). (2021). *Mental health in elite sport: Applied perspectives from across the globe*. Routledge.

Pichler, E.-M., & Claussen, M. C. (2020). The relationship between professional sports and suicidal behaviour. *Sports & Exercise Medicine*. https://doi.org/10.34045/SEMS/2020/35

Rice, S. M., Purcell, R., De Silva, S., Mawren, D., McGorry, P. D., & Parker, A. G. (2016). The mental health of elite athletes: A narrative systematic review. *Sports Med, 46*, 1333–1353.

Roderick, M., Smith, A., & Potrac, P. (2017). The sociology of sports work, emotions, and mental health: Scoping the field and future directions. *Sociology of Sport Journal, 34*, 99–107.

Souter, G., Lewis, R., & Serrant, L. (2018). Men, mental health, and elite sport: A narrative review. *Sports Medicine, 57*(4), 1–8.

1

Key Media Moment #1: Michael Phelps

"I learned how to communicate when I'm 30. But I did. And it's better late than never."

It is difficult to articulate the degree of dominance Michael Phelps achieved in swimming. You take half of his 28 Olympic medals and he would still be the most decorated Olympic swimmer in world history. You could take half of his 23 gold medals and he would still possess more Olympic gold medals than any Olympian in any discipline in any nation in the world. He set new world records on 39 different occasions. At the peak of his dominance in 2008, when he won a record eight gold medals in Beijing, NBC Olympic host Bob Costas described him as swimming perfection personified:

> If you were to build the perfect swimmer, the finished product would look just like this. Michael Phelps stands six foot four with an enormous wingspan of 6'7", creating the elongated stroke that has broken 22 world records…His size fourteen feet might as well be flippers. Dinner plate sized hands grab water like a pair of paddles, and the flex of double-jointed elbows and knees adds an exaggerated range of motion. Phelps is also perfectly tall and short. He has the legs of man who stands only about six feet tall but the torso of someone about 6'8". His short sturdy legs provide ideal balance and a powerful kick, while a long upper body forms a sculpted 'V' shape that begins with wide shoulders and concludes with narrow hips and a flat backside. Put it together, and you've got a human speed boat skimming the water's surface.

If there were a word to encapsulate the machine-like excellence Phelps had accomplished, that word might be *bulletproof*—which made any of his personal struggles difficult for many to relate or feel empathy toward the athlete who most credibly could be argued to be living the "Olympic Dream".

His first arrest for drunk driving occurred in the months following his first foray into major Olympic success in 2004, largely treated in the media as lucky (that no one was hurt) and a youthful dalliance (which he could learn from). When a photo of him using a marijuana bong surfaced four years later, there were greater ramifications as he lost sponsors and received a three-month ban from USA Swimming. He retired from swimming in 2012, but then announced a return less than two years later. Within months, he was in trouble with the authorities again, charged with driving (and speeding) under the influence, and issued a six-month ban from competition.

It was during his subsequent eight weeks in an Arizona treatment facility that Phelps came to recognize the root of his issues. While he had long been an advocate for healthier lifestyles in swimming (starting his Michael Phelps Foundation in 2008 with those aims in mind), his definition of healthy had not expanded to mental spaces, resulting in significant depression, anxiety, and thoughts of suicide. He would later explain that he wanted to "get out in public and talk and say, 'Yes, I've done these great things in the pool, but I'm also a human.' I'm going through the same struggles as a lot of the people in this room" (Crouse, 2017, para. 15).

Getting out and talking about it he most certainly did.

Emerging Advocacy: From Private to Public

In some of the media moments shared in this book, a seminal, crystallizing date can be attached to when an athlete formally became an advocate for mental health awareness and support. One won't find an agreed-upon date for Phelps, as it instead seemingly emerged from a series of clues and disclosures that Phelps himself seemed to be deciphering in the process. However, in hindsight, a 2015 interview with *Sports Illustrated*'s Tim Layden seems to be the point of demarcation where Phelps became vulnerable enough to discuss mental health in the context of his recent troubles. Having exited rehabilitation and eyeing a 2016 Rio Summer Olympic return, Phelps admitted that there were moments where he was "in a dark place" and had a mindset of "not wanting to be alive anymore" (Layden, 2015, para. 9). He spoke of his time in rehabilitation, where he conceded that his solution was to treat his recovery as a another competition he could conquer. Then, he told Layden, he realized layers of his depression and anxiety that he had not put together before. He connected elements of his troubles to an estrangement from his father, a laser-like focus on meeting enormous athletic expectations, and a variety of other factors. He explains his rehabilitation revelation thusly:

> For a long time, I saw myself as the athlete that I was, but not as a human being. I would be in sessions with complete strangers who know exactly who I am, but they don't respect me for things I've done, but instead for who I am as a human being. I found myself feeling happier and happier. And in my group, we formed a family. We all wanted to see each other succeed. It was a new experience for me. It was tough. But it was great (Layden, 2015, para. 28).

Other prior aspects of his life formed within this crystallized, new narrative. For instance, Michael Phelps was formally diagnosed with ADHD when he was in the sixth grade, but the diagnosis became public in 2008 (Winerip, 2008). It was largely a story of a mother opting for medication to help her child excel, not that ADHD was a part of a larger mental health-oriented picture. The piece even concluded with the coda that "Too many adults looked at Ms. Phelps's boy and saw what he couldn't do. This week, the world will be tuned to the Beijing Olympics to see what he can do" (para. 25). Thus, a "solution" to a "problem" was borne.

As Leonhardt (2021) writes:

> American medicine often struggles with subtlety. It treats many conditions as binary: You have it, or you don't...This overly neat drawing of lines ends up serving people poorly...It imagines an illness is either real and can be addressed with a pill or treatment—or is strictly a psychological condition. Reality is often messier (para 7–9).

It wasn't for another decade that Phelps publicly connected his ADHD diagnosis to other aspects of his mental health. In 2017, he appeared in a video for Child Mind Institute's *Speak Up for Kids* campaign, first to talk about how ADHD should never limit one's dreams, but also as a way to talk about how medication was just one part of his treatment. He offered:

> I think the biggest thing for me, once I found that it was okay to talk to someone and seek help, I think that's something that has changed my life forever...Now I'm able to live life to its fullest (Dowd, 2017, para. 7).

The pieces started to come together more frequently that year. First it was talking in the video. Then it was joining the board of Medibio, mental health disorders organization. Then talking more openly about his own mental health to *The New York Times*, but doing so in the context of aiding other athletes experiencing some of the same things. As Jackson, Dirks, and Billings (2021) establish in a subsequent content analysis of his active vs. retired media personae, there was a significant shift from athlete to advocate. Yes, his 23 gold medals were still part of the context for the advocacy stories, but it was only to underscore a larger issue: if the greatest Olympian of all-time not only experiences mental health issues but also can speak about them vulnerably and publicly, so can others.

Adding Narrative Dimension: Painting a More Vivid Picture

By 2018, Phelps was known in the media as an athlete who could ably and (somewhat) comfortably speak about his anxiety, ADHD, and depression. However, he was also adding considerable nuance to the story, including that his thoughts of suicide were quite real. As revealed in a *CNN Health* article, he talked about how thankful he was that he did not commit suicide, but also acknowledged the importance of talking about it. "That's the reason why suicide rates are going up – people are afraid to talk and open up," said Phelps. (Scutti, 2018, para. 24). In the *CNN Health* piece, the public also received more details about what rehabilitation was like for Phelps. As Scutti (2018) articulated:

> His first morning in treatment, a nurse woke him at 6 a.m. and said, 'Look at the wall and tell me what you feel.' On the wall hung eight basic emotions, he recalled. 'How do you think I feel right now, I'm pretty ticked off, I'm not happy, I'm not a morning person,' he angrily told the nurse, laughing now at the memory. Once he began to talk about his feelings, 'life became easy...I said to myself so many times, 'Why didn't I do this 10 years ago?' But, I wasn't ready (para. 16–19).

It was in May of that same year that he announced his partnership with TalkSpace, an online/mobile therapy company that provides access to licensed therapists. Such an organization is increasingly crucial in modern society due to the rise of "care deserts," which are locations where in-person medical care is not available unless people travel many miles or across state borders. Such care deserts have become more frequent in rural and inner-city areas, particularly in states opting not to expand Medicaid as part of the Affordable Care Act (Jones,

2021). These disparities would later obviously be exacerbated when the COVID-19 pandemic emerged in early 2020.

Phelps' involvement managed to garner major exposure for the organization, particularly via an Associated Press interview that reached hundreds of individual (and often rural) markets. Phelps stressed his commitment to the cause: "I feel like with all the issues we have in this world, this is something where I can truly make significant impact" (Newberry, 2018, para. 18).

He also again recalled his darkest moments involving suicidal thoughts:

> I thought it would make things easier. I almost felt like it would be better for everybody if I wasn't there. But the more I thought about it, I wanted to find a different route. I wanted to see if I could find some help. I wanted to see if I could get better. (Newberry, 2018, para. 11).

Perhaps most importantly, he stressed the degree to which mental health is something one has to continually maintain on a daily basis:

> I still go through times that are very challenging. I do break down and maybe have a bad day, where I'm not in a good mental state. I understand that. It's who I am. I guess that will always be something that's a part of me (Newberry, 2018, para. 15).

Thus, by the end of 2018 and then continuing into 2019, Phelps' mental health advocacy had been cemented. He had spoken with considerable detail about his own experiences, his Phelps Foundation was stressing mental health elements even more prominently, and he now had the TalkSpace partnership that was reaching many of the inaccessible and secluded portions of America.

Pandemical America: A Nation Jointly Has a Mental Health Moment

Phelps certainly did not have the scientific background to be prescient about a coming pandemic, but one could not be faulted for believing so. Most of Phelps's work in 2019 appeared to be laying groundwork for larger mental health projects to be advanced in the coming years. Most notably, he was an Executive Producer and star of an HBO documentary, *The Weight of Gold*, that specifically highlighted mental health challenges that Olympians (and aspiring Olympians) face.

The documentary was noteworthy in a multitude of ways. It expanded his scope of advocacy to broader experiences he has faced, but also did so in a much more produced manner. Arguably even more important, however, was the building of community provided within the film itself. Phelps and his fellow producers were able to assemble a wide array of American Olympians—many of whom were household names for millions of Olympic fans—and able to advance a narrative that showed that while everyone's story deviated in certain manners, there was a common theme of a need for better mental health support that permeated each account. Athletes ranging from snowboarder Shaun White to figure skater Gracie Gold to track and bobsledder Lolo Jones to short track speedskater Apolo Ohno to alpine skier Bode Miller each shared their stories and, in the process, moved discussions from singular to plural. The critics lauded the effort, with the consensus on Rotten Tomatoes claiming that the film was "anchored by a disarmingly frank Michael Phelps."

Indeed, bluntness and straightforward honesty became the calling card of Phelps' increasingly frequent media interviews and discussions. In some of the media discussion surrounding the film, Phelps claimed that "treating people like humans" rather than medal-earning products could be a good first step, unabashedly calling it "frightening" and "scary" and concluding that "It breaks my heart because there are so many people who care so much about our physical well-being but I never saw caring about our mental well-being" (Myers, 2020, para. 16–17). The film (combined with a pandemic that brought mental health issues to the foreground, led to the International Olympic Committee (IOC) saying it "recognizes the seriousness of the topic" with a working group of experts being created, webinars and forums being advanced, and a hotline being more formalized (Myers, 2020, para. 18).

In a *Time* magazine article, Phelps spoke to the empowerment he was now experiencing, noting that "For me, to be able to have that power, to have people listen to you and to open up and speak about things that are important to me whether that is mental health or saving water; that's amazing." He went on to explain his journey and the increasing confidence he has found in his advocacy:

> I never thought people would sit and listen to me, or care about what I was saying. It's pretty incredible to have that voice and be able to spread my message as loud as I can to get people to really open up, understand what is actually going on and what we are doing to the world we live in, no matter what it is (Park, 2020, para. 6).

When the pandemic hit, an amplified power was ascribed to Phelps in his willingness to admit that it caused reversion to past practices and fears, which people seemed to relate to far more than any notion of his "conquering" any mental health condition. His narratives appeared to be equal parts admitting personal bouts with mental illness combined with encouraging examples on how to journey through. Regarding the vulnerability on display, he candidly offered that he'd "be the first to admit my mental health has been scarier than it's ever been throughout all of this, so I can't even imagine what other people are going through" (Miller, 2021, para. 4).

Some of his comments struck a tone of advocacy, including that he could now identify "red flags popping up when I'm starting to go down that path," (Park, 2020, para. 4) leading him to share those warning signs with his support group, both formal (therapist) and informal (spouse). He synergizes these attitudes into a growing need for communication, as that is "something I really just learned, just to be completely wide open. I joke that I learned how to communicate when I'm 30. But I did. And it's better late than never" (Park, 2020, para. 4).

He also pointed to a much broader group of allies speaking about these issues than ever before, stating that "The fact that there are so many celebrities or so many people standing up and talking about the struggles that they have – I think that's a way for us to really break down that stigma" (Moniuszko, 2021, para. 9). There was a level of reflection that the pandemic seemingly hastened, with Phelps contending that:

> I think we've all learned there's so much more to mental health than we ever knew or ever wanted to talk about, and that was something I was very afraid of... it honestly destroys me every time I read (about suicide) because there are other outlets that we can take and we can try to learn more (Moniuszko, 2021, para. 5).

When trying to offer advice during this time, Phelps appeared to always want to start that notion with a feeling of community, advancing the argument that "for those who are struggling with mental health, know you're not alone: There are days where I want to curl up into a ball and sit in the corner" (Miller, 2021, para. 5). When those days occur, he offers small yet practical advice: "It's just taking a little step forward, taking a deep breath from time to time. It really helps" (Miller, 2021, para. 5).

He notes that for him, swimming still is his productive outlet, his "calming mechanism," He explains that whenever he experiences a red flag event, his inherent response it to "try to keep some touch of the water. I feel like it really connects everything in my body" (Miller, 2021, para. 12). Even if one is not a swimmer, competitive or otherwise, Phelps used the pandemic to advocate for having some common, focused touchstone. He explains that doing so helps to explain his past struggles as a useful heuristic for overcoming them in the present:

> You stack those bricks up one by one, then you're able to move forward and just keep going, going, going, and that's what I was able to do in my career. [Now] I'm just trying to make that transition from being submerged in water to taking a few steps on land (Miller, 2021, para. 17).

Tokyo 2020 (2021): Mental Health Hits Home

The drain of training for an Olympics has been well-documented, but in pandemic times that toll could be ascribed an entirely different meaning. It was not merely that the Tokyo Summer Games had been delayed an entire year due to COVID-19, it was also that athletes had to recalibrate their lives. Some had planned to turn the page toward other career and family pursuits. Some had budgeted just enough money to live meagerly and, hopefully, earn a medal in return for their spending austerity. Some were spending a fifth year of training at facilities far away from their families and friends. In short, it was not merely that the metaphorical 26.2 mile marathon had become the equivalent of over 32 miles in length; it was that these athletes had run that metaphorical marathon assuming they were about to finish, only to be informed that many additional miles were added to their journey. Emotional tanks were empty.

Phelps appeared to be able to see that crunch coming, but was cognizant that it would not just be athletes who were feeling the weight of the pandemic haze. In April 2021, Phelps gave an online speech to the Boys and Girls Clubs of America. "I want you guys all to be kind to yourselves," Phelps told them. "Treat yourselves like a good friend" (Bruton, 2021, para. 16). In this talk, Phelps clarified (and likely stunned some of the kids who were watching) when he claimed that his 23 gold medals still were secondary to his more recent achievements regarding mental health advocacy. He told them:

> Throughout my career, what I've done in the pool, it's been absolutely incredible, some of the greatest achievements of my life, but the goals I have outside of the pool in my life now are way bigger than anything I could have done inside the pool…I'm gonna try to really challenge myself and see how far I can take my imagination, my creativity. I never want to settle for less. (Bruton, 2021, para. 14)

Then, of course, the Tokyo Games began. Phelps was not even confirmed to be in Tokyo for the event, but was secured by NBC Sports after the Olympic trials. It proved to be an astute decision, as arguably the biggest story of the Games became the sporadic participation of legendary gymnast Simone Biles. After a disappointing (for Biles' standards) qualifying night of the team competition, USA Gymnastics utilized social media to disseminate the news that Simone Biles had withdrawn from the team final of the 2021 Tokyo Olympic Games, citing her need to "focus on her mental health" (Lewis, 2021, para. 2). Biles then used her own social media platforms to further explain that she was experiencing the "twisties"—a dissociative state affecting gymnasts, that tends to alter an athletes' bodily control particularly when airborne—a frequent requisite for nearly all gymnastics disciplines (Lewis, 2021, para. 1).

The case of Simone Biles will be discussed in detail within Chapter 4, but becomes relevant here because one of her strongest advocates proved to be Michael Phelps. As Finn (2021) encapsulated, "NBC was left in a complicated spot for an assortment of reasons, some beyond its control and some of its own doing" (Finn, 2021, para. 3). They then shrewdly turned to Michael Phelps who could speak about Simone while also speaking about Olympians, in general, evoking similar themes to what was the major motif of his documentary from a year ago, arguing that:

> The Olympics is overwhelming. I mean talk about 'weight of gold,' we need someone who we can trust. Somebody that can let us be ourselves and listen. Allow us to become vulnerable. Somebody who's not going to try and fix us. We carry a lot of weight on our shoulders and it's challenging, especially when we have the lights on us and all of these expectations that are being thrown on top of us. [Simone Biles withdrawing] broke my heart. But also, if you look at it, mental health is something over the last 18 months that people are talking about...Nobody is perfect. It is okay to not be okay. It is okay to go through ups and downs and emotional rollercoasters. But I think the biggest thing is that we all need to ask for help sometimes, too, when we go through those times. I can say for me personally that it was something that was very challenging (Finn, 2021, para. 6–7).

Phelps spoke with other media outlets, noting that the Biles situation, while heartbreaking, also provided an opportunity to "jump on board and to even blow this mental health thing even more wide open" (*Athletic* Staff, 2021, para. 4, 8). Nicole Auerbach, Senior Writer for the *Athletic*, underscored the power of Phelps' advocacy for Biles in that moment:

A lot of the bad-faith criticism of Biles over the past 18 hours came from those without elite athletic backgrounds. Their voices should be drowned out by the greatest Olympian in history. He and Biles talking about their struggles amid such success should be an eye-opener for all (*Athletic* Staff, 2021, para. 9).

As the will she/won't she compete dilemma continued to permeate NBC's Olympic coverage, the network—to its credit—continued to make use of Phelps as the voice of the veteran who could most closely relate to the feelings Biles was likely experiencing. Phelps—to his credit—obliged. NBC even offered special focused content on mental health via its social media platform, Peacock, with host Mike Tirico having an in-depth conversation with Phelps.

In an exclusive NBC Olympics interview, the swimmer did not hold back on grievances he had with the International Olympic Committee, noting that "one of the things I've been frustrated about is the lack of change and lack of support we have for mental health both during competition and post-competition" (NBC Sports Group, 2021). He acknowledged that the pandemic had exacerbated concerns, but also stressed that actions needed to be immediate, asking the question:

> How many athletes are we going to lose? We already lost a handful to suicide. How many more can we lose? It breaks my heart. I'm one that knows exactly what that feels like. I know what it feels like to not want to be alive, and the ups and the downs and roller coasters that everyone's gone through over the last two years, I'm afraid. I'm afraid for everybody else (NBC Sports Group, 2021).

He commented that while "Simone and I are the best in the world at what we do," there were still "many other millions of people are out there going through the same exact thing. I hope they're watching right now...This is real" (NBC Sports Group, 2021). His admission to having some darker days even while working at the Tokyo Olympics showed how there is no panacea ensuring positive mental health, but also expressed optimism that "maybe we'll see change. Maybe we'll actually be able to help athletes" (NBC Sports Group, 2021).

In the special, Michael Phelps seemed to be issuing a clarion call, specifically evoking the other major media moments this book will chronicle, listing athletes Kevin Love, Naomi Osaka, and Simone Biles specifically. In it, Phelps seemed to want to crystallize the moment, to show how change can be enacted with much greater immediacy than other systemic problems in the Olympic system. In what could be seen as his most holistic form of mental health activism to date, Phelps issued a call to action:

We need support. We need to be able to find a safe place…I think the biggest thing is understanding it and accepting it…People are standing up and talking about it left and right and that's what we need. We need more of that because I think, if we can do that, then we can break down this wall. The stigma can be gone, relieved, finished (NBC Sports Group, 2021).

References

Athletic Staff (2021, July 28). Michael Phelps on Simone Biles, mental health: 'It's OK to not be OK.' *The Athletic*. Retrieved at: https://theathletic.com/news/michael-phelps-on-simone-biles-mental-health-its-ok-to-not-be-ok/nVaL238ANGo7/

Bruton, M. (2021, Apr. 23). Michael Phelps' message to kids: Mental health is just as important as physical health. *Forbes*. Retrieved at: https://www.forbes.com/sites/michellebruton/2021/04/23/michael-phelps-message-to-kids-mental-health-is-just-as-important-as-physical-health/?sh=59c95bb6100a

Crouse, K. (2017, Sept. 17). Michael Phelps: A golden shoulder to lean on. *The New York Times*. Retrieved at: https://www.nytimes.com/2017/09/21/sports/michael-phelps-grant-hackett-tiger-woods.html

Dowd, M. E. (2017, Apr. 28). Michael Phelps opens up about ADHD struggles. *Sports Illustrated*. Retrieved at: https://www.si.com/olympics/2017/04/28/michael-phelps-opens-about-adhd-struggles-teacher-told-me-id-never-amount-anything

Finn, C. (2021, July 28). NBC got the Simone Biles saga right by turning to Michael Phelps for his insight. *The Boston Globe*. Retrieved at: https://www.boston.com/sports/media/2021/07/28/nbc-got-the-simone-biles-saga-right-by-turning-to-michael-phelps-for-his-insight/

Jones, A. (2021, June 7). Millions of Americans live in 'care deserts'—Here's what that means and why it's a huge problem. *Health*. Retrieved at: https://www.health.com/mind-body/health-diversity-inclusion/care-deserts

Layden, T. (2015, Nov. 9). After rehabilitation, the best of Michael Phelps may lie ahead. *Sports Illustrated*. Retrieved at: https://www.si.com/olympics/2015/11/09/michael-phelps-rehabilitation-rio-2016

Leonhardt, D. (2021, Nov. 11). When modern medicine doesn't cure chronic pain, what comes next? *The New York Times*. Retrieved at: https://messaging-custom-newsletters.nytimes.com/template/oakv2?campaign_id=9&emc=edit_nn_20211111&instance_id=45145&nl=the-morning&productCode=NN&regi_id=73415824&segment_id=74113&te=1&uri=nyt%3A%2F%2Fnewsletter%2Fc7dd41c8-b6a2-5d03-9595-3dea53a0a74f&user_id=84155ed03985fcf350f3f454f670996f

Lewis, S. (2021, July 30). Simone Biles opens up about withdrawal from Olympic competitions: 'I don't think you realize how dangerous this is'. *CBS News*. https://www.cbsnews.com/news/simone-biles-olympics-gymnastics-withdrawal-twisties/.

Miller, A. M. (2021, Jan. 12). Michael Phelps says his mental health has been 'scarier than it's ever been' during the pandemic. Here's how he's coped. *Business Insider*. Retrieved at: https://www.insider.com/michael-phelps-mental-health-scarier-than-ever-during-pandemic-2021-1

Moniuszko, S. M. (2021, Mar. 24). Michael Phelps on the pandemic's impact on mental health struggles: 'It honestly destroys me'. *USA Today*. Retrieved at: https://www.usatoday.com/story/life/health-wellness/2021/03/24/michael-phelps-meghan-markle-mental-health-amid-covid-pandemic/6967418002/

Myers, A. L. (2020, Aug. 10). Michael Phelps opens up about mental health struggles in new doc. *The Associated Press*. Retrieved at: https://www.detroitnews.com/story/entertainment/television/2020/08/10/michael-phelps-apolo-ohno-open-suicide-documentary-hbo/112875854/

NBC Sports Group Press Box (2021, Aug. 2). New Olympic special: 'Sports and mental health: A conversation with Michael Phelps' streaming now on Peacock, NBCOlympics.com, and NBC Sports app. Retrieved at: https://nbcsportsgrouppressbox.com/2021/08/02/new-olympic-special-sports-mental-health-a-conversation-with-michael-phelps-streaming-now-on-peacock-nbcolympics-com-and-nbc-sports-app/

Newberry, P. (2018, May 22). Michael Phelps opens up about his struggles with mental health: 'I still go through times that are very challenging.' *The Associated Press*. Retrieved at: https://www.boston.com/sports/olympics/2018/05/22/michael-phelps-depression-mental-health/

Park, A. (2020). Michael Phelps opens up about retirement and mental health awareness: 'I struggle through problems just like everybody else'. *Time*. Retrieved at: https://time.com/collection/davos-2020-mental-health/5402066/michael-phelps-mental-health-activism/

Scutti, S. (2018, Jan. 20). Michael Phelps: 'I am extremely thankful that I did not take my own life.' *CNN Health*. Retrieved at: https://www.cnn.com/2018/01/19/health/michael-phelps-depression/index.html

"The Weight of Gold" (2020). Rotten Tomatoes aggregate reviews. Retrieved at: https://www.rottentomatoes.com/m/the_weight_of_gold

Winerip, M. (2008, Aug. 8). Phelps's mother recalls helping her son find gold-medal focus. *The New York Times*. Retrieved at: https://www.nytimes.com/2008/08/10/sports/olympics/10Rparent.html

2

Key Media Moment #2: Kevin Love

"I've never been more comfortable in my own skin."

It was November 5, 2017. Early afternoon.

Kevin Love and the Cleveland Cavaliers hosted the Atlanta Hawks for the first time during the regular NBA season. Love and the Cavaliers entered the game 4–5, frustrating fans and players who were coming off the team's first championship the year before. His team—also featuring future Hall of Famers Dwyane Wade and LeBron James—hoped to get back on track by beating the Hawks, a team limping through the early stages of 2017.

In the first quarter, Love missed a 25-foot step-back jump shot from the three-point arc and a hook shot just outside the paint. Love tried again in the second quarter, driving the lane and attempting a floater—but it was blocked by Luke Babbitt, a 6'9 journeyman forward for the Hawks. Love missed another 20-foot jumper, but managed a layup under the rim.

As the first half wound down, Love sat on the scorer's table, chewing his mouthpiece. He pulled his jersey over his head, blocked his face, and walked over the bench, where he ripped open the jersey near the number 0 on his chest. "That's not a good look," one of the announcers laughed, as Love walked toward the locker room, seemingly deciding on an early and personally-extended halftime break.

He returned for the third quarter, but it did not go much better. Three minutes in, Taurean Prince made a three-pointer to put the Hawks up 62-53 over the Cavs. Love tried to respond with his own three but missed the shot. The

Hawks grabbed the rebound and ran down court, where Babbitt squared up and knocked down another three-pointer for the Hawks. The Cavs called timeout.

In the huddle, as the team reviewed defensive strategies to help stop the six-point run, Love felt his heart race. He could not breathe.

"Everything was spinning, like my brain was trying to climb out of my head," he recalled.

Love spun out of the huddle. Tyronn Lue, the head coach, approached.

"I'll be right back," Love blurted. He fled to the locker room, where he ended up on the floor.

"What can I do for you?" a trainer asked. "What can I do for you?"

Love did not respond, instead thinking to himself, "You're about to die."

When the final buzzer sounded, the Cavs had fallen to the Hawks by one bucket, 117-115. Love had never returned to the game. Instead, he ended up spending an hour under evaluation at the Cleveland Clinic, a local hospital, where he received fluids through an IV. He had struggled through 18 minutes and 29 seconds of playing time, finishing with four points, four rebounds, and four fouls. Teammates, coaches, and fans were flummoxed by his sudden departure. It was not in character for the NBA veteran.

"He has an illness and that's all we know right now," Lue told reporters after the game (Vardon, 2017, para. 5). Even the anonymous sources—the old staple of sports journalism—had no clue. "All I know is he really wasn't feeling well," one team insider told the local newspaper (para. 6).

Fans, athletes, and the talking heads on sports television picked apart the performance and, quite predictably, developed lay theories about what happened. "Love's illness wasn't disclosed, but it's a good sign for the Cavs that it wasn't serious enough to warrant an extended stay," one fan site reported (Villas, 2017, para. 4–6). Now, the armchair expert contended, "...If only there was a hospital out there who could also cure the Cavs' defensive woes."

Even Love was not sure what happened.

One day later, surrounded by reporters in the gym, Love shook his head. "I just wasn't feeling right," he said (Kaskey-Blomain, 2017, para. 5). "Stomach, shortness of breath. They sent me to the hospital for a routine check, and I was in and out of there."

As he stood near the wall, towel draped around his neck, Love seemed to be trying to sort out what happened himself. "I was kind of feeling all out of sorts. I can't truly explain how I felt, because I've never really felt like that" (ESPN, 2017).

He was not trying to be evasive.

Turns out, Love had experienced a panic attack.

Finding an Answer

In the days that followed, Love returned to form on the court. The day after his interview with the media, he scored 32 points in a game against the Milwaukee Bucks. He scored 17 points on Nov. 9 against the Rockets, and then he led the team with 29 points in a Nov. 11 victory over the Dallas Mavericks. Off the court, Love became preoccupied with a question. Why, he wondered, was he so worried about people finding out he had a panic attack?

As the stories in this book illustrate, athletes often confront a two-prong struggle when it comes to mental health. First, elite athletes such as Love face the symptoms of mental illness, such as extreme anxiety, depression, and, at the extreme, suicidal thoughts. Second, athletes navigate stigma. The world of elite competition has traditionally endorsed mottos such as "no pain, no gain," "suck it up," and "tough it out." Mental illness can be perceived as weakness in the locker room, facilitating a culture where caring for oneself can spell professional trouble.

Can coaches and teammates trust a person disclosing mental illness to perform when their own money, fame, and games are on the line? As the case of Houston Rocket Royce White indicated, that was definitely in doubt.

Can you step away from your spot for a couple games without losing it to another player forever? As former New England quarterback Drew Bledsoe could attest, the answer was no if the player waiting to take your place was Tom Brady.

Will the competition use your mental health against you? Baseball pitcher Zack Grienke disclosed social anxiety disorder in 2006...and yet still was taunted by Yankees fans during the playoffs a decade later.

Athletes, including female competitors, also buy into traditional notions concerning masculinity. Being strong means not complaining about pain. You don't share emotions.

Well after the panic attack, during a roundtable interview with *CBS This Morning* in September 2021, Love joined 6-time NFL Pro Bowler Brandon Marshall and WNBA player DiDi Richards in describing the need for vulnerability in sport. Love described the traditional approach to mental health in sport: "I was taught to compartmentalize, I was taught to not speak about it, not show weakness," Love said (Powell, 2021). "I think as athletes we can all understand that in a way."

In the period following his panic attack, Love recognized the old approach would no longer work for him (Love, 2018). He could not just tough it out alone. He connected with a therapist, walking into the first session with suspicions. The therapist talked about things other than basketball, and Love began to relax.

It changed his life. But it took time—and two other unexpected events—for Love to speak out.

First, the Cavaliers faced the Oklahoma City Thunder in January 2018. "Struggle" would be an understatement for the Cavs' performance that night. One Cleveland sportswriter used the word "crushed" to describe the game in which the Thunder scored 148 points, tying the record for the most points allowed by the Cavs in a regulation game, ever (Vardon, 2018). "Welp, Kevin Love lasted about three minutes in the first quarter," local journalist Joe Vardon wrote (2018, para. 2). Two months after Love's initial panic attack, sports writers—and teammates—were still in the dark about his mental health. LeBron James bemoaned the score, saying he never gave up that many points even in video games (Withers, 2018). James told reporters he looked forward to the next day's practice, when the team could break down the many things that went wrong.

The next day, Love didn't show up to practice.

Players openly insulted Love and demanded answers. Players accused Love of malingering, making up "an illness," the phrase used by journalists to explain the reason Love left the game early.

In the locker room, Lue shared the news about Love's mental health.

Teammates now knew, so their demand for answers stopped.

The public did not know, so their demand for answers continued.

An Inspiration in Toronto

The second event occurred in the early morning hours of February 17, 2018, when Toronto Raptors star DeMar DeRozan shared a seven-word statement on Twitter. "This depression get the best of me..." he wrote, quoting the lyrics of a song by Kevin Gates called "Tomorrow" in which the rapper says, "I'm in my thoughts I don't want to talk until tomorrow." More than 1,000 people responded by morning, offering the California native support and encouragement. DeRozan had been in his home state preparing for the All Star game, and his post about depression did not directly come up in the morning's interviews. DeRozan did tell reporters, "At the end of the day we are not just athletes, we are human beings just like everyone. And if we have a platform to help and put something out and put that knowledge to help, we should" (Smith, 2018, para. 23).

DeRozan's platform reached millions of people that day—including Love.

It is difficult to overstate the role of the media in Love's mental health. His first panic attack occurred in the middle of a professional basketball game, before

20,000 in-person spectators and tens of thousands more watching from home. Love has admitted (2020a) that exposure to social media and news can trigger his anxiety. And it was social media—through DeRozan—that inspired Love to share his personal experience with anxiety and depression. As he has embraced his role as an advocate for mental health, Love has followed DeRozan's advice and used his platform to educate the public.

Perhaps the most reverberant media moment for Love came on March 6, 2018, when he wrote an essay for *The Players' Tribune*, a digital publication in which professional athletes share first-person stories. Love started, "On November 5th, right after halftime against the Hawks, I had a panic attack" (Love, 2018, para. 1).

And just like that, the public knew.

The essay, titled "Everyone is Going Through Something," ultimately became a watershed moment in the history of mental health and sport. It was not the first mental health disclosure in the basketball world, or even in *The Players' Tribune*, but coupled with DeRozan's disclosure, it inspired a mental health movement in professional sports. Love and DeRozan became the faces of mental health in the league, leading the National Basketball Association to pick up the baton—as will be discussed in Chapter 6. Love encouraged other athletes to come forward and share stories of depression, suicidal thoughts, and anxiety everywhere from the soccer pitch to the basketball court, the baseball diamond to the football field. People conversed about mental health—and stigma—on social media, driven by the disclosures. *The Players' Tribune* now devotes an entire section to mental health; as of January 2022, featured stories from more than 40 elite athletes representing every major U.S. sport can be found in the expansive section.

In the years since the initial disclosure, Love has became a vocal advocate for mental health care by sharing resources, challenging stigma, and educating others through YouTube videos, morning talk shows, news articles, and even a podcast in which he interviews mental health professionals. "If you're suffering silently like I was," he told readers in the essay, "then you know how it can feel like nobody really gets it. Partly, I want to do it for me, but mostly, I want to do it because people don't talk about mental health enough" (para. 3).

In his essay, Love challenges those traditional notions of what it means to "be a man." Being silent doesn't work, he tells readers, but discussing mental health can.

A Lifetime of Basketball—and Looming Dread

Basketball runs in the family for Love, whose father, Stan, also played in the NBA. Love, a top prospect out of high school in Oregon, played one year of college ball for the UCLA Bruins. He joined the NBA following the 2008 draft. His career (so far) has included time on two teams, the Cavaliers and the Minnesota Timberwolves. Love has enjoyed tremendous success, helping the Cavs earn an NBA championship in 2016, appearing on five All-Star teams, and winning a gold medal on the United States National Team during the 2012 Summer Olympics.

Although Love relishes the game of basketball, his desire to play was also spurred by an ulterior motive, a realization that occurred to him when COVID-19 provided the space for him to reflect. During the pandemic, Love realized basketball was a longstanding way to escape intrusive thoughts. He would work himself to the point of physical exhaustion, hoping his mind would switch from its default setting of dread. "That's just the way I've been wired since I was a kid," he recalled. "It's like there's a constant, low-level threat that I can sense in the pit of my stomach from the moment that I wake up in the morning" (Love, 2020a, para. 5).

Success in elite sports—whether college or the pros—requires time-consuming dedication. It is common for athletes to experience depression when the competition ends. Olympic athletes are afflicted with the so-called "post-Olympic blues," regardless of whether they win medals. While head trauma is often blamed, depression among retired NFL players may be attributed at times to the sudden end of a lifelong pursuit. "What now?," they might ask. For Love, basketball represented a distraction from poor mental health maintenance. He lost basketball several times because of injury and the 2020 pandemic shutdown, and the experience forced him to confront Kevin Love the human rather than Kevin Love the 5-time All Star. Love admits he placed too much stock in basketball, adopting the sport as his entire identity "in a really unhealthy way" (2020b, para. 6).

"Thank you for being a real man!"

Fans largely supported Love following his disclosure in the *Tribune* and social media. Parrott et al. (2020) systematically examined how social media users commented beneath Love's post and the disclosure by DeMar DeRozan (Parrott et al., 2020). Of 3,366 comments found that fans often applauded the basketball stars, called for an end to stigma, and, importantly, disclosed their own experiences with depression, anxiety, and other mental illnesses. One commenter told Love, "I might actually go to a counselor now because of this," while another wrote, "Thank you for being a real man and talking about this openly. I am a real man too…it's time the stigma stops!" In addition to praising Love, commenters disclosed their own challenges and triumphs related to mental health. One commenter told Love he experienced anxiety for more than two decades. "I didn't want to talk about it and not willing to show my weakness until I saw DeMar and you are willing to share your issues," the man wrote. "Thank you both. Now I have realized that I need to face it and (I am) willing to talk with my family."

The comments illustrate a compelling phenomenon in mass media: parasocial relationships (Hoffner & Cohen, 2012). There is slim chance the social media users personally know Love through friendship, work, or direct acquaintance. Still, they felt enough connection to (a) inform this stranger about their shared experience with mental illness, and (b) model Love's behavior by opening up to family and friends. The reaction illustrates the power of elite athletes in shaping public understanding of mental health, despite the fact they lack expertise beyond personal experience. It also illustrates how a counter-stereotypical narrative can snowball into a larger stigma-busting discourse about mental health.

Indeed, journalists joined the public ovation for Love and DeRozan. Charlotte Wilder, a columnist for Fox Sports, called the *Tribune* essay "so important" and Love's description of the panic attack as "spot on" before using Twitter to share her own experience with anxiety. Seek help, she told her social media followers, because confronting mental illness "is the bravest thing you can do" (Wilder, 2018). In another study on the subject, Parrott et al. (2019) determined that journalists generally framed the basketball stars' disclosures as displays of strength and open challenges to an athletic atmosphere in which mental illness is stigmatized. In news stories, journalists often permitted Love and DeRozan to directly "speak" to readers, heavily quoting the athletes as they described coming out, being well-received by teammates, and the need for an end to stigma. In some cases, journalists were even inspired to share their own stories, as Wilder (2018) illustrated.

As noted, the majority of social media users who responded to Love's disclosure offered support. Still, others were not so kind. Love encountered a refrain—not common but present in sports—from social media users who questioned whether professional athletes could really experience depression and anxiety given their professional success. For example, Love competes (and succeeds) at the highest level of professional basketball, and he has been able to make millions of dollars while playing a game for a job. One fan simply told Love to "suck it up," repeating the misgiving that financial and professional success equates happiness. As *Time* magazine's Sean Gregory advanced in Chapter 5, this is a major theme when athletes seek empathy for personal matters. A minority of fans sounded similar comments when Simone Biles withdrew from the 2020 Tokyo Olympics, as described in Chapter 4. Nonetheless, other social media commenters came to Love's defense, and in interviews, Love directly challenged the idea himself. While speaking to student athletes from UCLA, he said, "Success is not immune to depression. Anybody can experience it. Having these tough conversations is going to help move stuff out of the shadows" (Love, 2020).

"You are not alone!"

Love's essay elicited praise from fellow athletes, too. LeBron James, his teammate in Cleveland, retweeted Love's post with emojis for a fist, muscle flex, and praying hands. "You're even more powerful now than ever before!!!" he wrote (James, 2018). Praising Love for his essay, point guard Jeremy Lin—himself the subject of intense media gaze at one moment (Park, 2014)—called for people to express more empathy toward others. Even "Nature Boy" Ric Flair, the legendary wrestler known for his flamboyance and gravitas, described himself as "someone who has suffered from anxiety and panic attacks," and assured Love "you will get through this, and you are not alone!" (Lee, 2018).

In addition to praise, Love received delayed apologies from the teammates who accused him of faking illness during the Thunder blowout. They included Dwyane Wade, who expressed regret in an interview while acknowledging he and Love were estranged (Leweck, 2021, para. 3): "I didn't know that he dealt with or suffered from any mental health issues...I didn't know what he was dealing with mentally. So we had a very ugly incident..."

Love often receives credit for the swelling conversation concerning mental health in sport (Lavelle, 2021). He challenges the notion, pointing back to DeRozan's disclosure as inspiration. Indeed, other athletes came forward previously and discussed mental health, including Royce White, whose career in the NBA floundered because of mental illness and the league's attitude toward mental health during the early 2010s. Love's disclosure also followed first-person essays from more than one dozen other athletes from professional hockey, football, and even basketball who shared their experiences in the *Tribune*. The athletes—male and female, retired and active—shared stories about drug addiction, alcohol abuse, depression, and suicide. Since Love's essay, dozens more elite athletes (e.g., Troy Deeney, Colin Wilson, Kayla McBride) joined the public conversation, challenging traditional "tough it out" attitudes in sports.

The month Love's essay appeared in the *Tribune*, another prominent figure on the Cavaliers stepped away from the team for two weeks because of anxiety: Head Coach Tyronn Lue. Lue told ESPN he needed the break because he had starting experiencing chest pain, shortness of breath, and sleep loss—symptoms similar to Love during the build-up to his in-game panic attack. As he prepared the Cavs for the NBA Finals in May 2018, Lue told ESPN he felt great after starting anxiety medication and changing his diet (Bieler, 2018). When he retired from professional basketball, Wade also told reporters he would seek therapy to help with the adjustment.

Light After Midnight

Since the disclosure, Love has embraced the role of mental health advocate. He has granted dozens of interviews with news organizations and penned additional essays for the *Tribune*. He has also fielded questions about treatment from other athletes, both publicly and privately, and he says people talk to him more about mental health than basketball. He has gone beyond media-based mental health advocacy to launch the Kevin Love Fund, which challenges stigma through education, research, and advocacy. The program provides educators resources so they can teach children to talk about emotions, empathize with others, and develop other tools to support their mental health.

Love thinks it is ironic he became known for the moment in 2017 on the court when he experienced the panic attack. It was the only time he experienced an anxiety attack so publicly, he says, but it also represents "the tip of the iceberg" in relation to his mental health (Love, 2020a, para. 17). He recalled a period in which he plummeted into the depths of depression when he injured his hand early in his professional career, losing the ability to compete. He would stay in his bedroom, shades drawn, the lights and television off. "It felt like I was on a deserted island by myself, and it was always midnight," he says (2020a, para. 18). In those depths, Love started questioning how he could make the pain go away. A good friend ultimately helped pull him out of the despair, and today he continues to tell people: Speak to others about mental health.

Love eschews the label of "Success Story for Mental Health" (2020a, para. 38). Mental health is constant work, he says, and for him the combination of therapy, medication, and speaking out has been helpful—and empowering. Love told NBC that he has noticed young players on the Cavaliers using the team's designated therapists. "These guys are buying in and understanding the mental side and these micro-gains," he said. "Whether it's something at home or within your personal life, there's stuff to work on. The better you understand yourself and who you are, you're going to feel more comfortable in your own skin" (Scipioni, 2021, para. 23, 24).

During the COVID-19 pandemic, Love engaged student athletes from UCLA—his alma mater—in conversation about mental health. Love and the student athletes discussed the challenges brought about by the pandemic and methods for coping. Video of the panel, called "To Anybody Going Through It," appeared on the *Tribune* site (Love, 2020b). Losing competition during the pandemic, he said, was like seeing an emotional crutch disappear. One of the student athletes, a basketball player named Lauryn Miller, told Love that the male and African American communities share taboos about mental health. Miller asked Love how he found the strength to speak out, and Love pointed back to DeRozan.

He described his disclosures as "paying it forward," adding "you know, opening up and seeing how I could connect the dots looking backwards, allowed me to move forward…I've never been more comfortable in my own skin."

References

Albertie, Q. S. (2017). LeBron James was referring to Kevin Love on Sunday. https://kingjamesgospel.com/2017/11/06/cleveland-cavaliers-lebron-james-calls-out-kevin-love/

Bieler, D. (2018, May 31). Cavaliers' Tyronn Lue says anxiety caused him to step away. Washington Post. https://www.washingtonpost.com/news/early-lead/wp/2018/05/31/cavaliers-coach-tyronn-lue-says-anxiety-caused-him-to-step-away/

ESPN (2017). Kevin Love addresses sudden illness during Cavaliers' game. https://www.youtube.com/watch?v=mk0IHnpwhFU

Hoffner, C. A., & Cohen, E. L. (2012). Responses to obsessive compulsive disorder on Monk among series fans: Parasocial relations, presumed media influence, and behavioral outcomes. *Journal of Broadcasting & Electronic Media, 56*(4), 650–668.

James, L. (2018, March 6). You're even more powerful now than ever before. Twitter.

Kaskey-Blomain, M. (2017, November 6). Kevin Love says he 'wasn't feeling right' against Hawks. 247 Sports. https://247sports.com/nba/cleveland-cavaliers/Article/WATCH-Kevin-Love-says-he-wasnt-feeling-right-against-the-Atlanta-Hawks--110062201/

Lavelle, K. (2021). The face of mental health: Kevin Love and hegemonic masculinity in the NBA. *Communication & Sport, 9*(6), 954–971.

Lee, B. (2018). WWE legend Ric Flair sends message to Cavs' Kevin Love. *CavsNation*. https://cavsnation.com/cavs-news-ric-flair-sends-message-to-kevin-love/

Leweck, S. (2021, August 6). Dwyane Wade expresses regret for challenging Cavs' Kevin Love during his private mental health battle. Cavaliers Nation. https://cavaliersnation.com/2021/08/06/dwyane-wade-expresses-regret-for-challenging-cavs-kevin-love-during-his-private-mental-health-battle/

Love, K. (2018). Everyone is going through something. The Players' Tribune. https://www.theplayerstribune.com/articles/kevin-love-everyone-is-going-through-something

Love, K. (2020a). To anybody going through it. A discussion on mental health. The Players' Tribune. https://www.theplayerstribune.com/posts/kevin-love-mental-health-discussion

Love, K. (2020b). To anybody going through it. The Players' Tribune. https://www.theplayerstribune.com/articles/kevin-love-mental-healt

Park, M. K. (2015). Race, hegemonic masculinity, and the 'Linpossible': An analysis of media representations of Jeremy Lin. *Communication & Sport, 3*(4), 367–389.

Parrott, S., Billings, A. C., Hakim, S. D., & Gentile, P. (2020). From# endthestigma to# realman: Stigma-challenging social media responses to NBA Players' mental health disclosures. *Communication Reports, 33*(3), 148–160.

Parrott, S., Billings, A. C., Buzzelli, N., & Towery, N. (2021). "We all go through it": Media depictions of mental illness disclosures from star athletes DeMar DeRozan and Kevin Love. *Communication & Sport, 9*(1), 33–54.

Powell, T. B. (2021, September 29). Kevin Love, DiDi Richards, and Brandon Marshall emphasize the importance of mental health and vulnerability. *CBS News*. https://www.cbsnews.com/news/kevin-love-didi-richards-brandon-marshall-mental-health-vulnerability/

Scipioni, J. (2021, November 18). NBA star Kevin Love on finding success while struggling with mental health. *NBC*. https://www.cnbc.com/2021/11/18/nba-star-kevin-love-on-mental-health-struggles-success-getting-covid.html

Smith, D. (2018, February 17). DeMar DeRozan's tweet stirs social media support. Toronto Star. https://www.thestar.com/sports/raptors/2018/02/17/innocuous-demar-derozan-tweet-stirs-social-media-support.html

Vardon, J. (2017, November 5). Kevin Love sent to Cleveland Clinic to determine illness that knocked him from Hawks game. https://www.cleveland.com/cavs/2017/11/kevin_love_sent_to_cleveland_c.html

Vardon, J. (2018, January 18). Cavaliers reach wrong milestones in 148-124 blowout loss to Oklahoma City Thunder. https://www.cleveland.com/cavs/2018/01/cavaliers_thunder_lebron_james.html

Villas, R. (2017, November 5). Kevin Love went to the hospital after early exit from game versus Hawks. Cavs Nation. https://cavsnation.com/cavs-news-kevin-love-hospital-early-exit-versus-hawks/

Wilder, C. (2018, March 6). This piece is so important. I've dealt with anxiety and panic my whole life and Kevin Love's description of a panic attack is spot on. *Twitter*. https://twitter.com/TheWilderThings/status/971031094815608833?ref_src=twsrc%5Etfw

Withers, T. (2018). Thunder thump Cavs 148-124, keep LeBron shy of 30,000 points. Associated Press. https://apnews.com/article/324e080e96f248128fdb76393d68d6d3

Wojnarowski, A. (2018, January 22). Sources: Kevin Love takes heat from Cavs over illness, absence. https://www.espn.com/nba/story/_/id/22184066/kevin-love-target-ire-cleveland-cavaliers-meeting

3

Key Media Moment #3: Naomi Osaka

"Each of us is a human being and subject to feelings and emotions."

On May 26, 2021, in the build-up to the French Open, tennis champion Naomi Osaka shared a statement with her one million followers on Twitter. Starting with a heart emoji and well-wishes, she declared she would do no press conferences or interviews during Roland-Garros, the world's premier clay court tournament held in Paris—one of the four comprising tennis' Grand Slam. "I've often felt that people have no regard for athletes' mental health and this rings very true whenever I see a press conference or partake in one," she wrote (Osaka, 2021a).

Athletes are often required to answer questions that "bring doubt into our minds and I'm just not going to subject myself to people that doubt me" the then-reigning United States and Australian Open champion wrote. Osaka, 23, recalled athletes breaking down in tears during press conferences, describing the treatment as "kicking a person while they're down."

Tennis is a game of shifting surfaces. Each court alters one's style and paths to victory. Osaka was a hardcourt master, winning her four Grand Slam titles on that surface. Other surfaces seemed much more foreign to her, as she struggled equally on the fast grass of Wimbledon and the slow-paced clay of Roland-Garros. Osaka did not play in the 2020 French Open because of an injured hamstring. However, the press conference following her third round defeat against Katerina Siniakova in 2019 is illustrative of the type questioning tennis players encounter: "Naomi, you don't seem like you've particularly enjoyed this tournament," one reporter asked. "Is that just the pressure of having the No. 1 next to your name or has there been something else?" "Um," Osaka responded, as camera shutters clicked. "I just feel like there's been a weight on me, kind of...yeah, it hasn't been the happiest of times..."

A second reporter asked what could help lift the weight off her shoulders, outside of the journalists peppering her with questions.

Osaka laughed, and then she explained that losing the tournament could be the best thing for her, because it reiterated for her the challenge of winning. If it was easy, she reminded herself, then anyone could do it. She needed to train hard and put herself in the position to win.

She added, "but for now, I'm peacing out of this tournament. I'm going home, like bye, I'm sorry I'm not going to miss you guys." She and the reporters laughed.

It looked like she would not be seeing them in 2021, either. The Grand Slam represents the pinnacle of international tennis competition, featuring four competitions: the Australian Open, French Open, Wimbledon, and U.S. Open. Each tournament's rulebook requires players to attend post-match news conferences unless they are physically injured or unable to appear. The obligation comes in addition to the media attention preceding the tournament, the cameras clicking as competitors transition from streetcar to court, the fans snapping selfies and reaching out to touch their hero athletes from the stands. An athlete who fails to show for the presser can be fined up to $20,000 for each failed appearance. Osaka acknowledged she would be fined for missing the press conferences at Roland-Garros in 2021, and was willing to live with that consequence; she hoped the fines she ultimately paid would go toward a mental health charity. She challenged French Open organizers and professional tennis in her social media post (Osaka, 2021a):

> If the organizations think that they can just keep saying, 'do press or you're gonna be fined,' and continue to ignore the mental health of the athletes that are the centerpiece of their cooperation, then I just gotta laugh.

Her stance drew swift condemnation from tennis organizations and even fellow players, who described press conferences as part of their professional responsibilities (e.g., Young, 2021). Meanwhile, the entire episode embodied the duality of the relationship between mass media and elite athletes. Media attention can help launch careers, lock down prosperous contracts, advertise political causes, lead to endorsement deals, and carry other perks. At the same time, the attention can erode privacy and increase stress, feeding negative outcomes related to mental health.

Talent obviously matters in professional competition, but international attention helps promote and cement an athlete's legacy. "Without the press, probably we will not be the athletes that we are today," 13-time French Open champion Rafael Nadal said in the wake of Osaka's protest (Young, 2021, para. 2). "We aren't going to have the recognition that we have around the world, and we will not be that popular, no?" Indeed, Osaka was and is the highest-paid female athlete in the world, making $57 million in 2021 primarily through sponsorship deals with Nike, Luis Vuitton, and other corporations (Blasi, 2022). She also has an amplified platform for advocating social justice causes, including her work related to Black Lives Matter, anti-Asian prejudice, and the COVID-19 pandemic.

However, celebrity also translates into increased personal and professional pressure for Osaka and other elite athletes. The curtain often ends up stripped away from an elite athlete's private life, as the tabloid press advertises athletes' romantic lives and other personal details. Professionally, the attention means Osaka and other athletes must perform in public and, at times, help reporters critique and deconstruct the shortcomings within the day's performance. For people who judge themselves based on winning, the dissection is inherently frustrating (to say the least). The performance, meanwhile, can be two-fold: winning and losing competitions on the court, but also playing the role that managers, endorsement partners, media, and fans expect. Like Michael Phelps, Osaka has described feeling like two people: her true self, and then a public persona in which she is expected to be quiet and nice. The image runs contrary to her protests for mental health and Black Lives Matter, which she advocated by wearing a different pandemic mask each day of the U.S. Open that bore the name of a Black person killed by police.

The tennis champion's mental health disclosure uniquely captures the darker side of the relationship between elite athletes and the mass media. Osaka sought to avoid the mental anguish of enduring another press conference. In doing so, the spotlight of the international press shone exponentially brighter. By seeking to protect her mental health, Osaka ultimately faced a decision to publicly share her mental health or risk being misunderstood.

"This isn't a situation I ever imagined..."

The reservations Osaka expressed about press conferences are often misinterpreted as an all-or-nothing confrontation between elite athlete and the journalists who cover her. Such an interpretation is oversimplification. Osaka estimates she granted more interviews with reporters than her older contemporaries during her career, in which she rose to fame as a teenager by defeating her idols with superb skills and a serve that registered a blistering 124 miles per hour. Osaka describes herself as an aggressive baseline player, the person who dictates the direction of the match, as opposed to a counter-puncher, one who rolls with the competition's shots until a moment for striking presents itself. In 2018, she defeated Serena Williams in the U.S. Open to become the first Japanese player to win a Grand Slam singles title, fulfilling a "Bucket List" ambition from the time she was a child training for eight hours a day on public courts. Since that contest, she won a singles title in four consecutive years, and in 2021 she became the first tennis player to light the Olympic cauldron to signal the beginning of the Summer Games. She has also experienced intense pressure, including a personal ambition to be the best player in the world, and, as her agent admits in the 2021 documentary *Naomi Osaka* on Netflix, pressure from family, friends, sponsors, coaches, and over one million people on social media. She also shoulders pressure to be a role model for her gender and nationality—her mother is Japanese, while her father is Haitian.

In news conferences, she often smiles, demonstrates rapport with reporters, and appears pensive, and frank, a direct attitude she attributes to being homeschooled alongside her sister, Mari, who also played professional tennis. In addition to endorsements, her advocacy for social justice issues such as Black Lives Matter has earned her recognition as one of the 2020 *Sports Illustrated* sportspersons of the year and *Time* magazine's list of 100 most influential people in the world. Part of her advocacy includes writing an essay against police brutality for *Esquire* magazine, and her media appearances even include a featured role in a manga series published in Japan. To put it mildly, the mass media are ever-present in Osaka's career.

Therefore, her demand to skip post-match press conferences, accompanied by an explanation, should not be conflated as an overall attitude toward the media. Osaka described her intentions as a method of protecting her mental health instead of being peppered with negatively phrased questions about her shortcomings in the match. Her experience is common among professional athletes; YouTube has collections of poorly phrased and insulting questions from press conferences for tennis and other professional sports, and the Hidden Game of Tennis kept a running tab of "Dumb U.S. Open Press Conference questions" asked of Osaka. In "Osaka Edition, Part III," from 2017, the following back-and-forth appeared:

> Reporter: Time and again, you seem so open, so fun-loving, so straightforward, sort of American-type traits, I think.
> Osaka: Oh.
> Reporter. Yet you say you feel like you're Japanese in spirit or your traits are Japanese.

The HGOT moderator quips, "I'm regretting numbering these, as the dumb questions are pouring in now" (HGOT, 2017).

Four years before the French Open fiasco, when Osaka was still in her teens, *USA Today* featured a story headlined "Tennis player handles 'stupid question' perfectly" in which writer Adi Joseph described an interaction between Osaka—a "wonderfully talented" person who "may well be one of the sport's next great players"—and a reporter (Joseph, 2017, para. 1).

> Reporter: Stupid question. Why did you win today?
> Osaka: I didn't win today.

Much like Olympic gymnast Simone Biles, Osaka experienced pressure to disclose her mental health to the general public after journalists, fans, and others demanded an answer to "Why?" At times, elite athletes choose when to disclose personal experience with mental illness without formal outside pressure. At other times, teams, coaches, and authority figures strip the athlete of the power to determine what they will disclose, how, and with whom. Osaka encountered a combination: She could determine whether to disclose, but the decision was made urgent by pressure from the international tennis world, French Open organizers, fans on social media, journalists, and thousands of others offering up unsolicited pontifications about her rationale. To not comment on why she would be skipping press conferences would be delaying the inevitable, all while ceding autonomy on how to shape and understand the story.

Five days after saying she would do no interviews, Osaka again used social media to bypass journalists and reach out directly to fans. She announced she would be formally withdrawing from the tournament to avoid being a distraction, describing the situation as one she "never imagined or intended." Osaka made the announcement before the second round of the tournament—she had already won her first-round match.

"More importantly I would never trivialize mental health or use the term lightly," she said. "The truth is that I have suffered long bouts of depression since the U.S. Open in 2018 and I have had a really hard time coping with that."

Osaka described herself as a "natural introvert," explaining that she experiences "huge waves of anxiety" before speaking to the world's media. "I get really nervous and find it stressful," she wrote.

Looking back, her admission did not represent the first time Osaka spoke about mental health (Baer, 2021). In 2018, after winning her first Grand Slam title at the U.S. Open, she spoke to *Teen Vogue* about the ease with which elite athletes can become depressed. "Usually, if you play sports, you think that one match or one game is very important, and when you lose it, you think your whole world is over" (Bauer, para. 11). Without hindsight, the earlier comments could be construed as figures of speech, as one might call an experience depressing but simply mean deeply saddening. That was not the case, it turned out. With her disclosure on Instagram and the controversy swirling the French Open, Osaka became a face of mental health in athletics. She took on the role, albeit hesitantly.

Two months after her Instagram post, Osaka wrote an essay for *Time* magazine about her experience with depression. She appeared on the cover in a black-and-white photo, staring at the camera, accompanied by the phrase, "It's OK not to be OK." She described learning two important lessons during the French Open. First, you cannot please everyone. Second, we are all affected by mental illness through personal experience or the trials of someone we know.

In the article, Osaka explained that she has an excellent relationship with many journalists and the press, in general, but she found press conferences problematic at times and the general formatting out-of-date. She acknowledged the off-the-court responsibilities that accompany playing professional tennis, yet also wondered: "Perhaps we should give athletes the right to take a mental break from media scrutiny on a rare occasion without being subject to strict sanctions" (para. 12).

Most professions would not require an employee to divulge personal symptoms to employers, she wrote, but she felt pressure to share "frankly because the press and the tournament did not believe me" (para 15). "I do not wish that on anyone and hope that we can enact measures to protect athletes," she wrote, "I also do not want to have to engage in a scrutiny of my personal medical history ever again."

Describing herself as a "natural introvert," Osaka said she felt uncomfortable suddenly becoming a spokesperson for athlete mental health. Still, she wrote, "I do hope that people can relate and understand it's OK to not be OK, and it's OK to talk about it. There are people who can help, and there is usually light at the end of any tunnel."

Osaka returned to competition for the Australian Open in 2022. She was knocked out of the tournament by an unranked American tennis player. During the press conference that followed—her first since the controversy—Osaka said the first thing she would do when she returned home would be to delete Twitter and Instagram—at least for a couple of weeks. Again, she was illustrating the duality of the athlete/media relationship. "I'm not God," she explained. "I can't win every match" (Sutelan, 2022, para. 3).

The idea emerged again during a news conference the previous August, when a reporter from the *Cincinnati Inquirer* asked Osaka, "You're not crazy about dealing with us, especially in this format, yet you have a lot of outside interests that are served by having a media platform? I guess my question is how do you balance the two? And also, do you have anything you'd like to share with us about what you did say to Simone Biles?"

"Um, when you say that I'm not crazy about dealing with you guys, what does that refer to?" she asked.

"Well, you said that you don't especially like the press conference format, yet that seems to be the most widely used means of communicating to the media and through the media to the public."

"I would say that the occasion—like when - to do the press conference is the most difficult, but." She paused for 20 seconds before a moderator interrupted, saying they could move to the next question. Osaka stopped the moderator and said, "No, I'm actually very interested in that point of view."

After asking for the question to be repeated, she explained:

> I can't really speak for everybody. I can only speak for myself, but ever since I was younger, I've had a lot of media interests on me and I think it's because of my background as well as how I play. In the first place I'm a tennis player and that's a lot of why people are interested in me. I would say that in that regards I'm quite different than a lot of people and I can't really help that there are some things that I tweet or some things that I say that create a lot of news articles. I know that it's because I've won a couple Grand Slams and I've gotten to do a lot of press conferences that these things happen. But I would also say that I am not really sure how to balance. I'm figuring it out at the same time as you are.

As the press conference wore on, she started to wipe away tears. She bowed her head so her visor blocked the view of the cameras. A reporter asked about her training for the Summer Hard Court Swing and her tweet about "what's going on in Haiti." A 7.2 magnitude earthquake had killed more than 2,200 people in Haiti, destroying 137,000 buildings and representing the worst national disaster of 2021. Osaka's father is from the Caribbean country, and in the *Netflix* documentary, Osaka visited the country with her family.

"Sorry," the reporter said.

"No, you're super good," Osaka responded, fighting back tears.

The moderator stopped the press conference.

"She's an example I would show my children."

Athletes such as Michael Phelps, Kevin Love, and DeMar DeRozan encountered primarily positive responses when they publicly shared experience with depression. The response was notably mixed when it came to Naomi Osaka, in a way mirroring the public response to Simone Biles. A writer for the *Telegraph* in England described Osaka as demonstrating "diva behavior" (Hassan, 2021, para. 2). A right-wing television host cited the behavior of Prince Harry and his American wife, Meghan Markle, writing that Osaka had followed "the Meghan and Harry playbook of wanting their press cake and eating it" (para. 3).

The New York Times described fans in Japan as offering support after the French Open. But that script flipped when Osaka fell short of securing Olympic gold for the country in the Tokyo Games. The *Times* described critics as "pouncing" and Osaka as taking "a drubbing" (Rich, 2021, para. 1). On Japanese social media, people questioned whether Osaka should represent the country (given her upbringing in the U.S.) and used her mental health disclosure as ammo for personal attacks.

An argument could be made that the responses to Osaka and Biles were swayed by the circumstances. Biles was actively competing in the Olympics, an event in which the limited number of competitive slots leaves other outstanding athletes unable to compete. Osaka was bucking long-standing tradition by removing herself from press conferences. Given the inherent conflict, it is understandable each decision would elicit praise and condemnation. Still, the circumstances also raise questions concerning gender, race, and nationality. Indeed, an Olympics advisor told *The New York Times* that Osaka encountered negative comments that were "exaggerated because of the gender issue, her being a woman" (Rich, 2021, para. 19). In the *Netflix* documentary, Osaka describes being shunned by African Americans when she chose to compete for Japan (rather than the U.S.) in the Tokyo Olympics. In Japan, people wondered whether she should truly represent the country because of her lack of fluency in the Japanese language.

Gender stereotypes perpetuate notions of women being weaker than men, and the world of elite sports amplifies sexist lines of thinking. To illustrate, Osaka lit the Olympic torch at the 2020 Summer Games in Tokyo, an important moment for the native of Japan. At the same Games, though, the male organizing committee president joked about women speaking too long in meetings. Michaela Kilgallen and a team at Relative Insight used its language processing technology to examine how male and female journalists covered Osaka's decision to step away from press conferences. Female journalists pushed for change in relation to the treatment of mental health in sport, using action-oriented words such as *prioritize, sacrifice, dedicate*. Meanwhile, male journalists were more inclined than female peers to use terms such as *shocked* and *stunned*. Tumaini Carayol, a sportswriter for *The Guardian*, called the French Open response to Osaka "a shameful moment," writing that her decision "was received with a clear lack of empathy from many quarters" Carayol added (2021, para. 4):

> For some players, their thoughts and discomfort in the press room follow them home and it is logical that it can affect their mental health. Osaka is also a black and Asian woman charged with fielding questions to an audience of majority white men, a dynamic that has led to numerous uncomfortable questions over the years.

Other media personalities—whose business models depend on generating controversy—accused Osaka of being a hypocrite for pulling out of the French Open but appearing on the covers of magazines such as *Sports Illustrated* and *Vogue*. Osaka responded to one critic, Megyn Kelly, via social media, saying a journalist would understand the lead time for magazines and the fact she shot the magazine covers the preceding year (Cooper, 2021). The critic responded that she guessed Osaka was "only tough on the courts." It should be noted that Kelly has been called "racist and ignorant" by coworkers and lost her poorly-rated NBC show after questioning the problem with White people wearing Blackface on Halloween (Koblin & Grynbaum, 2018).

Contrasting the reaction from tennis officials, celebrities and athletes offered Osaka support and encouragement after her decision (and disclosure; Thompson, 2021). American Coco Gauff, another tennis star, told Osaka to stay strong, saying she admired her vulnerability. Osaka had offered Gauff similar encouragement and invited the teenager to do a joint interview after the superstars met in competition and the Osaka emerged the victor. Viola Davis, the Oscar-winning actress, tweeted, "As one who also deals with social anxiety, I admire your courage and stand in solidarity with you." The singer Pink used social media to tell fans she applauded Osaka for putting her health first. "She's an example I would show my children," Pink wrote. "You can work hard to master your craft, but you do it on your own terms, and screw anyone if they don't get it." Tennis player Martina Navratilova wrote on Twitter that, "As athletes we are taught to take care of our body, and perhaps the mental and emotional aspect gets short shrift. This is about more than doing or not doing a press conference."

Throughout interviews, elite athletes have described the need to be recognized as more than competitors—as humans. Kevin Love discussed the happiness he felt after walking through a door for the first time as Kevin Love human instead of Kevin Love NBA star. Michael Phelps described a comparable sensation when he realized he could shed the image of Golden Boy Olympian for the real Michael Phelps. Eric Deggans, a critic for National Public Radio, saw such an internal battle in the *Naomi Osaka* documentary. Deggans (2021, para. 8) described the documentary as "one of the best arguments yet for Osaka's decision earlier this year to step away from post-game press conferences to protect her mental health," adding: "Watching how intensely she worries about so much, revealing her thoughts through introspective monologues, it is easier to understand why she refused to participate in press conferences" (para. 9).

In her *Time* magazine essay, Osaka described the public reaction to her disclosure as enlightening. "It has become apparent to me that literally everyone either suffers from issues related to their mental health or knows someone who does," she wrote (para. 4). "I think we can almost universally agree that each of us is a human being and subject to feelings and emotions."

References

Baer, J. (2021). Naomi Osaka announces French Open media blackout, citing mental health concerns. *Yahoo Sports*. https://sports.yahoo.com/naomi-osaka-french-open-media-blackout-mental-health-tennis-233117050.html

Barnes, A. (2022). Naomi Osaka says she's deleting Twitter, Instagram after Australian Open exit. *The Hill*. https://thehill.com/changing-america/enrichment/arts-culture/590803-naomi-osaka-says-shes-deleting-twitter-instagram

Blasi, W. (2022). Naomi Osaka is No. 1 again with over $57 million in earnings. *MarketWatch*. https://www.marketwatch.com/story/the-10-highest-paid-female-athletes-naomi-osaka-is-no-1-again-with-over-57-million-in-earnings-last-year-11642184134

Carayol, T. (2021). French Open's response to Naomi Osaka is a shameful moment for tennis. *The Guardian*. https://www.theguardian.com/sport/2021/jun/01/french-open-hastened-naomi-osaka-exit-but-also-refused-tricky-questions-tennis

Cooper, S. (2021). Naomi Osaka clapped back after Megyn Kelly accused her of hypocrisy for her Vogue and Sports Illustrated cover shoots. *Insider*. https://www.insider.com/naomi-osaka-hit-back-megyn-kelly-criticism-media-appearances-2021-7

Deggans, E. (2021). Timely Naomi Osaka docuseries explores the inner emotional world of a champion. *National Public Radio*. https://www.npr.org/2021/07/16/1016511444/naomi-osaka-netflix-review-tennis-mental-health

Hidden Game of Tennis (2017). Dumb US Open Press Conference Questions - Osaka edition. https://www.usatoday.com/story/sports/ftw/2017/09/02/naomi-osaka-handled-the-stupidest-question-of-the-us-open-perfectly/105238816/

Joseph, A. (2017). Tennis player handles 'stupid question' perfectly. *USA Today*. https://www.usatoday.com/story/sports/ftw/2017/09/02/naomi-osaka-handled-the-stupidest-question-of-the-us-open-perfectly/105238816/

Osaka, N. (2021a). Hey everyone - Hope you're all doing well, I'm writing this to say I'm not going to do any press during Roland Garros. *Twitter*. https://twitter.com/naomiosaka/status/1397665030015959040

Osaka, N. (2021b). Hey everyone, this isn't a situation I ever imagined or intended when I posted a few days ago. *Instagram*. https://www.instagram.com/p/CPi9kJHJfxO/?hl=en

Osaka, N. (2021c). It's OK not to be OK. *Time Magazine*. https://time.com/6077128/naomi-osaka-essay-tokyo-olympics/

Rich, M. (2021). Critics pounce on Naomi Osaka after loss, denting Japan's claim to diversity. *The New York Times*. https://www.nytimes.com/2021/07/27/world/asia/naomi-osaka-olympics-loss.html

Sutelan, E. (2022, Jan. 21). Naomi Osaka loses to unseeded American in Australian Open: 'I'm not God.' *The Sporting News*. https://www.sportingnews.com/us/tennis/news/naomi-osaka-loses-australian-open-im-not-god/f4bfjgkb4itj1pk6lj65xfu0f

Thompson, E. (2021, June 4). Naomi Osaka exits French Open for mental health: Serena Williams and more celebs react. *US Weekly*. https://www.usmagazine.com/celebrity-news/pictures/naomi-osaka-exits-french-open-celebs-athletes-react/

Young, R. (2021). Rafael Nadal, others react to Naomi Osaka's French Open media blackout. *Yahoo!Sports*. https://sports.yahoo.com/rafael-nadal-others-react-to-naomi-osakas-french-open-media-blackout-221059950.html?guccounter=1

4

Key Media Moment #4: Simone Biles

"I don't think you realize how dangerous this is."

(Lewis, 2021, para. 1).

Many sports never have an athlete possessing a clear-cut "greatest of all-time" moniker. Men's basketball perpetually has a Michael Jordan vs. LeBron James debate. Soccer fans dispute athletic superiority within their own nation, pitting Mia Hamm against Abby Wambach and Michelle Akers—all before even considering their relative comparison to Brazil's Marta Vieira de Silva or England's Kellie Smith. Even the man credited with the quote for being "the greatest of all-time," Muhammad Ali, is frequently ranked below No. 1 in the greatest heavyweight boxers of all time.

However, Simone Biles was considered the greatest gymnast ever long before the Tokyo Summer Olympic Games in 2021. She already had four signature moves named after her. Imagine a gymnast saying they aspire to complete a "Biles" and not knowing which signature maneuver was being referenced. In floor exercise, there is even a distinction between the "Biles" (double layout with a half twist) and a "Biles II" (triple-twisting double-tucked salto backwards). That, by any measure, represents the epitome of athletic dominance.

The transcendent career arc of Biles was invariably altered during the Tokyo Olympic Games, even as she added a pair of medals to her already impressive ledger. On July 28, 2021, USA Gymnastics tweeted that Biles, regarded by many as the greatest Olympic gymnast ever, would be withdrawing from the team final of the Games, citing her need to "focus on her mental health" (Lewis, 2021, para. 2). Biles later clarified that she was suffering from a condition called the "twisties," a mental malady in which one's spatial awareness becomes off-kilter. In gymnastics, such a problem can be catastrophic given the acrobatics that are completed in mid-air within fractions of a second. Biles attempted to unpack the degree of physical harm that this mental state could create for an Olympic gymnast, educating a public that is generally less than fully literate about the inner workings of gymnastics that "I don't think you realize how dangerous this is" (Lewis, 2021, para. 1). As later explained by Park and Gregory (2022):

> Biles is all about control. Her life is about micro-managing every possible element—her diet, her training, her sleep—that goes into performing, so when the lights are brightest, and the stake are highest, little is left to chance. But for Biles, control isn't just about winning; it can be the difference between life and death (para. 2).

Having already competed in the team preliminaries—noticeably not as her dominant self—Biles' week-long respite ended with her competing in a single individual event final, earning bronze on the balance beam, the one gymnastic apparatus that did not require Biles to be in the air for a substantial portion of the time.

Media narratives regarding Biles were overwhelmingly positive, likely informed by the media moments that have been discussed in the immediately preceding chapters about Phelps, Love, and Osaka. The recognition that mental health in sporting contexts was, at a minimum, having a moment, was something that seemingly underscored virtually all of the coverage of Biles and her experiences in the Tokyo Olympics. Thompson et al. (2023) conducted a content analysis of media coverage surrounding Biles' mental health disclosure, finding that the most prevalent themes regarded the impact on her individual and team fortunes and legacies, her heroism, and, intriguingly, her gender. Moreover, Biles' gender was frequently paired with discussions of her African-American heritage when heroism themes emerged. American sources were uniquely focused on the racial component, with international news sources diminishing that potential framing of the story.

Still, such a quantitative analysis only tells part of the Biles story. The themes that emerge when qualitatively focusing on how media discussed Biles' disclosure dovetail considerably, yet reveal new insights. Thus, this chapter will focus on some of those storytelling choices.

Understanding the Timeline

Before one can understand how media told the story, one must first comprehend the daily nature of it. In stark contrast to an athlete experiencing a physical injury that typically is accompanied by a timeline for recovery, mental health related maladies have no fixed timeline. Given the pressing timeline of an Olympics that would only have gymnastics medals awarded in the next weeks' time period (and then not again until 2024), the media gaze weighed heavily on Biles' potential recovery and return. A physical injury typically becomes a one-day story (Athlete X has suffered an injury Y with timeframe for return Z); a mental health-related absence becomes a daily check-in for any news and information, problematically extending the media spotlight on an athlete that almost always seeks privacy.

Thus, one should understand the timeline in which the Biles Tokyo Olympic experience, such as it was, unfolded. Nine key dates can illuminate such a context:

1. July 22: At a podium practice, Biles appears ready for all-around dominance at an Olympics again. She lands her trademark Yurchenko double pike vault, a choice that was widely seen as unnecessary for her to still secure gold in the event.
2. July 25: At team preliminary qualifications, Biles makes several uncharacteristic mistakes while still qualifying for the finals in all four individual apparatus competitions as well as the team and individual all-around. Even clearly at less than optimal levels, Biles appears to be on a path to securing six more medals.
3. July 27: Biles withdraws from the team final, citing mental health concerns. Her team—previously favored to earn gold—instead wins silver in a final lacking the sport's "greatest of all time."
4. July 28: Biles withdraws from the next night's all-around competition (teammate Suni Lee ultimately earns a gold in Biles' absence).
5. July 30: Biles utilizes social media in an attempt to clarify what her issue is (the "twisties") along with explanation on how such a spatial block can dramatically hinder gymnastic performance.
6. July 31: Biles withdraws from the finals on vault and uneven bars that were set to be contested Aug. 1.

7. Aug. 1: Biles withdraws from the finals in the floor exercise that was set to be contested on Aug. 3, leading to postulation that an appearance on the balance beam final (also on Aug. 3) was still a possibility.
8. Aug. 2: USA Gymnastics affirms that Biles compete on the balance beam.
9. Aug. 3: Biles earns bronze on the balance beam in a less than characteristic performance that she nevertheless calls the "most meaningful" of her career (Fieldstadt, 2021).

The compressed time period yielded heightened focus on Biles and the public discussion pertaining to mental health. In contrast to a Kevin Love (who revealed his panic attacks two months before the NBA playoffs would begin) or Naomi Osaka (whose withdrawals from the French Open and Wimbledon tabled the discussion to some degree), Simone Biles became Story A for what is always an enveloping and glaring Olympic media spotlight. By the end of the year, Biles was promisingly reporting that the entire experience had a silver lining as she could say "I know who I am now" (Finan, 2021, para. 1).

However, media coverage largely did not have that sense of perspective. As stalwart sports columnist Christine Brennan once observed about Olympic media: "You go from an ember to a wildfire in a very short amount of time. And then often you cool back down to that ember status and move on" (Billings, Moscowitz, & Yang, 2016, p. 48). The remainder of this chapter will focus on the primary themes one can extract from that wildfire Brennan references, noting that Biles was primarily discussed in terms of: (a) justifiable withdrawals, (b) unjustifiable abandonment, (c) celebrity support, and (d) ties to the broader "OK not to be OK" movement.

Justifiable Exit

When compared to a physical injury that is often accompanied with a timeline in the prognosis, mental health injuries adopt more nebulous temporal areas. Even beyond this, Biles presented a unique quandary for media to report, as most likely would have agreed that panic attacks or suicidal inclinations would warrant withdrawal. However, because Biles' malady came with an unfamiliar name (the "twisties"), leaving reporters to educate themselves about what the "twisties" constituted and then convey that to a lay audience. When they did become familiar with it, their conclusion was that Biles' withdrawal seemed exceedingly justified. As Stephanie Gosk (2021) explained on NBC News: "With the awe inspiring thrill of gymnastics also comes serious risks. The sport can be dangerous, especially if you are not one hundred percent mentally focused, which can lead to catastrophic injuries."

Christine Brennan was even more direct in her account relayed on CNN's program with host Wolf Blitzer (2021), employing a useful comparison for audiences to comprehend:

> If you're a basketball player, you can kind of go through the motions and at the very at least we hope you not injured yourself seriously. What Simone Biles, the greatest of all time, does in those routines [is a] high flying, high-wire act. Those twists and turns in the air could be very dangerous if her mind is not into this (Blitzer et al., 2021).

Brennan helped to explain that while the "twisties" were a health hazard for any gymnast, they were particularly impeding for Biles, who twists, turns, and flies in the air in larger times and degrees than any of her predecessors. Thus, reporters not only were able to identify harm, but a unique and elevated degree of harm inflicted upon Simone Biles.

Bolstering such claims was the conception that the "twisties" disorient a gymnast when in the air; thus, Biles' ultimate choice to participate in the balance beam apparatus final justified claims that the disorientation was real. By illustrating that the beam required less time in the air than other events, reporters explained how one could feel adequate enough to compete within one discipline and not another.

Even beyond the explanation of Biles' unique malady, there was also a strain of justification because of the unique stressors imparted by both (a) the pandemic and (b) Biles' unique past history. Regarding the former, the notion that the Games were contested in the shadow of a pandemic led to schisms in regard to many elements of society, certainly including mental health (see Billings, Wenner, & Hardin, 2022). As Lindstrom (2021, para. 5) explained: "The coronavirus has exacerbated mental health struggles, especially for teens and young adults. It is in no way shameful to speak up and seek help; in fact, it is extremely brave."

However, more serious elements of Biles' past as a survivor of sexual abuse were also imbued within the media conversations of her exit. Convicted rapist and former U.S. gymnastics team doctor Larry Nassar had over 500 victims, but only one of them was still actively competing in Tokyo: Simone Biles. Thus, the compounded burden of court testimony, the pandemic, and being considered the greatest of all-time became a narrative that not only legitimized her exit, but underscored that the ethical recourse for journalists seeking a story was to leave Biles alone to recover on her own timeline. Former gymnast Andrea Orris offered in a statement that she believed Simone Biles "has endured more trauma by the age of 24 than most people will ever go through in a lifetime" (Anderson & Lankston, 2021, para. 1.) The seeming immutability of such an argument largely quelled the majority of potential criticism that could have been levied toward Biles.

Abandonment

Of course, in a modern era of splintering and niche media, not all potential critics of Biles' decision were stifled. Conservative talk show host Charlie Kirk labeled Biles a sociopath and a shame to the country (Beer, 2021, para. 1). Meanwhile, notorious and controversial Piers Morgan (2021) authored an op-ed article in the *London Daily Mail*. The title?: "Sorry Simone Biles, but there's nothing heroic or brave about quitting because you're not having 'fun': You let down your teammates, your fans, and your country" (para. 1).

In an era in which virtually anything is debatable no matter how one-sided an argument should be, such vitriolic takes seemingly were inevitable. So too were the defenders, which often included the athletes that were argued to be harmed by Biles' decision. Teammate Jordan Chiles affirmed unity within the team in advancing that "She is Simone for a reason…She is not a quitter. You will never see Simone just go out there and not do what she knows she can do" (Butler, 2021, para. 1-2).

Still, the verbiage utilized in this theme was telling, with detractors arguing that Biles abandoned her teammates, "two of whom were forced to take her place in the three other events at the last minute" (Anderson & Lankston, 2021, para. 2). In contrast, Robach (2021) used the phrasing of "stepped in" to describe the two American athletes inserted into Biles' emptied slots in the event finals. Such terms still likely mitigated some actual feelings of the situation; media reports did not wish to show teammates capitalizing on Biles' exit. Nevertheless, one must presume that MyKayla Skinner was fairly pleased to "step in" and earn a silver medal on the vault when she otherwise would not have qualified to compete in the finals until Simone Biles withdrew.

In the end, teammates helped to advance a message of comradery (Jordan Chiles posted on Instagram that they won silver medals together). This was largely embraced by the media in capturing the notion that "it is so beautiful to see how this team supports one another, and really Simone's showing us what strength truly is" (Robach, 2021). As for the criticism from the overly vocal minority, strong voices like former ESPN anchor and host Jemele Hill largely subdued those sentiments. Hill argued that "walking away from competition now wasn't an indication that Biles was weak. It was an indication that she was strong enough to admit that she couldn't push through the problems she was facing" (Hill, 2021, para. 7).

Celebrity Support

While columnists such as Jemele Hill are expected to weigh in on contemporary topics of import, many reporters must advance information through the lens of objectivity. As has been the case in other progressive topics focusing on inclusion, acceptance, or support, one way a reporter can claim objectivity while also shifting frames to champion an athlete's perspective involves using other celebrity words of support (see Billings et al., 2015). Social media now facilitates this type of journalism to an unparalleled degree and was used as a primary theme to advance nearly uniformly positive positions about Biles' decision.

Unsurprisingly, many of the forms of celebrity support advanced in articles about Biles' withdrawal came from the sports world. The most frequently-mentioned voice in this regard was swimmer and mental health advocate Michael Phelps, seemingly at least in part because his comments were not limited to 280 characters on Twitter but, instead, could be conveyed over several minutes during NBC's nightly Olympic broadcasts. However, other athletes were utilized in many forms. While the majority of these athletes that were quoted were female (e.g., tennis legend Billie Jean King, gymnast and former teammates Aly Raisman and Laurie Hernandez, tennis player Coco Gauff), many other athletes and sports figures were also inserted into such articles (Olympic skater Adam Rippon, soccer star Landon Donovan, NFL quarterback Dak Prescott). Each were nuanced; each ultimately thanked and praised Biles for her decision.

Interestingly, the celebrity support did not stop there, though. People within Hollywood (actresses Beth Behrs and Uzo Aduba, media personality Andy Cohen, and morning news host Hoda Kotb) offered praise in the media as well. These figures outside of sport seemed to disproportionately have their full social media posts cited. For instance, former First Lady Michelle Obama tweeted: "Am I good enough? Yes, I am. The mantra I practice daily. @Simone_Biles, we are proud of you and we are rooting for you. Congratulations on the silver medal, Team @USA!"

Meanwhile, comedian Chelsea Handler spoke to issues beyond the competition: "@Simone_Biles drew a boundary for herself and her health on the world stage. This is real superhuman strength, setting an example for all of us."

However, the most-often cited quote of celebrity support came from pop star Justin Bieber, who compared Biles' decision to his prior decision to prematurely end a tour in 2017. He offered to his over 200 million Instagram followers: "Nobody will ever understand the pressures you face! I know we don't know each other but I'm so proud of the decision to withdraw" (Anderson & Lankston, 2021, para. 1).

Each reverberation bolstered the legitimacy of Biles' decision, while also cementing that the world was experiencing a collective moment regarding mental health.

Mental Health Advocacy: This Is the Moment

These celebrity sentiments fed into the final (and most all-encompassing) theme: the notion that mental health advocacy is bigger than Simone Biles, the Olympics, or sport itself. Biles may not have been as successful as was anticipated in terms of adding to her Olympic medal pile, but in terms of getting others to speak about mental health, she again appeared to be earning gold. As Graves (2021, para. 1-2) contended, "Simone Biles didn't plan for her second Olympics to become a flashpoint in the evolving conversation about the role proper mental health plays in all levels of sports. Then again, she's hardly complaining. If anything, she's leaning into it."

USA Today's Nancy Armour (2021) offered an even wider perspective:

> Though some athletes had already started opening up about the importance of mental health and the intense pressure they're under—Michael Phelps has made this his mission in retirement—Biles' decision to withdraw from the Olympics elevated the conversation. Athletes in all sports expressed their support for her while sharing their own experiences, and general society began discussing with more seriousness the importance of it being OK to not be OK (para. 8).

Connections to previous athletes—including the three media moments already encapsulated in this book for Phelps, Love, and Osaka—were often made with a sense that society was finally understanding the importance of embracing and talking about mental health. The legitimacy of the issue now seemed abundantly clear, showing that this collection of athletes had collectively accomplished a larger aim. "Their outspoken candor has made refreshingly inarguable the short-hand formula that says: mental health = health. The two are inseparable." (Malone et al., 2021, para. 2).

Reverberations were argued to range from the micro to macro levels. For instance, within Biles' chosen sport, Gleeson (2021) believed that "particularly at the youth level, Biles has planted a seed of courage in a culture that's long had a dangerous definition of mental toughness" (para. 13).

Within sport writ large, the insertion of mental elements of health and performance were now argued to be fully substantiated:

> One of the world's top athletes revised the language of greatness, positioning it as something to be tended to and mindfully maintained, not drawn on ad nauseam. Her most telling words rejected the false dichotomy between personal well-being and professional excellence, instead pointing to the former as a precondition of the latter. Biles has spoken in the run-up to the Olympics about the pressures of fame, the isolation of these particular Games, and her experiences in therapy. Yesterday, Biles said she felt 'lost in the air' [and that] "'I tried to go out here and have fun but once I came out here I was like, 'No, mental's not there,'" (O'Connell, 2021, para. 2).

The ramifications beyond the sports world seemed to be particularly resonant amongst college newspapers, many of whom wrote effusively to praise Biles and speak to larger struggles their age demographic was/is facing. McDonald (2021) believed that Simone Biles "challenged our perception of what an Olympic role model should be" (para. 1), while Duregger (2021) made a case for Biles' patriotism:

> So, no, Biles is neither weak nor unpatriotic. She is quite the opposite. She was strong enough to prioritize her mental health so that she did not jeopardize her physical health later on. By doing so, she avoided further injury…She was patriotic enough to leave the competition to the rest of her team, who ended up earning a silver medal (para. 5)

Brennen (2021) advanced an argument based on the "bravery of quitting" (para. 1) all while connecting back to an Olympic moment from 25 years earlier that likely should not have been embraced in the manner it was:

> Growing up, I was inspired by the story of Kerri Strug, who at the women's team final in the 1996 Olympics severely sprained her ankle on her first attempt at the vault, but completed her second vault anyway, landing on one foot before needing to be carried off the mat. Looking back at this event through a new lens, this teenager should not have been encouraged to risk her long-term health in exchange for a gold medal. However, she did not have much of a choice with the world watching and famous gymnastics coach Bela Karolyi insisting 'you can do it' (para. 4).

In advancing such narratives, the fusion of the physical and mental sides of health seemingly are intertwined in ways that were not frequently advanced in previous years. Still, some articles acknowledged that while awareness may be the first step, true actions to improve mental health still must be enacted. As advanced in a *Business Insider* editorial:

> Biles is right: Everyone should have the right to quit harmful situations that are detrimental to their mental health. But no matter how many infographics I see on Instagram that tell me my mental health is the most important thing in my life, the rhetorical affirmation that I deserve to be well won't change my current material inability to slow down and get the treatment I deserve. We need concrete ways to care for ourselves and our minds, and that requires major structural changes in our places of work and in how we make our money ("Simone Biles deserves all the praise for prioritizing her mental health", 2021, para. 17).

The Value (and Limitations) of Media Moments

Thus, even with each of these landmark media moments along with dozens of moments that likely were of measurable influence to demonstrable swaths of people, there are nevertheless limits to what athlete disclosures can do. When athletes are singularly focused on near-impossible pursuits, the tunnel vision is likely both the facilitator of that dream and harbinger of mental health imbalances to come. When athletes step aside to focus on their own mental health, time and events do not stand still. When Naomi Osaka withdrew from Wimbledon, Ashleigh Barty emerged victorious, cementing her world No. 1 status that Osaka previously enjoyed; when Biles withdrew from competition, Sunisa Lee stepped into the void and emerged with a hard-earned gold medal.

Finding ways to helpfully and organically infuse the mental with the physical remains elusive, with no media moment likely to singularly enact wholesale change to systems that have evolved over many decades and, in some cases, centuries. Nevertheless, each media moment built on the prior: Phelps informed Love who informed Osaka who informed Biles. In the process, an American public was informed as well. By the time Biles had explained her decision, there was little question that larger deliberations (in the sports world and beyond) would follow. As Rothschild (2021) postulated, "Biles sparked a bigger conversation about mental health than either Prince Harry and Meghan Markle's interview with Oprah or Naomi Osaka's withdrawal from the French Open—both of which generated significant international interest" (para. 3).

References

Anderson, N., & Lankston, C. (2021, July 28). 'Simone has endured more trauma than most will go through in a lifetime': Biles hints that sexual abuse by Larry Nassar is behind her mental health issues and withdrawal from the individual all-around as she retweets powerful message from fellow gymnast. *MailOnline.* https://advance-lexis.com.libdata.lib.ua.edu/api/document?collection=news&id=urn:contentItem:637N-G541-DY4H-K1R6-00000-00&context=1516831.

Armour, N. (2021, August 31). Biles says that it's OK to ask for help. *USA Today.* https://advance-lexis-com.libdata.lib.ua.edu/api/document?collection=news&id=urn:contentItem:63GX-JF61-DYRR-928F-00000-00&context=1516831.

Beer, T. (2021, July 29). I'm more than my accomplishments: Outpouring continues for Simone Biles as she acknowledges support. *Forbes.com.* https://advance-lexis.com.libdata.lib.ua.edu/api/document?collection=news&id=urn:contentItem:6383-X6R1-JBCM-F1TM-00000-00&context=1516831

Billings, A. C., Moscowitz, L. M., Rae, C., & Brown-Devlin, N. (2015). The art of coming out: Traditional and social media frames surrounding the NBA's Jason Collins. *Journalism & Mass Communication Quarterly, 92*(1), 142–160.

Billings, A. C., Moscowitz, L. M., & Yang, Y. (2016). Frames of the Olympic host: Media coverage of Russia's anti-gay legislation. In R. Lind (Ed.), *Race and gender in electronic media: Challenges and opportunities* (pp. 38–54). New York: Routledge.

Billings, A. C., Wenner, L. A., & Hardin, M. (Eds.). (2022). *American sport in the shadow of a pandemic: Communicative insights.* New York: Peter Lang.

Blitzer, W., Nobles, R., Ramsey, C., Coates, L., Gangel, J., Collins, K., Todd, B., & Brennan, C. (2021, July 27). Officers attacked at the Capitol testify at insurrection hearing; CDC urges masks in schools nationwide and indoors in COVID hot spots; Biden's infrastructure deal in peril, Dems push to wrap up talks; Interview With Sen. Dick Durbin (D-IL); Select committee shows never-before-seen video of January 6 attack; Simone Biles cites mental health struggles after pulling out of Olympic team gymnastics final. Aired 6-7p ET. *CNN.* https://

advance-lexis-com.libdata.lib.ua.edu/api/document?collection=news&id=urn:contentItem:637N-CX81- JB20-G2B0-00000-00&context=1516831.

Brennen, M. (2021, September 8). The bravery of quitting. *The Hawk: Saint Joseph's University.* https://advance-lexis-com.libdata.lib.ua.edu/api/document?collection=news&id=urn:contentItem:63JP-W421-DY7P-T23R 00000-00&context=1516831.

Butler, A. (2021, July 28). U.S. teammates relate to Simone Biles: 'She's not a quitter'. *United Press International.* https://advance-lexis-com.libdata.lib.ua.edu/api/document?collection=news&id=urn:contentItem:637R-8PP1-JBT2-310G00000-00&context=1516831.

Duregger, G. (2021, Sept. 21). DUREGGER: Prioritize your mental health - Simone Biles did. *Cavalier Daily: University of Virginia.* https://advance-lexis-com.libdata.lib.ua.edu/api/document?collection=news&id=urn:contentItem:63NF-V361-JBSN-3550-00000-00&context=1516831.

Fieldstadt, E. (Aug. 3, 2021). Simone Biles says Tokyo bronze means more than all her golds. *NBC News.* Retrieved at: https://www.nbcnews.com/news/olympics/simone-biles-says-tokyo-bronze-means-more-all-her-golds-n1275804

Finan, E. (2021, Dec. 1). For Simone Biles, the mental health journey is never over: 'But I know who I am now.' *People.* Retrieved at: https://people.com/sports/simone-biles-people-2021-person-of-the-year-mental-health/

Gleeson, S. (2021, August 19). Biles gives mental health courage to youth. *USA Today* https://advance-lexis-com.libdata.lib.ua.edu/api/document?collection=news&id=urn:contentItem:63DB-X531-JC8N-K1YN00000-00&context=1516831.

Graves, W. (2021, August 19). Biles: Mental health advocacy part of post-Olympic tour. *Associated Press International.* https://advance-lexis-com.libdata.lib.ua.edu/api/document?collection=news&id=urn:contentItem:63DC-WH91-DYMD-63GX00000-00&context=1516831.

Guthrie, S., Kotb, H., Gosk, S. (2021, July 28). Simone's decision overnight to now withdraw from the individual all-around final here in Tokyo. *NBC News.* https://advance-lexis-com.libdata.lib.ua.edu/api/document?collection=news&id=urn:contentItem:63K3-TVB1-JB20-G0M5-00000-00&context=1516831.

Hill, J. (2021, July 29, 2021). Simone Biles's critics don't understand this generation of athletes. *Atlantic Online.* https://advance-lexis.com.libdata.lib.ua.edu/api/document?collection=news&id=urn:contentItem:63K1-FM41-JCG7-V2CR-00000-00&context=1516831.

Lewis, S. (2021, July 30). Simone Biles opens up about withdrawal from Olympic competitions: 'I don't think you realize how dangerous this is'. *CBS News.* https://www.cbsnews.com/news/simone-biles-olympics-gymnastics-withdrawal-twisties/.

Lindstrom, S. (2021, Sept. 17). Not just Simone Biles, but Simone: "The GOAT" sets a new kind of example. *The Scarlet: Clark University.* https://advance-lexis-com.libdata.lib.ua.edu/api/document?collection=news&id=urn:contentItem:63MJ-P5M1- JBSN-32GD-00000-00&context=1516831.

Malone, P., & Associates (2021, August 4). Olympians offer golden insights on the importance of mental health for all. *Newstex Blogs JD Supra.* https://advance-lexis-com.libdata.lib.ua.edu/api/document?collection=news&id=urn:contentItem:6397-GHX1-F03R-N50X00000-00&context=1516831.

McDonald, C. (2021, August 8, 2021). MCDONALD: Simone Biles reaffirms GOAT status regardless of medal count. *The Hoya: Georgetown University*. https://advance-lexis-com.libdata.lib.ua.edu/api/document?collection=news&id=urn:contentItem:63B8-M6R1-JBSN-336Y-00000-00&context=1516831.

Morgan, P. (2021, July 28). Sorry Simone Biles, but there's nothing heroic or brave about quitting because you're not having 'fun': You let down your teammates, your fans, and your country. *London Daily Mail*. https://www.dailymail.co.uk/news/article-9835069/PIERS-MORGAN-Sorry-Simone-boast-GOAT-selfishly-quit.html

O'Connell, R. (2021, July 28). What Simone Biles understands about greatness. *Atlantic Online*. https://advancelexis-com.libdata.lib.ua.edu/api/document?collection=news&id=urn:contentItem:63K1-FM41-JCG7-V2C9-00000-00&context=1516831.

Park, A., & Gregory, S. (2022, Jan. 3). Athlete of the year: Simone Biles. *Time*, p. 74.

Robach, A. (2021, July 28). Simone Biles' stunning exit; gymnast withdraws to focus on mental health. *ABC News Transcript*. https://advance-lexis-com.libdata.lib.ua.edu/api/document?collection=news&id=urn:contentItem:639N-5R31-JC85-K2DR-00000-00&context=1516831.

Rothschild, N. (2021, August 4, 2021). Simone Biles' exit brings global attention to mental health. *Newstex Blogs Axios*. https://advance-lexis-com.libdata.lib.ua.edu/api/document?collection=news&id=urn:contentItem:6396-2VT1-JCMN-Y1BM-00000-00&context=1516831.

"Simone Biles deserves all the praise for prioritizing her mental health" (2021, July 30). Simone Biles deserves all the praise for prioritizing her mental health. And it's a good reminder that many Americans can't afford to take time off when they need it. *Business Insider US*. https://advance-lexis-com.libdata.lib.ua.edu/api/document?collection=news&id=urn:contentItem:6384-G8Y1-JBG6-50JK-00000-00&context=1516831.

Thompson, K., Carter, G., Lee, E., Alsharmani, T., & Billings, A. C. (2023, in press). 'We're human too': Media coverage of Simone Biles' mental health disclosure during the 2020 Tokyo Olympics. *Electronic News*. https://doi.org/10.1177%2F19312431221095207.

White, A. (2021, July 27). Hollywood rallies around Simone Biles following Olympics event withdrawal: 'Protect your peace.' *The Hollywood Reporter*. https://www.hollywoodreporter.com/news/general-news/hollywood-support-simone-biles-olympics-1234988848/

5

The Storytellers: Marking a Moment

"It's neither heroic nor is it something to be ashamed of. It's simply reality and athletes should be treated with respect, dignity, and understanding when discussing that reality."

— Bob Costas

Sports journalists and broadcasters are used to competing for a story; there's a reason why a "scoop" and "exclusive" have infiltrated even the general public's conscience. Nevertheless, the moment that was unfolding regarding mental health and sport was different from most other stories in many ways. First, of course, there were new competitors in the media space: the athletes themselves. From Kevin Love's first-person narrative in *The Players' Tribune* to Naomi Osaka's shaping of her mental health message via Instagram, media professionals now had to acknowledge that breaking a story was not always something a writer/reporter for a major media conglomerate could garner. Second, though, was that these stories lacked the typical sports story arc: athlete experiences obstacle, athlete attempts to overcome obstacle, journalist bears witness and assesses the degree to which the obstacle was overcome. This book has likely already made the mental health journey abundantly clear in that there is no finish line, but improvement and acknowledgments of meaningful turning points could still be documented. Finally, media storytellers could acknowledge that there was a "moment" going on in regard to mental health, yet it would be an impossible task to determine when such a moment would end—or even if the moment could instead become part of the infrastructure of future sports. Could mental health be subsumed in the larger continual assessment of physical health in sport?

To gauge a sense of how sports media storytellers interpreted and rendered the growing fountain of athlete mental health stories, four key interviews were conducted: (a) former *New York Times* journalist Karen Crouse, who told many of these stories—including, most tellingly, the details of Michael Phelps' journey, (b) legendary broadcaster Bob Costas, whose chronicling of stories can now be witnessed in his monthly HBO program, *Back on the Record with Bob Costas*, (c) *Time* magazine Senior Sports Correspondent Sean Gregory, who regularly wrote on mental health in sports, which culminated in the summer 2021 *Time* cover story written by Naomi Osaka herself, and (d) *USA Today*/CNN/ABC News/NPR veteran and award-winning reporter Christine Brennan, who wrote and discussed these issues, particularly those impacting the 2020 Tokyo Summer Olympics with Simone Biles.

Each of these four media thought leaders acknowledged that something was changing, but were reluctant to deem it a formal turning over of a new leaf for the sports world. As Karen Crouse contends, the stories journalists were telling were unquestionably improving, but "the nuances of mental illness are still being lost. There's no easy fix. You live with it day by day and do the best you can. It's never behind you." There was a recalcitrance to the sports world that each acknowledged needed to be challenged not only in the current mental health stories, but in the future ones as well. Sean Gregory explains that:

> It's been there as long as I can remember: you've got to be 'mentally tough', and there's a stigma around, not being 'mentally tough.' That implies some level of self-control, and these athletes were challenging that, saying 'you can't control these kinds of things.'

The inability of athletes to open up about any level of struggle for fear of being perceived as lesser is seemingly baked into the cake of each mental health story. Crouse asks any sports fan to "think of all the sporting mantras: *when the going gets tough, the tough get going; grit it out; no pain, no gain*" and then realize "that doesn't give people permission to be vulnerable."

Walking on Eggshells While Capturing a Moment

None of the journalists questioned that the stories being shared were important, nor did they push back upon the notion that the stories were significant in magnitude. Christine Brennan simply summarized that "there's no question this is a watershed moment for sports journalists covering the issue" and argued that the sheer number of athletes telling these stories underscored their gravity. "Each of these athletes have led us to very important conversations that we needed to go to as a society," Brennan explains, believing that "we need to be thankful that they did. They took us there in their own way."

A sense of victory in the desire to infuse mental health into sports stories seemed premature, though. As Bob Costas advanced: "It would be naive to say that the *culture* of all sports has embraced that same outlook, especially in the sports that tend to be more hyper-masculine." Still, each believe they could (and should) play a crucial role in advancing the cause of illuminating mental health into the sports celebrity stories. To be able to challenge the "sports heroes have it made" argument was something that the media could do better than the athletes themselves. Crouse explains how her life experience informed her desire to shed light on cracks in the invincibility narratives that were far too often assumed in sports culture:

> I was a walk-on swimmer at USC, training daily with Olympic gold medalists and world record holders and national champions. I quickly learned that these people who were projected as winning the life lottery, were so talented and gifted—and also were the most miserable people I've ever been around. I truly felt such empathy for them. I was obviously nowhere near as good as a lot of my teammates I learned that I was absolutely fine with that. If that's what it takes to be an elite athlete, I would prefer to be what I am.

Therefore, she explains, her "goal became to give athletes the breathing room to be themselves and not feel like they have to these plastic people, these cardboard figures." She found the space to tell such stories to be less crowed because "this type of writing was much less celebrated." Still, she could garner an audience interested in "demystifying elite sports by showing people how the sausage is made." At least for Crouse, this approach proved to be liberating. She explains what would become her philosophy at *The New York Times*: "I would go left when everyone else was going right. I would write the story that nobody else would write. I would talk to the people that nobody else would talk to."

Such stories are not easy to advance, particularly because the public has a difficult time believing them. Despite *Us Weekly* magazine's repeated mantra that "Stars: They're Just Like Us!", many sports fans cannot grasp that this is the case, particularly when they are well compensated for playing a sport fans love. Gregory explains the inherent friction:

> You have to fight that aspect that gets baked into these stories that they're millionaires and that millionaires athletes, of course, have the best lives. Most of the athletes know they have privilege, and know they're paid very well to do this stuff. That fight gets harder as the years progress. When I was a kid, it was 'these athletes make *thousands* of dollars,' but now it's 'these athletes are making *millions* of dollars.' You have to fight that belief that the more money you make, the less room you have to complain.

Crouse concurs. She believes elite athletes experiencing mental health challenges are "trapped in this box" as "everyone envies them for this gift that they absolutely hate." Athletes expressing vulnerabilities risked being perceived as ungrateful, meaning that a journalist like Crouse must "give voice to their troubles and insecurities." Even more than that, while most of her colleagues were chasing the story about the latest triumph or celebrity coupling, Crouse could carve a fairly unique niche: "I decided I wanted to be a journalist that could tell their stories in a more honest way. I wanted to show that so that these people have gifts that may elevate them but, in more ways than not, they're like everybody else."

In many ways, this amounted to countering part of the notion of the American Dream. Gregory could assess the landscape and see how tilted it was toward an athlete believing they should just be grateful—another form of the "shut up and sing" or, in the sports world, "shut up and dribble" mantra that had become part of the class politics of the modern era. Gregory explains that:

> The money gets played against them for everything. 'How dare a millionaire athlete disrespect the flag?' or 'how dare an athlete talk about stress.' Just because an athlete makes X amount of money doesn't mean they shouldn't have an opinion. That's where we've had progress with mental health. It's been this realization that just because Kevin Love is paid so much money doesn't mean he can't have a panic attack.

Complicating matters was the fact that each of the athlete stories being advanced were coming from athletes a generation (or more) younger than many of the storytellers. Costas believes age becomes an integral aspect of how mental health is understood in the sports world, because:

> You're talking about one of the few walks of life—some aspects of entertainment might be another—where people peak when they're very young. When they're doing the best work they can do is when they're also under the most scrutiny. Greater levels of maturity and insight may be years away, but in the meantime whatever level of anxiety exists is only amplified and, in some cases, distorted in a social media world. Drop a pass at a key moment and you're not just criticized, you're vilified. That's difficult I would think for anybody, let alone someone in their early twenties to deal with.

Thus, to be able to responsibly tell these types of stories in a compelling manner, storytellers need editors and upper-level management who see the value in zigging when everyone else zags. Crouse believes she was "lucky to have editors who I believe would have let me hold the story until an athlete is ready." She postulates that this "enables you to earn the trust of the subjects that you know the people you're talking to, because then they know you're not going to burn them."

Sometimes, that means acknowledging that a story in which a media storyteller places hours of time may ultimately be left untold. Crouse lived such an experience, recalling a story that never even ran. Even in such circumstances, she recalls that "the athlete said just the process was helpful. She said 'I have lost 20 pounds since we talked. I feel physically lighter by unburdening myself.' Just the process can be transformational."

Overall, these storytellers each recognized that mental health was enjoying an elevated position within the sports media ecosphere. Costas contends that the biggest difference is not the stories themselves, but the lack of stigma that now appears to be attached to such disclosures. He now believes that sports media storytellers generally accept that "it's not weakness to say that you have anxiety or depression or other issues that fall under the broader umbrella of mental health. By and large, the media is now sympathetic to it."

Nevertheless, Crouse believes that if mental health is now in the spotlight, it means that earlier stories could have been elevated more, as much of the public perceives recent stories as revelatory. "Simone Biles came out at the Olympics talking about struggles and, story after story, it was 'we need more athletes to do this' and 'she's such a pioneer. A trailblazer," she offers. However, she then questions: "What about Michael Phelps in 2015? How about Kevin Love? That gave me pause, because it told me that this area isn't quite as open as we think because people still thought Simone was the first to do this."

The Pre-Phelps Media Landscape

Of course, Phelps and Love were not the first to offer personal stories related to mental health in sports, either. Many names were invoked as earlier pioneers that made diminished stigma possible. Many prominent athletes were mentioned; Costas recalls John McEnroe being particularly willing to speak about it. Gregory believes some of the forebearers to the mental health disclosures were not even speaking about mental health but, rather, making the case for the athlete as being defined as more than merely their performance. He recalled the role of NBA MVP Steve Nash when he began work two decades ago. "It was rare to hear an athlete talk about anything other than sports," he remembers. "So, when Steve Nash spoke out against the Iraq War in 2003, it was a huge thing. An athlete spoke out about a big controversy. He was seen as some radical."

Gregory also believes there were stories of mental health that were not labeled as such at the time, for a variety of reasons. "Mental health is so broad," he admits. Thus, he believes *Time* magazine (among many others) were already telling these stories, but with different labeling:

> We did one of the first big cover stories about concussions in football, over a decade ago. That's a mental health story. We have done stories about athletes and body image. That's a mental health story. What about grieving families? Or parents still trying to find time to train? To some degree, all of these are mental health stories.

Crouse believes she has advanced many stories that, while not formally about mental health, were about the removing of the veil of secrecy around the life of the celebrity athlete, believing that such stories will naturally unfold if "the media gives people the freedom to ask questions that would be considered completely inappropriate in normal conversations." She recalls that a story she once worked on with swimmer Amanda Beard (who is profiled in a case study in Chapter 12 in this book) where the story was initially to be one about athletes being human, too, but quickly became something more. When it did, Beard initially had considerable reticence to relay that message to the media. Crouse explains:

> To give you an idea of the mindset of these athletes, I sat down with [7-time Olympic medalist] Amanda Beard. She was cutting herself and taking all kinds of recreational drugs and she was bulimic. She'd posed for *Playboy* magazine. From the outside, it looked like she had it made: world-class swimmer, very attractive, great personality. She was also miserable. We were set to run a story about some

of these personal issues and, a couple days before, I get a text from her saying: 'I just don't know if I can. I just don't want people to think I'm weak.' That's the problem in a nutshell: being fully human is seen as a weakness in the world of elite sport.

Each story is delicate, and Costas concedes that he once tried to tell a story that had too many tentacles for the time he was allotted. The case involved 25-year old Kansas City Chief Jovan Belcher, who murdered his girlfriend and then drove to the Chiefs facility, where he died by suicide. The story was about so many things: mental health, gun culture, and—it was learned a year later—head trauma and a formal diagnosis of CTE. Costas used a halftime moment to quote a column from Jason Whitlock, which advanced that there were many prongs to the story, but that if Belcher did not have a gun, the deaths would not have occurred. Whitlock (2012) wrote:

> In the coming days, Belcher's actions will be analyzed through the lens of concussions and head injuries. Who knows? Maybe brain damage triggered his violent overreaction to a fight with his girlfriend. What I believe is, if he didn't possess/own a gun, he and Kasandra Perkins would both be alive today (para. 17).

Costas concedes he was inartful in trying to cover these bases, but also believes it revealed something larger about the response to such stories at the time:

> I shouldn't have tried to cover so much ground in a minute and 15 seconds. That's on me. But what's not on me is the media culture who felt it was useful to have a boldface name as a target. I clarified and further contextualized it almost immediately and did so in prominent places. Not backpedal, but to provide a clearer and more accurate understanding of the issues involved. Of course, none of that was of any use to Fox News or right wing talk radio because they always need a straw man. They need a villain.

Costas strives for "nuance and texture," but then asks when such discussions should best occur. For instance, in the case of Belcher, he believed at least the potential for CTE needed to be part of this tragic story. Costas contends that particularly in football, there are mental health issues because brain trauma, especially to the prefrontal cortex. Depression can be amplified and impulse control diminished by head trauma and then when you add the possibility of PEDs, painkillers, and alcohol you have a witches brew of dangerous elements." Therefore, Costas says, such issues need to be addressed in their totality where they may apply when dealing with mental health stories.

The mindset of the athlete in the earlier era (largely pre-Michael Phelps) appeared to be one of steadfast adherence to invincibility. To discuss a personal focus on mental health was seen as tantamount to weakness, many of the storytellers explained. However, they also felt that mental health was not the only aspect of wellness that would be shunted to the side by an elite athlete. Crouse, for instance, explained that any form of physical challenge was something that most athletes she encountered would go to great lengths to hide. She uses a 2013 interaction with Tiger Woods as an exemplar, as it was the five-year anniversary of one of his most stunning achievements: winning the 2008 United States Open Championship (including a 19-hole playoff) on what amounted to a broken leg. Still, Tiger was reluctant to play any card that would, in his mind, be exhibiting weakness. She recollects:

> Tiger kept saying the hardest part of that was not the actual walking, but rather hiding it from everybody. I had to ask: why was it so important to you that nobody knew that you were injured? He looked at me like I had asked him why the sun sets in the west and said, 'because I couldn't get my competitors that advantage.' *That's* how the greats are wired. They hold everything extremely close to the vest and they don't want you to know that they have any frailties.

Alternatively, sometimes athletes were sending signals about mental health even before they knew it themselves. For example, Brennan recalls what she believes was a telling conversation with figure skater Gracie Gold (whose case study is illustrated in Chapter 10). She recalls a press conference after a rough performance at Skate America in 2016. It had encapsulated a difficult few years for what Brennan called "the skater of her generation" and, fairly off the cuff, Gold started speaking about the need for leanness in the sport. "No one had asked about her weight. No one. But she brings it up" Brennan remembers. Gold explained that:

> You don't often see—there aren't that many—you just don't see overweight figure skaters for a reason. It's just something I've struggled with this whole year and in previous seasons. It's just difficult when you're trying to do the difficult triple jumps. It's something that I am addressing but it's obviously not where it should be for this caliber of competition (Brennan, 2016, para. 6).

Brennan recalls being taken aback by the focus on size because "I've got a slender young woman in front of me, and she thinks she's overweight. She said it completely unprovoked." In her mind, there was something highly concerning about this focus, so much so that she "immediately went to someone within U.S. Figure Skating and asked: 'Are you handling this?' because that's how much I was concerned."

Brennan remembers being not the only one to challenge the line of thinking. When another reporter questioned Gold about labeling herself overweight, the response was: "Oh, that's lovely, thank you. It's just not what's required for this sport. It's a lean body sport and it's just not what I have currently, but, thank you." (Brennan, 2016, para. 9). Less than a year later, Gold would be in a treatment facility for anxiety, depression, and an eating disorder. However, in this moment, Brennan wrote about how disorienting Gold's comments were:

> I've covered sports involving young women for years, but this was the first time I had ever heard one of them speak so jarringly about her weight in public. I echoed my colleague's compliment, but Gold was not comfortable accepting any praise at that moment (Brennan, 2016, para. 10).

Sometimes signs of mental health challenges are there, but these storytellers could only probe so much. That is, until prominent athletes started voicing mental health messages much more emphatically.

Phelps and Beyond: A New Era

The Michael Phelps revelations seemed to be a turning point in the eye of most storytellers we interviewed. However, the magnitude of the moment and the ability to advance it via a variety of voices was still not evident. Brennan believes her earlier criticisms of Michael Phelps were fair, but that once she heard his discussions about mental health and how own personal experiences, those added post hoc texture to the stories. "There were very valid questions to ask about Michael," she argues, contending that "there were legitimate issues to write about. But I didn't put together what seems obvious now: this was a young man crying for help. Now have a name for that. We didn't then."

Partly because of her experience telling these types of stories, Crouse felt prescient in the angles she was presenting to the public about Phelps. She recalls:

> After the bong photo and, even more so, after 2014 DUI, I wrote pieces asking: at what point are we going to pay attention to Michael Phelps the person and not just the performer? It was not well-received from Michael or his team at the time.

But, years later, I was able to tell him: 'See, I was way ahead of the curve here. I was seeing you as a person before you saw yourself as a person.'

The stories were starting to come from the athletes, but the language, structure, and nature of telling these stories were still unfolding. Brennan does not have regret for how she covered the Phelps story ("never did it occur to me that there was a larger issue at play. I still stand by my stories I wrote. He was a very public figure and I'm a journalist"), she concedes that "of course, I'd tell that story differently now." At the time, though, "Phelps was partying, enjoying his fortune—but he was breaking laws in the process. You can't condone that, even if mental health is part of the story." Thus, the new stories with mental health infused seemed it be rebalanced with what she terms "a little more concern and a little less criticism. Certainly more empathy."

"Rehabilitation" was often part of the process of telling these stories but because it is such a broad conception, it was difficult to label it in any more specific manner than that. Part of it was because there would often be a confluence of issues that collectively led to treatment, but part of it also was because there was nothing concrete in which to report, and a media opinion leader seeks to first not get the story wrong. Explains Brennan:

> I don't believe I even referred to Michael's issue in terms of mental health. It wasn't labeled that way. He went to a rehab center; I'm not sure we separated out the issues requiring rehabilitation the way we would now. Tiger Woods went to rehab a few years before that, but we didn't really know what was being rehabilitated there, either.

However, what Phelps unlocked perhaps better than anyone was that not only could an athlete tell these stories without losing respect, but they could also enhance their legacy to some degree. Crouse felt a floodgate was opened once Phelps had led the way because "after being completely vulnerable, he was *more* popular in the eyes of corporate America and even global corporations." More than that, as witnessed in Phelps' case in Chapter 7 in this book, Phelps felt better after talking about it. And he felt even more improved when discussing it a second, third, or fourth time. Soon, Crouse notes, Phelps was a conduit for other athletes to reach out: "From Tiger Woods to Grant Hackett, Michael's become sort of the unofficial therapist to celebrity sports stars."

Each time an athlete speaks about something delicate, Crouse believes they are "blown away by how positive the reaction is." This included some incredibly dark and personal stories. Crouse uses one as exemplar:

Even when [former NFL wide receiver] Laveranues Coles was talking about being sexually assaulted, he internalized the worst possible consequences of their secrets coming out. How horrible the reaction will be. And then, to the person, the reaction becomes the opposite of what they expected. It lifts a burden.

Thus, she claims, there is an augmented responsibility that must be exacted within media's telling of these types of admissions. First, Crouse argues, journalists need "to avoid the narratives that are neat and tidy." These are problematic because they ring untrue, yet seem to be endemic to the sports media narrative: athlete encounters obstacle, athlete overcomes obstacle, athlete experiences glory in perpetuity. Countering those easy, streamlined stories becomes essential, but also takes more tact, and often more time and space. Crouse explains how storytellers have to buttress against the story of some form of easy victory over a mental health challenge. It's important not to render a narrative in which:

Michael Phelps was depressed and had anxiety. He had suicidal ideation. And then he goes to rehab, and he comes out, happy, and transformed. He's living happily ever after. The end. It's not that simple. It's not a linear journey.

The other safeguard media has to enact, Crouse contends, that the more positive stories of navigating and managing cannot always take precedent. "For every Michael Phelps story, there are the Kelly Catlin's of the world," she says. "Silver medalist in cycling at the Rio Olympics who dies by suicide just a few years later. We have to tell those stories, too, no matter how difficult they may be."

The Pandemic—and Two Prominent Women Athletes—Further Escalate the Conversation

Revelations from Kevin Love, DeMar DeRozan, and many others continued the conversation in the coming years. However, once people had lived in isolation and uncertainty for over a year, it seemed the public was primed for broader and more nuanced conversations. Two athletes who were at or near the top of their fields, one tennis star and one legendary gymnast, were willing to provide the fodder for that elevated conversation. Gregory postulates that "Phelps, Love, and DeRozan took the conversation to a four, but then Osaka and Biles took the conversation to a nine or ten." As explained in the two media moments about Naomi Osaka and Simone Biles (in Chapters 3 and 4 of this book), each story was huge, but Naomi's happened first.

Perhaps the most unique angle of Osaka's case was that she initially positioned the media as part of the problem itself, with the need to "feed the beast" being portrayed as the foundation of her apprehension. Brennan bristled at such a characterization: "I have so much empathy for her, but to frame it as journalists *causing* this was unfortunately and, frankly, counterproductive." She believes Osaka unwittingly facilitated the political right by being seen as anti-media, something she clearly would not wish to do given her earlier progressive stances for issues such as #BlackLives Matter. Gregory recalls the juxtaposition as well: "Naomi had just come out of her shell on social justice. She had a whole new following. A whole new wave of people. That raised her profile, but also made her a lightning rod." Brennan explains:

> I appreciated the situation that Naomi was in. Total respect from me as a journalist. The press conferences were negatively affecting her mental health, and I could see that. However, it was important that she later came out to clarify her attitudes about many of us in the media because, unfortunately, I think she may have inadvertently fed into the anti-media sentiment fostered by Donald Trump.

Thus, she believes that "in a perfect world, Naomi would have talked about it weeks earlier. She could have gone to the French Open and asked if there was a way to work this out." Since the story was already Topic A at one of tennis' four Grand Slam events, some level of damage control needed to occur: "When she blamed the press conference, she derailed the focus that should have been on mental health. Osaka tapped into Trumpism. There's no way she intended that, so she apologized." Brennan also believed there were other aspects to the lack of press conference availability that should have and needed to be covered more. One of the conversations came from retired men's tennis player James Blake who claimed that not doing press conferences was a competitive advantage. Brennan thought this type of angle had to be part and parcel of the larger Osaka story: "That player has an extra hour to get a massage, take a nap, work out, or prepare. I'd never thought of that, but it was a good point."

There was something about the tone of the Osaka coverage that seemed off to Crouse, and she felt the fact that this press conference argument was coming from a woman was at least partly responsible:

> She was halfway to a Naomi Slam [having won two of the four major Grand Slam titles consecutively]. Next was clay court season and the French Open. She struggles on clay and doesn't like to be reminded of how much she struggles on clay. Things spiral. With both Naomi—and later Simone—there was this

undercurrent of: 'oh these poor little women. We need to be nicer to them.' I worried about that because we were almost incentivizing women, encouraging journalists' lens to be trained differently on female athletes than with male athletes who talk about this.

Any notion of infantilizing a superstar like Osaka seemed to be anathema to what Crouse believed needed to be the major focus. "Naomi's the breadwinner of her family for goodness sakes. She's had to be old beyond her years so to infantilize her like that does her no good." Still, she saw these stances on the Osaka case continually percolate. She wishes she could be surprised, but was not because "it's just way too nuanced for the culture in which we find ourselves right now. People don't seem ready for anything but a single mental health narrative."

Gregory's role in the Osaka story was an intriguing one, because he would write initial stories for *Time* based on her Instagram posts and other witnessable portions of evidence. However, Osaka then inserted herself into the media story. She had already shaped every word of her stance on social media, but now Osaka wanted to lay out her case in more detail via a first-person *Time* cover story. Gregory did not see that prospect as a major compromising of journalistic principles, because "for journalists, there's less supply of 'big gets' because athletes can do their own "get"; I mean, it's not like those options are going away." More than that, if you wished to advance the Osaka story with the most intricacy, he believed this was, indeed, the best way to accomplish it:

> In the case of Naomi Osaka, once it was clear she wanted to write her own story for *Time* Magazine, you still have to welcome it. We'd rather see them do it with us than in short Twitter bursts. Meanwhile, athletes get more room to tell their stories and still have the ability to reach a global audience. They have every right to want to tell their own story in their own way and the media outlet has every right to decide if they wish to provide that platform. In the case of Naomi Osaka, we felt it was absolutely worth it and even very worthy of the cover. It's still a 'get' for us; it's just a different 'get.'

Osaka could control how her story was told, but ultimately could not control the narrative—particularly in the social media space. Gregory recalls some people—mostly men—who were telling Osaka to "suck it up" or responding with "give me a break." Then, when Osaka seemed fully capable of attending to other aspects of her professional and social life, those criticisms swelled. Gregory incorporates a specific case: "Naomi Osaka was at the Met Gala in September—months after the French Open issue. Still, some of the reactions were 'she suffers from anxiety, but she can wear this to the Met Gala?'" Gregory firmly believes that Osaka embodied his believe that "there's a different undercurrent when women athletes are involved."

And then, later that summer, came Simone Biles. The story was, again, about mental health, but with much more direct ties to her physical health and performance. Brennan contends that the mental health pot was already near boiling before the Olympics' most recognizable star entered the equation:

> Simone's case comes after Naomi's, and that timeline is important. The media and the public opinions changed even in the course of those weeks in between. Add in the Olympics—a stage unlike any other—and people are even more ready to have the conversation about Simone. Everything is heightened, which is why people care about the Olympics, and that also made the spotlight shine even brighter on Simone Biles.

The magnitude of the moment was part of the story, but could also be connected to Biles' struggles. Explains Costas: "If you're talking about an Olympic athlete like Simone Biles—athletes whose biggest moments come once every four years and are compressed into mere moments or seconds, the pressure and the expectation peaks differently than for other sports. Expectations escalate exponentially. The mental and physical aspects become intertwined."

Biles again was providing another unique angle to the case, one in which even the most veteran journalists covering the game had to quickly gain expertise. Explains Brennan:

> For Simone Biles, the story was different than some of the others because it was immediately and directly physically dangerous for her to compete. It was initially reported that she was getting "lost in the air." Later, we got the term "twisties" that seemed to be more specific, at least in the gymnastics world.

Again, the public response appeared to be fairly (but not overwhelmingly) positive, even when the lack of peak-Biles performances resulted in a silver (not gold) team gymnastics medal. Gregory thought that regardless of one's stance about Biles, the intense media focus was foundational for moving mental health to a higher echelon of conversation. He offers:

> With Biles, the whole world is watching. It's the summer. The Olympics are on all the time. I was covering the Tokyo Games and remember asking people what people are talking about and the response was basically it's all Simone Biles. People praising her. People hating on her. The whole gamut. The pandemic was

still keeping people home, so people were focused and hunkered down right when Simone announces, 'I've got to take care of myself.' It was a huge thing.

The combined summer of 2021 led to a variety of athlete posts, podcasts, and even books that shared vulnerability. These two athlete stories seemingly were the direct cause. As Gregory expands: "Anybody who speaks out about this is taking a huge step. There were a lot of conversations happening about Simone Biles and Naomi Osaka and most of them weren't happening in a psychotherapist's office."

Mental Health in 2022: A Frank Media Assessment

Thus, one finds the interviews with the media storytellers assessing not merely the past but also the current landscape of mental health in sport. Each feels the general stance on how such issues are approached have been permanently altered. Assesses Brennan "The approach for journalists is changing, and it should be. Years ago, perhaps you wouldn't ask 'what's wrong with you?,' but you probably would just vaguely writing that an athlete was 'clearly having issues.'"

Both Costas and Gregory reiterated that such narratives cannot be forced and likely need to happen organically and, as Costas phrases it, "when you have both the platform and the time that allows you to do justice to the topic." From years of experience, Gregory explains what needs to be evident at the outset when speaking about such delicate matters with an athlete:

> You have to make that clear: we don't have to talk about this. If you do, you don't have to talk about it again if you don't want to. Once you do that, you'll see people approach it in different ways. Some people will never talk about it at all. We won't get those stories, but that's OK. We're not entitled to them.

Such an approach, he argues, is most fruitful because of their organic nature. To anyone who would disagree, Gregory counters: "We just can't have the expectation: 'Tell me your worst moment. Tell me your worst moment. What's wrong with you? Why aren't you telling me your worst moment?'" Such a sentiment coincides with how Costas says he approaches the issue: "You tell those stories, generally speaking, if the person opens the door." He cites Michael Phelps as a "prime example of an athlete that opened the door and, thus, there was a lengthy conversation prior to the 2016 Rio Olympics."

Still, Costas claims, there sometimes can be signals where thoughtful probing could be warranted. For instance: "Let's say a person has had extremely erratic, emotional behavior that has happened in public view. And let's also say it's happened repeatedly. Then it would be appropriate to broach the subject."

Of course, there are more athletes volunteering, which aids the media storyteller tremendously. Gregory summarizes that he doesn't "get the sense that there's a reluctance to tell stories to media outlets. There are just different ways to do this." A recent example for his was track star Allyson Felix, who he profiled before the Tokyo Olympics issue. He explains that it became a collaborative endeavor in which "we wrote it, but since she wanted to talk about her struggles, motherhood, and sensitive things about her Nike contract, we gave her some latitude. But that was still a journalistically reported version of her story."

He believes there is a space for journalists to play critical roles, even if athletes themselves are embracing the role of media producer:

> I understand the impulse for athletes to want to control, and now with social media they can skip us, and we understand that. But I think in a perfect world, you can have it both ways. Write that first person essay, but then have a conversation with a trusted journalistic outlet. Have that back and forth talk and the follow ups. Get your story out even more. Basically, do what Kevin Love did: first person story followed by an interview with Jackie MacMullan.

Nevertheless, each storyteller interviewed for this chapter had areas for media improvement. Crouse was "concerned that we aren't writing the feel-good profile for women. It was always capturing women at their most vulnerable, instead of celebrating their strength." Meanwhile, Costas stressed the need to differentiate between the varying realities being advanced:

> The stories need to have nuance and, quite frankly, many in society right now don't want nuance. They want a story with a consistent theme: OK, we've had another athlete with a mental health disclosure. They're automatically a hero, or to some, an object of scorn. But that's a story painted in primary colors. In some quarters these days, shades of grey don't play well, but they are essential if we are going to understand the complexities involved.

Many lamented the potentially destructive role that social media can play, even while also providing a lifeline for people to connect and discover they are not alone. "The Twitter scrolls are not the greatest place for nuance," Gregory emphasizes, noting that "as a reporter, you want to be nuanced, but you also don't want to question when someone says they're having a panic attack. It's not our job to rank people's experience based on how serious we think it is."

Thus, as Costas illustrates, one has to safeguard against "the tendency to want to create a soap opera." He believes there is a line each media entity much walk so they can determine for themselves: "If there's something legitimately there, fine. If it's just a chance to tap into cheap emotional narratives, I think we can do better than that." To anyone who believes all mental health stories must inherently be tales of heroism and optimism, he counters that "when someone acknowledges they have a mental health issue, I don't think building a statue in their honor is nearly as respectful or useful as being well-informed and understanding about their situation." Elevating truth and authenticity instead becomes paramount. Costas expounds:

> You have to thread the needle very carefully sometimes because the general narrative in the media becomes reporters and commentators trying to show they are properly sympathetic to the person or the issue in general. Thus the impulse to label everyone a hero. And yes, there are often elements of bravery involved, but in most cases—especially as we move forward—it's neither heroic nor is it something to be ashamed of. It's simply reality and athletes should be treated with respect, dignity, and understanding when discussing that reality.

Even with more voices, platforms, and ways to disseminate the message, each media storyteller sees traditional media platforms as central to how mental health is acknowledged and discussed in the future. As Gregory contends: "I don't think we're obsolete. We're still telling stories. Still, for sure, athletes know they have levers that they didn't have before and they're going to use them."

References

Brennan, C. (2016, Oct. 22). Gracie Gold addresses issues of weight, physical shape, in skating. *USA Today*. Retrieved at: https://www.usatoday.com/story/sports/columnist/brennan/2016/10/22/gracie-gold-addresses-issues-weight-physical-shape-skating/92618094/

Whitlock, J. (2012, Dec. 1). In K.C., it's no time for a game. *Fox Sports*. Retrieved at: https://www.foxsports.com/stories/nfl/in-kc-its-no-time-for-a-game

6

Organizational Synergy: Teamwork in Making Mental Health Work

> "We know we are not mental health experts…but we know the power of the brand."
>
> —Ashley Powell, Indianapolis Colts

It was Head Coach Tyronn Lue who first sensed something wrong with NBA All-Star Kevin Love when he experienced a panic attack in a game between the Cleveland Cavaliers and Atlanta Hawks (Love, 2018). A member of the Cavs organization accompanied Love to the Cleveland Clinic for tests as he sought to figure out why his body told him, "You're about to die" (Love, 2018, para. 12).

When NHL goaltender Corey Hirsch could no longer take the "dark, dark, dark, dark, dark" thoughts of obsessive compulsive disorder, he turned to an athletic trainer on the Vancouver Canucks for help (Hirsch, 2017).

And when U.S. Olympians Katie Uhlaender and Michael Phelps continue to lobby for better mental health care for Olympic athletes, they direct the calls toward the U.S. Olympic Committee (see Chapters 7 and 14).

These are just a handful of examples illustrating the importance of organizational responses to mental health in the world of elite athletic competition. Athletes often spend more time around teammates, coaches, and team personnel than family and friends because of demanding schedules for training and travel. Given their proximity, team members often appear on the front end of the response to an athlete in crisis. Therefore, appropriate understanding, empathy, and policies can either translate into an athlete finding help or remaining silent about the challenges they are experiencing.

Beyond such emergencies, these teams, leagues, and news outlets bear responsibility for the health and well-being of their employees. Organizations can be pro-active by nurturing environments in which athletes, coaches, and other personnel feel comfortable talking about mental health. Such organizations do so by implementing healthy guidelines, lending support, encouraging advocacy, and other means. Conversely, organizations can (both overtly and covertly) nurture unhealthy environments by perpetuating stigmatizing attitudes, behaviors, and policies.

The present chapter highlights how three groups of stakeholders—the team, the athletic association, and the sports media conglomerate—can be instruments for the good in advancing mental health initiatives. More specifically, we will use interviews with employees of the Indianapolis Colts football team, the National Basketball Association, and the ESPN newsroom as exemplars of how larger mental health progress can be achieved. Each organization is challenging the stigma of mental illness in sport through community partnerships, the development of healthy guidelines, and open conversations about mental health.

These organizations' examples provide a fairly stark contrast with the behavior and attitudes common in sport during the 1990s and 2000s. Mental illness has long been stigmatized in elite athletics. As illustrated in this book, athletes can feel hesitant to disclose an issue for fear of losing playing time or becoming socially and professionally marginalized. In the 2000s, the NBA witnessed the example of Royce White, whose personal battle with anxiety and fear of flying significantly complicated his relationship with the Houston Rockets and the NBA (e.g., Chiari, 2018). White advocated for mental health policies in the league, which he described as ignoring the issue (Chiari, 2018). Meanwhile, Chapter 13 highlights the experiences of Corey Hirsch, whose relationship with teammates suffered because of his severe anxiety and the silence surrounding mental illness. "A tough place to be" when struggling with mental health was the way one teammate described the NHL locker room (Canucks, 2017). "It's an unforgiving place," Hirsch argued.

Teams and leagues have witnessed changes in the ensuing years as elite athletes disclose personal experience with depression, anxiety, and other conditions, and organizations adopt proactive approaches to nurture healthy environments. Hirsch describes the environment surrounding mental health in the NHL as improved, but notes there is room to grow. Some of that growth has now penetrated the organizational sphere. The NBA expanded the scope of its mental health resources with the 2018 launch of its Mind Health initiative in 2018 after NBA stars DeMar DeRozan and Kevin Love disclosed experience with mental health conditions (Love, 2018; Shama, 2019). As highlighted here, organizations are increasingly recognizing the importance of mental health for professional athletes and their fanbases.

The Team Response: Getting Communities Involved— and Growing New Ones

In 2020, the Indianapolis Colts launched "Kicking the Stigma," an initiative in which the professional football team partnered with the local and state communities to promote mental health literacy and the work of mental health professionals. You could say the timing was prescient, as the initiative's launch accompanied the COVID-19 pandemic that claimed the lives of 23,000 residents of the Hoosier State and threatened residents' mental health through social isolation, unemployment, and the exacerbation of other risk factors. Despite the pandemic—or perhaps partly because of it—Kicking the Stigma raised $4.5 million for local mental health organizations during the Colts' first fundraiser for the cause. The fundraiser was one of several successes to result from the Kicking the Stigma initiative, says Ashley Powell, the Director of Community Relations for the Colts.

The program focuses its efforts on raising awareness about mental health and expanding treatment and research. Toward growing awareness, the Colts produced a series of nationally televised public service announcements featuring professional athletes, musicians, actors, and other celebrities. On September 19, 2021, the team dedicated its home game against the Los Angeles Rams to educating fans about mental health. Coaches and players also wore T-shirts during pre-game warmups with positive mental health messages such as "You are enough" and "Vulnerability is a strength." Meanwhile, the Colts and its owners, the Irsay family, have contributed millions of dollars to area mental health organizations, including a $3 million gift to Indiana University for a new institute whose goal is to become a research leader of the stigma attached to mental illness. The initiative illustrates the myriad ways in which professional athletic organizations can advocate for mental health.

"It was something that, from inside the organization from the top down, was really a personal and important topic," Powell says. "We felt we needed to help and use our platform as an organization to bring more awareness to mental health."

Kicking the Stigma amplified the stories of professional football players, team personnel, and even the Colts' ownership when they shared experience with mental illness. The Irsay family owns the Colts, and at least two members have openly discussed their personal mental health. Jim Irsay was addicted to painkillers, and his daughter, Kalen Jackson, has experienced anxiety since childhood (Nye, 2021).

Jackson, the vice chairman/owner of the Colts, told reporters the initiative sought to tell "everybody that it is OK to not be OK, and really by starting with our own issues within ourselves and our family and things that we've gone through, to really utilize our platform to kind of lay that out for everyone to see it's OK to talk about" (Nye, 2021, para. 4).

Players have also embraced the initiative. Darius Leonard, a linebacker for the Colts, suffered depression and anxiety after his brother was killed (Daniels, 2021). Leonard adopted a lead role on Kicking the Stigma. "I knew I needed help, and for a long time, I didn't reach out," Leonard said (Daniels, 2021, para. 3). "Once I did reach out, I knew that's what made it better for me."

Powell says the team and its players appreciate the influence they exercise over fans, athletes, and even other football organizations. "We always remind our team and our guys of the powerful platform they have as a professional athlete," Powell says. "What they do off the field is just as important as what they do on the field."

In addition to disclosures from active players, alumni of the Colts have addressed the importance of mental health. The spokespeople include Hall of Fame quarterback Peyton Manning, who described the initiative as incredibly important:

> because they're shining a light on an issue that a lot of people struggle with every single day. It's important to remove the stigma associated with mental health because it's really the first step in getting people the help that they need (Colts, 2022).

Powell says the Colts knew from the beginning that the initiative would be a community one. "We know we are not mental health experts, we are a national football organization," Powell says. "But we know the power of the brand as well, so we really leaned heavily into local experts and organizations in this space before we even came out with Kicking the Stigma."

Community partnerships permitted the Colts to better understand gaps and barriers to mental health in Indianapolis and the greater Indiana area. The conversations permitted the team to focus on numerous areas, including behavioral health workforce development, equitable access to treatment resources, and anti-stigma initiatives. While the COVID-19 pandemic could be seen as a challenge, Powell says the timing of the initiative actually worked out fairly serendipitously: More people realized the importance of mental health during the pandemic, helping the team's messages resonate.

The Colts hope Kicking the Stigma can become a league-wide initiative. Organizers have crossed competitive lines to spotlight the stories of athletes on other teams. Leonard, the Colts linebacker, joined the Atlanta Falcons' Hayden Hurst and Las Vegas Raiders' Solomon Thomas and Darren Waller for a roundtable on mental health (Daniels, 2021). Teams within the league are demonstrating camaraderie when it comes to mental health, Powell says, because "it's not about who started it, it's just about continuing that conversation and making it a core focus".

The League Response: Mental Health All the Time—Not Just Times of Crisis

While DeMar DeRozan and Kevin Love are the faces of mental health in the NBA, Dr. Kensa Gunter is one of the representatives on the clinical side. Gunter, an Atlanta-area clinical and sport psychologist, helps spearhead the NBA's programming and policy-making related to mental health.

Contrasting previous decades, the NBA recently adopted a proactive approach to mental health both publicly and behind-the-scenes. Commissioner Adam Silver expressed surprise while speaking to the MIT Sloan Sports Analytics Conference in 2019, blaming social media and players who choose to listen to music on headphones rather than interacting with teammates. "When I meet with them, what surprises me is that they're truly unhappy," Silver said (Delaney, 2019, para. 2). In the 2019-2020 season, the NBA required teams to add a licensed mental health professional, such as a psychologist or counselor, to the staff. Teams must also retain a licensed psychiatrist (Shama, 2019). Meanwhile, public initiatives used social media, websites, and other platforms to illustrate the experiences of NBA stars who have experienced depression, anxiety, and other conditions.

Through Mind Health, the NBA adopted a four-pillared system for advocating mental health among players and fans. Mind Health advocates an approach in which mental health is treated along a continuum rather than yes/no, either/or approach in which an individual experiences mental illness or does not. People navigate a range of emotions day-by-day, so an NBA point guard (or businessman, or high school student) could feel great in the morning but poorly in the afternoon. The league advocates for a holistic approach to mental health in which a wide range of individual, social and systemic factors are taken into account when negotiating one's emotions, including money, family, friends, and communication. Communities are important for maintaining mental health, and an individual can contribute to his/her own mental health and the mental health of others by nurturing communication, empathy, and positive emotions. Finally, mental health is as important as physical health when it comes to athletic competition (or work, or school, etc.). Therefore, maintaining balance helps elite athletes succeed.

"Our aspirational vision is to humanize mental health and to position mental health as an essential element in excellence on and off the court," Gunter says. "We really want to humanize the conversation and move beyond talking about signs and symptoms to really thinking about the person that is at the core of these conversations."

The NBA initiative is framing mental health as important for all-around well-being and success. Just as elite athletes physically work out to build muscle, increase speed, and nurture agility, so, too, can they enjoy additional success by adopting healthy mental behaviors, she says.

Gunter stresses the importance of elite athletes and journalists consistently focusing on mental health rather than solely discussing it during times of crisis. Toward this end, the NBA is adopting a holistic approach to mental health. In addition to addressing illness, the league is encouraging athletes to take a proactive approach to establishing and maintaining their mental wellness

"As we are talking about mental health in the world of sport, we are really talking about competitors, people who are trying to perform," Gunter says. "We want to focus on helping them to elevate their performance—not just on the field of play, but off the court as well. If you have a healthy person, you're more likely to have a healthy athlete." Athletes are central to the initiative, Gunter says, because "we're trying to respect the lived experience, and the way we try to do that is by listening to those we're serving." She reveals that, "I think oftentimes experts have ideas on what's helpful—and we need that—but we also need to listen to the people that we're serving to make sure that what we're doing is relevant and relatable."

Gunter joined the program in 2020, and says she already has noticed positive results from the NBA initiative. Players' attitudes toward mental health mirror those of larger society, she contends. As attitudes of the elite athletes progressed, so too did societal attitudes. This was especially the case during the period surrounding COVID-19, when professional basketball temporarily shut down before reopening within the so-called "bubble." The bubble permitted the NBA to continue competing by quarantining teams in Orlando, Florida, to prevent the spread of COVID-19. Athletes missed family and friends—and also social protests following the deaths of citizens at the hands of police officers. As the NBA prepared for the bubble, she says, mental health professionals sought to anticipate how athletes would respond—and how they might help. Among other resources, they consulted the research literature related to military veterans on deployment, Gunter says.

Through its initiatives, the NBA is attempting to generate a fairly dramatic cultural shift. Rather than a weakness, a request for help should instead be seen as a strength. Athletes are being encouraged to adopt different perceptions of mental health. Rather than focusing on dualities—mental illness is present or absent—Gunter says mental health occurs along a continuum. Athletes can train and elevate mental health similar to how they lift weights and condition to reinforce physical health.

The shift also requires alternative narratives in the news media. The message from athletes has been clear, whether voiced in the public view or behind-the-scenes, Gunter argues, because "They want to be seen as people, and they do not want their humanity to be diminished at the exclusive focus on their skills, their performance, and their talents."

Gunter says a news story about mental health need not only focus on an athlete's personal journey of illness, treatment, and recovery. Other story ideas abound. For example, professional competition requires physical and mental resiliency on the part of the athlete; a journalist could highlight the methods that athletes adopt to succeed. Gunter says she encourages athletes to recognize "that adversity is a part of the success journey." Mental health skills can provide athletes with the skillset to successfully navigate adversity.

In addition to COVID-19, professional athletes face numerous mental health challenges uncommon among typical Americans. Athletes often make substantial sums of money, but the financial success can translate into additional pressures and problems. Athletes also dedicate their lives to competition. At some point the competition ends, and an athlete can be left in their mid-20s or 30s without the fanfare, structured schedule, and identity that has dominated their lives since childhood. These challenges feed into the NBA's holistic approach for mental health, extending beyond simple mental health literacy. "Thinking about how we can help them to develop a more well-rounded identity, one that is not just exclusively defined by their performance, is a really big thing," Gunter says.

In the end, she believes that professional athletes are at an age when many people are discovering themselves; the difference is their journey appears in the public spotlight. "They're trying to live in their own skin," she says, "and they're doing all that publicly. So it's like this fishbowl effect where they're just trying to swim in the waters while the world is scrutinizing how they're swimming."

Mind Health is attempting to revamp the way athletes are treated. Rather than focusing on the "performance," Gunter says, we need to focus on "the performer, the person."

In some newsrooms, the approach is already changing.

The Media Response: Shifting the Media Narrative— On and Off Screen

Melissa Rawlins's day job is photographer for ESPN, the self-monikered "worldwide leader of sports." Within the organization—and its parent company, Disney—Rawlins is also a mental health advocate. Rawlins serves on a committee whose goal is to ensure ESPN (and other Disney companies) treat mental illness with compassion and accuracy in the stories they tell. The team also works to support the mental health of ESPN employees by providing training seminars, advocating for mental health-friendly policies, and nurturing an environment in which people are free to talk about mental health.

"We really saw a need for people in the company to have support with mental health, but also have the company as a whole, with the content, understand how to properly represent mental health," Rawlins says. "We were not only here for the employees. We're also here to make sure that content was represented properly."

The ESPN initiative remains in its infancy, but Rawlins describes the results as "remarkable." She describes the openness:

People are disclosing their own lived experiences on our internal platforms, people are stopping me in the hallways and talking to me, saying, 'I feel like I can actually say something. I don't have to say that I'm sick or I can't come in because my kid is sick,' when there really is just a mental health situation going on.

On the content side, ESPN began incorporating additional content about mental wellness—not just moments of crisis—into its reportage. For example, during Mental Health Awareness Month, the ESPN website highlighted stories in which athletes discussed mental illness, treatment, recovery, and other mental health-related subject matter. In addition to specialty content, ESPN journalists are reaching out to Rawlins and her peers in advance of stories about mental health to ensure the wording and content are respectful. In the past, she says, stories might use phrases such as "committed suicide," which mental health advocates consider problematic because it implies fault. Now ESPN journalists use the phrase "died by suicide," following recommendations of the World Health Organization (2017). "I think those little words mean everything and they are the biggest change in our storytelling," Rawlins says. "It's the way we represent people."

Similar to athletes, Black journalists faced mental health challenges while covering social justice stories for ESPN, including the death of George Floyd at the hands of police. During COVID-19, Asian Americans reported an increase in prejudice as a result of the pandemic's origin in China. Rawlins says the journalists must live through the trauma while explaining stories to viewers. At ESPN, Rawlins and her colleagues work to direct coworkers to resources that are relevant for specific circumstances, such as racial justice and COVID-19. Rawlins says the group recognizes that someone's lifeboat might be overflowing at home even if they do not show it at work or on television. "Everybody experiences life differently," Rawlins says. "Especially during COVID, people didn't want to speak up because they felt anxiety for the first time." People would come to the group's open sessions and say, "I'm not supposed to be falling apart like this. I've dealt with bigger things, and I can't believe this is happening," Rawlins says.

The mental health program's implementation garnered attention outside the ESPN newsroom. Employees from the larger parent company, Disney, approached the group for recommendations regarding creative content and employee health. The group has also extended its work beyond mental health to launch an "inclusive content committee" to "make sure all of the content, not just mental health but every group, has the right representation," Rawlins says.

She echoes Gunter from the NBA when recommending journalists adopt broader approaches to telling stories about mental health. Rather than focusing on times of crisis, journalists can convey the broad role of mental health in professional athletics—and society. "I really hope that it's something that people really start to understand, that mental health is just as important as physical health," Rawlins says. "With COVID, everybody has experienced something and before not everybody did. Different athletes—and people in general—now have a better understanding and empathy. They can really understand it—and respect it."

The increased understanding and respect comes in part from elite athletes, sports teams, and news organizations putting a spotlight on mental health. The advocates from the Colts, NBA, and ESPN hope the light doesn't dim anytime soon.

References

Canucks. (2017). Corey Hirsch's story of struggle and recovery. YouTube. https://www.youtube.com/watch?v=0D8URDg0lKI

Chiari, M. (2018). Royce White urges NBA to update mental health policy on 'The Last Renaissance.' *Bleacher Report*. https://bleacherreport.com/articles/2782606-royce-white-urges-nba-to-update-mental-health-policy-on-the-last-renaissance

Colts (2022). Kicking the Stigma: Peyton Manning. https://www.colts.com/video/kicking-the-stigma-peyton-manning

Daniels, T. (April 14, 2021). Darius Leonard opens up about anxiety, mental health struggles after death of brother. *Bleacher Report*. https://bleacherreport.com/articles/10001470-darius-leonard-opens-up-about-anxiety-mental-health-struggles-after-death-of-brother

Delaney, J. (2019). Adam Silver: NBA players are 'truly unhappy.' *Basketball Forever*. https://basketballforever.com/2019/03/02/adam-silver-nba-players-are-truly-unhappy

Hirsch, C. (2017). Dark, dark, dark, dark, dark, dark, dark, dark. *The Players' Tribune*. https://www.theplayerstribune.com/articles/corey-hirsch-dark-dark-dark

Love, K. (2018). Everyone is going through something. *The Players' Tribune*. https://www.theplayerstribune.com/articles/kevin-love-everyone-is-going-through-something

Mickle, S. (2018, February 27). Dwyane Wade thinks he was depressed last few days with Cavs. *Clutch Points*. https://clutchpoints.com/heat-news-dwyane-wade-thinks-he-was-depressed-last-few-days-with-cavs/

Nye, R. (2021, May 3). Colts owners "Kicking the Stigma" of mental health illness. WTHR. https://www.wthr.com/article/news/health/colts-owners-kicking-the-stigma-of-mental-health-illness/531-77fd2c8e-106d-4cf4-8f58-fb7900661b51

Shama, E. (2019). NBA adopts new rules requiring teams to add full-time mental health staff for 2019-2020 season. *CNBC*. https://www.cnbc.com/2019/09/19/nba-now-requires-teams-to-add-full-time-mental-health-staff.html

Windhorst, B. (2018, May 31). Cavaliers coach Tyronn Lue says he's being treated for anxiety. ESPN. https://www.espn.com/nba/story/_/id/23659954/cleveland-cavaliers-coach-tyronn-lue-reveals-being-treated-anxiety

World Health Organization. (2017). Preventing suicide: A resource for media professionals. https://apps.who.int/iris/handle/10665/258814

7

Case Study: Michael Phelps, Olympic Swimmer

"Little by little, it's just going to get bigger and bigger."

Michael Phelps cannot remember which question prompted his admission, one that would change his life and chart another course for the 23-time Olympic gold medalist. Later, he would even reach out to Tim Layden, the senior writer for *Sports Illustrated*, to see if he could recall. Phelps just remembers walking into an interview, one of those "typical lead up, how is your preparation going" pieces that would function as a precursor for the Rio Olympics. By the time the story came out in the November 16, 2015 issue of *SI*, Phelps and his loved ones had all opened up about the mental health challenges of the world's most successful and decorated Olympian. "It wasn't set up to be my coming out party for mental health," Phelps recalls. "After it was over...I felt like a new person. I felt relief." He recalls being somewhat surprised by himself as well as the immediate lift he felt to his mindset. "When something is holding you back for so long, and then you just drop it and keep walking...," Phelps pauses to consider "...that's what I felt like. 'This is awesome. That's how easy it is.'"

Though the disclosure felt easy in hindsight, the personal struggles he shared were anything but. As chronicled in this book (Chapter 1), it had taken years to collect hundreds (if not thousands) of life moments, incidents, and struggles and place them into a narrative that he could coherently understand himself. It would take even longer for him to feel confident enough in that understanding to express those feelings with Layden, knowing that he was sharing those feelings with millions of people around the globe.

In the story, Phelps detailed how he contemplated suicide after his second arrest for driving under the influence of alcohol, how his family and friends convinced him to pursue rehabilitation at a facility in Arizona, and how he discovered the man behind the myth of the "Golden Child" athlete in a support group where people judged him not for his athleticism but for the human being who wanted to feel better. Phelps knew that when people initially think about Michael Phelps, images come to mind of a chiseled swimmer pumping his fists in the air in triumph, or appearing on magazine covers draped in gold medals, or eyes focused beneath a swim cap bearing his surname and the Stars and Stripes. His steely glare before his 2016 200-meter butterfly semifinal against Chad Le Clos was so viral it became a viral meme; *USA Today* exhibited the top 27 memes built from the image (Kerr-Dineen, 2016), with the comments section still listing many more worthy candidates that the journalist had excluded.

The *SI* cover was decidedly less intense. Phelps, who like other swimmers usually appears cleanly shaven, instead sported a beard. He smiled, eyes bright, standing in a white V-neck T-shirt. He was flanked by two quotations pulled from the interview: "I was in a really dark place. Not wanting to be alive anymore," one read. The other: "I look back now. I lived in a bubble for a long time."

The story was headlined, "The Rehabilitation of Michael Phelps."

Antecedents to a Media Revelation

Nearly a year had passed between when Phelps had exited rehab and when he candidly spoke with Layden. He spent 45 days in rehab, entering the treatment program after a state trooper clocked him driving 84 mph in a 45-mph zone. He failed two field sobriety tests, and his blood-alcohol level was at .14 (Layden, 2015). Equally telling was the fact that family and friends sounded unsurprised. His mother Debbie, an educator in Baltimore, told Layden that her immediate thought was, "Oh, my God, here we go again. How terrible is the world going to be to my son?" (para. 4). A good friend described feeling disappointment. His long-time coach, Bob Bowman, had worried Phelps was going to die young. As he told Layden (2015) after Phelps' revelation:

> I had been living in fear that I was going to get a call that something had happened... Honestly, I thought, the way he was going, he was going to kill himself. Not take his own life, but something like the DUI, but worse (para. 7).

When Phelps emerged from treatment, family and friends described him as markedly different. Still, there were new avenues of himself to negotiate. For example:

> There were times after my second DUI where I didn't want to ask for a ride to the grocery store. I didn't have a license, so I couldn't do anything. I was ashamed. But eventually I got over that. I started asking for help. Recognizing that I could not do it by myself was extremely important.

He was gradually learning the importance of conveying his emotions to others. "I learned to communicate at the age of 30," he frequently jokes. That may explain the reason he shed the myth in his interview. "I just decided to open up right there. I blurted everything out. Just like a word vomit," he recalls. He also remembers the abrupt manner he took to talking about these issues. "I was kind of just like 'fuck it.' Let's just get it all out in the open. I didn't care. Clean slate. Let's go." The result of his opening up in the interview with Layden? The veteran sports writer concluded his profile with the lines, "A familiar face. But a new man."

Coming out of rehab, Phelps says, "I was ready to just show the real me, and the Michael Phelps that I am. I am not this perfect Golden Child. I'm a human being. I might make mistakes. I go through ups and downs. But hell, it's part of life." The treatment facility had a crystallizing effect for Phelps, because "I realized that my mental health struggles weren't just going to go away," he says. "I wasn't going to be able to drop them like a bad habit. They were a part of who I am. And they are. They are and will be a part of who I am for the rest of my life."

From Acknowledgment to Advocacy

Although Phelps did not anticipate his initial disclosure, he says he has embraced being a new man. In Phelps' life, the high moments include qualifying for the 2000 Summer Olympics at age 15 and becoming the youngest male to set a world record in swimming during the 2001 World Championship Trials. He won a record eight gold medals at the 2008 Summer Games. In all, he ultimately competed in 5 Olympic Games, winning 28 medals, becoming the most successful and decorated Olympian of all time...by a long shot.

And yet Michael Phelps' Twitter account describes him as a mental health advocate before he lists himself as a gold medalist. He has learned that labels matter. Order matters.

Thus, he cannot separate those aforementioned high points from the low points, including an arrest for driving under the influence at the age of 19. In 2009, a British tabloid ran a photograph of Phelps hitting a bong at the University of South Carolina, an image that generated public outcry and a three-month suspension from competition for Phelps. The second arrest for DUI, in 2014, led Phelps to treatment at The Meadows in Arizona.

As with other celebrities, Phelps' ups and downs are well documented in the news. There were headlines celebrating the swimmer's accomplishments in the pool, which included world records. But there were also stories about Phelps missing practice, partying, and getting into trouble with the law. Speaking with the *Today* show after the *Sports Illustrated* piece was released, Phelps described the 2014 arrest as a cry for help - but also a turning point in his life. "I sent myself down a downward spiral," he told interviewer Matt Lauer (Jackson, 2016, para. 4). "I think it was more of a sign than anything else. (A sign) that I had to get something under control, whatever it was. I look back at that night and everything happened for a reason."

These type of comments illustrate how frank Phelps has been with journalists through the years. He maintains privacy but also does not sugar coat the times he has felt down. After sharing his experience with depression in the media, Phelps says he adopted a "gloves off" attitude. "If anybody doesn't like me, it's not my problem," he says.

Public Embraces an Amplified Message

That's not the way it turned out, though. Instead, people applauded Phelps for demonstrating that anyone—even a storied Olympian—could experience mental illness. A common refrain from people explaining why they have not talked about mental illness or sought professional guidance is that the person feels like they shouldn't complain because their lives are so much better than the less fortunate. Phelps' admission shattered that narrative for many people: if a 28-time Olympic medalist could be honest about his darker days, others, presumably, could as well.

His personal stories embody the tenets of social learning theory (Bandura, 1963) in mass communication. In sharing, Phelps illustrates how therapy and mental health care can help people navigate life challenges. For example, when Phelps partnered with Talkspace, an online mental health care company, for a Mental Health Month video in 2018, he encouraged people who are struggling to seek therapy. In the advertisement, Phelps recounts his rock bottom moment in 2014, explaining that:

> I was one of the world's most successful athletes. 18 gold medals, the All-American dream come true. But I was lost. I hadn't left my room in five days. I questioned whether I wanted to be alive anymore…I realized I couldn't handle this by myself.

The video drew more than 2.1 million views on YouTube, where one viewer commented that, "this is the type of encouragement and awareness we need from celebrities and athletes. Mental health is extremely important, and I'm glad he is open enough to share with the world that it is never too late to seek help."

The ability to speak with multiple audiences in multiple manners gave his story the necessary nuance for those willing to assemble the different parts of Phelps' mental health journey. People often enjoy tying the narrative of mental illness in a neat bow, Phelps contends, with the desired narrative befitting the typical sports movie: a person experiences challenges, overcomes them, and completely recovers, end credits. That is far from the reality, he says. Clinical depression, chronic anxiety, and other illnesses can linger for extended periods, but therapy, medication, and other mental health-supportive steps can help. "My struggles are still constant," he says. "They're not going away anytime soon. I'm still going to fight for what I think is right, and I think we all need to look at mental health in a different way."

The ongoing struggles are also the reason he believes the blossoming movement for mental health in sport will not end anytime soon. Since Phelps shared his experience with depression, other celebrity athletes and Olympians have come forward to publicly share how they have been affected by depression, anxiety, eating disorders, and other conditions. Even when athletes opt not to talk about their mental health journeys in the media, athletes have nevertheless still opted to chat with Phelps about it. "I think the messages and the stories are only getting bigger and bigger," Phelps says.

The *Sports Illustrated* article was prescient, in a way. Phelps did indeed emerge a different man. Since his initial disclosure, Phelps has granted several dozen interviews in which he openly discusses his experience with depression, suicidal thoughts, ADHD, childhood bullying, and mental health in general. The stories on CNN, ESPN, *Sports Illustrated*, *People* magazine, and other outlets ultimately led to Phelps backing the production of an award-winning documentary called *The Weight of Gold*. In the HBO-distributed film, Phelps and other star Olympians describe their experiences with depression, anxiety, suicide, substance abuse, and a competitive environment in which elite athletes can feel completely alone, even underneath the glare of the international spotlight. The documentary includes deeply personal stories from Shaun White, David Boudia, Lolo Jones, Bode Miller, and other U.S. Olympians, including Katie Uhlaender, who is profiled in Chapter 14.

In the documentary, Phelps describes Olympians' experience following competition (regardless of victories). "If your whole life was about building up to one race, one performance, or one event, how does that sustain everything that comes afterwards? Eventually, for me at least, there was one question that hit me like a ton of bricks: Who was I outside of the swimming pool?"

In shepherding the documentary project, Phelps was pleased to develop what he sees as "one corner of a larger puzzle." Phelps says he experienced an epiphany while walking alongside other Olympians during Opening Ceremonies as he could see "people basically with messages written across the forehead that they're struggling." Immediately, he felt a kinship, even with athletes he had never met. "I don't know if it's the sixth sense or what, but I could feel something," he recalls. "I was like, 'I'm not alone. There are people going through the same exact thing. What can we do?' I think we've obviously seen that it isn't just an Olympic issue, it's across all sports. All walks of life."

Common Media Advice from an Uncommon Star

Phelps appreciates the role of the news media in spreading word about mental health, even though he acknowledges having negative experiences with the press. Sometimes stories "take on a mind of their own," he says. For example, Phelps recalls outlandish claims made about him and how futile it was to refute them all. He specifically referenced an erroneous 2012 story (London, 2012) in the *London-Daily Mail* that went viral:

> Think of those ridiculous storylines that everybody wrote about my eating habits. I never ate 12,000 calories a day. Never. Not even close. But the *Daily Mail* starts this bullshit and, of course, it takes off. To this day, people ask me if I really ate 12,000 calories a day. No, I didn't. But that's what they do. They take this little stuff and they twist it. I almost think of it as like clickbait. But now it's a part of me. Media is a part of what I do, so this becomes part of who I am.

Even after Phelps has debunked the rumor over and over again, the story lives (and is still posted, retraction-free, on the *Daily Mail* website).

Phelps understands the role media has played—and must play—in telling his story. However, he is cognizant of the pitfalls and troubles in the industry as well:

> I've been barbecued in the press multiple times for things that I haven't said. Things that are completely false. It makes it hard to be ourselves because we don't know who we can trust. They just want to get a bunch of clicks.

The inanity of the questions revealed odd motives in reporters. "I had this reporter who once asked me: do you feel bad for winning all those medals?," he recalls, "I was like, what the fuck are you talking about? Are you joking? And he is asking this with a serious face, so I have to say: "no, absolutely not." Moreover, he believes easy media narratives of "downfalls" followed by "triumphs" feed into public misunderstandings about mental health. For instance:

> Even now, when I do speeches or I have engagements that I have people who reference that I'm now free of mental health problems. I so want to ask them: how ignorant are you? Mental health is a sensitive thing because unless you go through it, or you struggle with it or you have somebody in your family you're close to that struggled with or you know somebody that's struggling with it, you don't really understand it.

His relationship with the press has always been complicated, as it is for most elite athletes. Other times, he believes the press is manufacturing questions to fit larger narratives, citing a reporter who wanted him to render practical advice for royals Harry and Meghan as an exemplar of questions that "drive me up the wall."

Social media seems to both help and hinder these processes, Phelps argues. He believes "social media has the opportunity to be an amazing tool, but it also has the possibility of destroying every single thing inside of the human being." Thus, some of his advice has been, first and foremost, "to try to be my authentic self as much as possible. If I want to post, I'll post. If I don't, I won't." He also says limiting engagements or attempting to resolve disputes via social media is likely ill-advised:

> I learned the hard way not to engage with comments. Somebody attacked my family and I decided to private message with that person. Not a good plan. Since then, I don't even look at (comments), because it's not worth my time. Time is such a valuable thing. Why spend it engaging with people who are hiding behind an alias, just throwing shade?

Phelps entered stardom as a teenage phenom, leading journalists he never met to ask inappropriate questions about whether he had a girlfriend and whether he had been kissed. An article on CNBC before the 2016 Rio Olympics quoted marketing experts who targeted the sponsorship value of the most decorated Olympian because of his arrests and bong photo. "Why Michael Phelps may not be as marketable as you think," it was headlined (Golden, 2016).

Put simply, the mass media can forget the human behind the stories—both when they are building up the myth of the golden athlete and when they are tearing the person down. Phelps appears to harbor no ill feelings, though, understanding the media attention comes with the territory. His goal is to tell parts of the stories that are not told as frequently for premier athletes. "Everybody thinks that it's this magical wonderland," he says, "and yeah, it obviously has upsides. There are a lot of amazing things that come with it, but there are downsides as well and sometimes those are magnified even more because of who we are."

All in all, he believes the stories should illustrate for younger athletes the pros and cons of sharing personal information in the news. "I could probably count on one hand the reporters I felt comfortable with because they were fair," he says. "They didn't always love me and make me out to be this hero, but they also didn't try to kick me every time I was down. They treated me like a person." Phelps specifically noted his continued relationship with former *New York Times* reporter Karen Crouse, who he respected because she was one of the few who could meet that criteria: "It's about how she writes. Karen can tell the story that reaches every single reader, not just your typical sports fan."

Becoming a Mental Health Advocate

The Weight of Gold, released in 2020, provided insight into the heavily publicized withdrawal of Simone Biles from the 2020 Tokyo Olympics, which happened in 2021 because of the COVID-19 pandemic. Biles, the most celebrated gymnast of all time, took herself out of several competitions for mental health reasons. Tokyo marked the first time Phelps had not competed in the Games since 1996, but he had already committed to being there as a guest commentator for NBC. He provided insight while speaking with NBC Olympics host Mike Tirico, saying, "You know, we carry a lot of things, a lot of weight on our shoulders. And it's challenging, especially when we have the lights on us and all of these expectations that are being thrown on top of us. So, it broke my heart" (White, 2021, para. 3).

Troubling to him, too, was the initial treatment of tennis star Naomi Osaka's disclosures. "In the first 24-36 hours, Naomi got thrashed by people who are going through the same exact stuff," he recalls. "That's not right. She did this on her own terms and gets barbecued for it." He also seeks more press understanding that athletes need to be given the space to tell their own stories in their preferred media venue at the time of their own choosing:

> For me, it is healing to talk about it, whether that's at home or in the media. Athletes like Simone and Naomi have talked, giving you a little anecdote or two. I think there's more there and when they're ready to share, they'll share. But you have to remember that everybody's mental health story is different, so everybody's going to have a different timeline.

Like other celebrity athletes, Phelps understands his potential influence over public attitudes. It is the reason he has appeared on boxes of Wheaties, Corn Flakes, Frosted Flakes, Reese's Cups, Rice Krispies treats, Club crackers - the list goes on. Those sponsorships are particularly important in the United States Olympic system, where athletes do not receive a check from the United States Olympic Committee—unless they win a medal. Obviously, those payouts came more frequently for Michael Phelps than any other athlete. Coupled with the sponsorships, Michael had financial room to advance his cause.

Ultimately, it was a $1 million bonus from a sponsor that provided the seed money for the Michael Phelps Foundation, through which Phelps advocated for children's water safety before expanding to feature mental health. The organization passes on to children an important lesson Phelps picked up in treatment. Every morning in the first week of treatment, he would be asked to talk about his emotions and the reason he felt the way he did. "For me, as simple as that was, it was pretty incredible," Phelps says. "You have to pinpoint every little thing you're feeling, and for me that opened up so many doors. It gave me so much freedom."

The Michael Phelps Foundation works to teach children to implement the behavior at an early age. Phelps says, "We've seen dramatic changes in children's behavior. It's been absolutely incredible." He also teaches his own boys, Boomer, Beckett, and Maverick, to talk about their emotions, even "where every single day is like WWE Monday Night Raw," he jokes. "We've learned a lot about how strong our emotions can be at times, and they've gotten to the point where they can talk about them and open up," Phelps says. "For me as a dad, it's incredible because hopefully you can give them so many more tools moving forward to be able to conquer more things."

This similar focus on emotions is one of eight lessons the Phelps Foundation shares with children. The foundation's educational initiative also teaches children steps for appreciating life, deep breathing exercises, mindfulness, and tips for handling sadness and nervousness. The final lesson focuses on helping others—and letting them help you. By discussing his own mental health, Phelps understands he can help others. Phelps recalls emails and letters of thanks he received after disclosing his mental health. Before the pandemic, Phelps spoke at an event at Microsoft. An employee stood up in front of 500 coworkers and, through tears, shared his own story of mental illness. "It was so moving," Phelps says. He says that reactions to the larger mental health in sport movement have "been absolutely incredible hearing," because he believes "it's almost like it's giving people a voice. I think that's the most powerful thing, because when you hold onto things and stuff things down, it just crushes you and it ruins you."

Thus, he argues that "the stories never grow old" because:

> It's OK to not be OK. It's OK to cry. Crying can be a scary thing, but it can also be such an amazing moment. It can give you so much knowledge, and you can learn so much just by taking that small step. I can't smile enough at all the amazing things that we've been able to do from the Foundation standpoint, helping people understand that they can talk about these things and they're not alone.

Navigating the Pandemic...and Beyond

Michael Phelps' personal story now embodies the reactions he received from family, friends, and fans following his disclosure. "I'm starting to see that we are making a difference, that people are getting over these obstacles and they're talking about their struggles," he says. "Little by little, it's just going to get bigger and bigger."

The COVID-19 pandemic exacerbated his mental health path, but he also found a silver lining in terms of public understanding. "It is unimaginable to see where the movement really has gone since the pandemic," he says. "I almost look at the pandemic and I'm thankful for it because it shed so much more light on these issues. We've had to get in our own shit and I believe that has been helpful in terms of understanding this stuff."

Phelps recommends younger athletes - everyone, really - be open about mental health: "I always say, if we're working on our mental health like we do our physical health, that makes us almost superhuman." His strategy is one he's enacted plenty before when he was swimming competitively:

For me to be able to get to where I was, it had to be one step at a time, one practice at a time, one year at a time. For me to be able to reach my true peak and be my best self, I knew I couldn't do that overnight. It's a process. So, when I when I talk about mental health, I apply the same strategies. I want to be able to be better than I am now, whatever that looks like. Keep moving forward.

By doing so himself, he did, indeed, become a different man in the years following the article. He got married, and he and wife Nicole now focus their attention on raising three boys. The oldest boy, Boomer, lounged on his father's lap one afternoon as Phelps discussed the reaction to his openness about mental illness in sport. And he is abundantly clear: openness should never be equated with "cured":

There are days where I feel like I just want to dive into a 10-foot hole and not see the light of day. But that's just how it goes. For me, I'm working through that in terms of how I can gain more knowledge and how can I be more prepared for what's going to come my way in the future.

Shedding the stereotypes that are ascribed to many elite athletes and, particularly to himself has been a parallel journey as well. "Throughout my career, I kind of had to be selfish. That meant compartmentalizing," he explains. "Now that I am a dad with three kids and a family, I'm not able to compartmentalize like that." He believes this is ultimately a good thing because it eliminates the cloak of invincibility that he often felt obligated to wear:

"I'm not the Energizer Bunny and I never was. I'm not only a swimmer. To be able to look in the mirror now and see myself as a human—after some of the obstacles that I had to climb—is a dream come true".

He foresees remaining as a mental health advocate for the foreseeable future. While noting significant progress, he also believes much work is left to be done. "When we are going through downward spirals, we feel alone," Phelps says. "And that's when suicide happens. That's when overdoses happen. So how can we avoid that?" he asks. "That's my mission. How can we save a life?"

References

Bandura, A. (1963). *Social learning and personality development.* New York: Holt, Rinehart, and Winston. Golden, J. (2016, August 12). Why Michael Phelps may not be as marketable as you think. *CNBC.* https://www.cnbc.com/2016/08/11/why-michael-phelps-may-not-be-as-marketable-as-you-think.html

Jackson, J. (2016). Michael Phelps talks Rio, rehab and retirement with TODAY's Matt Lauer. *NBC*. https://www.today.com/news/michael-phelps-talks-rio-rehab-retirement-today-s-matt-lauer-t88666

Kerr-Dineen, L. (2016, Aug. 9). The 17 funniest Michael Phelps face memes from the Rio Olympics. *USA Today: For the Win*. https://ftw.usatoday.com/2016/08/micheal-phelps-hilarious-tweets-memes-rio-olympics-swimming

Layden, T. (2015). After rehabilitation, the best of Michael Phelps may lie ahead. *Sports Illustrated*. https://www.si.com/olympics/2015/11/09/michael-phelps-rehabilitation-rio-2016

London, B. (2012, July 23). Michael Phelps reveals details of his 12,000 calories a day diet…and he doesn't look bad on it either girls. *The London Daily Mail*. https://www.dailymail.co.uk/femail/article-2177613/Michael-Phelps-12-000-calories-day-dont-doing-harm.html

White, A. (2021, July 29). Michael Phelps says Simone Biles' reason for Tokyo Olympics withdrawal "broke my heart." *The Hollywood Reporter*. https://www.hollywoodreporter.com/news/general-news/michael-phelps-simone-biles-toyko-olympics-mental-health-1234990243/

8

Case Study: Kearnan Myall, Premiership Rugby Union

"You can't talk about it if you don't understand it."

He had never known anything but rugby and sports culture. Like many elite athletes, heavy training had led to an early spotlight on his skills and potential. By the age of 15, Kearnan Myall had joined the prestigious Leeds Academy; three years later, he helped lead the team to athletic glory with a National Colts Cup. His career would include stops at Leeds Carnegie, Sale Sharks, and Wasps RFC. His career spanned a decade and a half and included designation on English national teams.

He was living the dream of many aspiring rugby players.

He was also lost.

In 2014 and 2015, Myall started experiencing what he later knew was depression. He was somehow still performing well on the pitch with his team, Wasps RFC, but was spiraling with no sense of why. Ultimately, it found himself clinging to the outside a 15th-floor balcony seeking to end his life. He later recalled that it was his teammate, Charlie Davies, who pulled him back and asked what was happening. Myall's response: "I don't know." He merely remembered a lack of caring about any aspect of his life. None of it mattered at the time. Later, he would recall that "I can't say if I was going to do it, but I was in a place where it wasn't a big deal. I'd already made my peace with it. It was…happening at some point in time" (Kitson, 2019, para. 3).

A failed drug test led to mandatory therapy, which led to a diagnosis of major depression disorder (MDD). Still, he kept all aspects of his mental health private—even to the exclusion of family, close friends, and his partner. Years later, he was approaching retirement and spoke "offhandedly mentioned that I'd experienced depression and I wanted to do something that was going to help athletes in a similar position." That experience got modest but universally positive response, which led to his becoming a major mental health advocate and, interestingly, a second career. Myall's case is about a person who "knew nothing" about mental health and yet eventually sought information to the point that he became a leading advocate and psychiatry doctoral student at one of the best medical schools in the world.

Timing the Disclosure

Kearnan felt that there was a world of difference between when he was at the height of his depression in 2014-2015 ("Nobody really spoke about it. At that period of time, it just wasn't a thing that anybody spoke about.") and the end of his career in 2019 ("Before I had zero understanding of mental health, but now I had something I felt I could contribute.") His pending retirement was cited as the key impetus for being able to discuss his own experiences with mental health because he had always presumed, rightly or wrongly, that such discussions could have repercussions.

Suddenly, with the end of career clearly in sight, "a weight was off my shoulders," he recalled, advancing that he could now "actually speak more honestly." There was no overt plan to become a sport-based mental health advocate, nor was there even the intent of infusing any interview with discussions of his depression. However, retirement allowed his emotions to move more freely simply by being less guarded. Without retirement on the horizon, he is confident that he "wouldn't have been this honest." This was true whether he was staying with Wasps RFC, but would have been particularly the case if he were seeking to move to another team. The possibility that such a disclosure could threaten career sustainability was prominent in his thoughts:

> I would have been concerned about people's perceptions of whether I was mentally weak, whether I couldn't hack it, whether I was going to be up and down at training and not be inconsistent in my performance. Could they trust that I was going to deliver on a weekend during games? Those would have been the questions instead.

Testing the Waters: Local Media

Myall was already comfortable in his post-career plans, which included working part-time on Ph.D. in Psychiatry while also working as a human performance specialist for GB Snowsports. Both dovetailed on topics relating to his experience juxtaposing sport and mental health, but he was asked to participated in a local newspaper interview in Coventry to discuss his career with the Wasps. He kindly obliged. After covering all of the reporters' requisite topics, the end of the interview took a turn. Recalls Myall:

> We were having a standard sort of media exit interview. He asked me what about what I would be doing in the future, so I explained I was going to do a Ph.D. in Psychiatry. That led to the questions of why. So I told him my personal story...and that became the headline.

Kearnan understood the journalists' desire to make the unique angle of his depression the focus of the article, reflecting: "Would I have done that if I was going to a new team? Probably not. But, given where I was in my career, I said it very matter of fact. Naturally, a journalist picks up on that." Myall said he was pleased with the way the article explained his depression, but the headline basically was "Kearnan Myall suffered with depression," which was not "what I would have intended it to be." Because of the focus on his depression, the story got picked up more widely than he would have anticipated. "My teammates understood me a bit better after the first article," Myall recollects, because "they started to understand that I wasn't just grumpy."

After dealing with what it meant for his partner, family, and close friends—all of whom were unaware of the extent of his depression—there was another nagging element to the story that remained with Kearnan: he hadn't said everything he wanted to say. Moreover, he wanted the opportunity to tell the story in the manner that best exemplified his experience. It was both the quantity and quality of the comments that he wished to amend and reshape in the media, with the overarching goal being to advance the issue for the public good, as well as for his fellow athletes. Myall explains:

> Over the sort of coming months, I realized I had only told a tiny part of the story. I wanted to clarify a few things. But the positive response gave me the confidence—even though I was incredibly nervous—to do the *Guardian* article because, obviously, it's a national newspaper so it was going to get picked up more

widely. I actually got in touch with the journalist from *The Guardian* myself, and that's when the story really got coverage.

Myall Goes National

The result of his work with Guardian journalist Robert Kitson was a story that was comprehensive by newspaper standards (over 1,700 words) and covered many bases. "I went back and forth with Robert Kitson the journalist quite a few times," Myall notes, "I probably could have pushed back harder on some things, but he did a nice job with it." Kitson's (2019) article covered the "human beneath the headguard," (para. 1) including the contemplation of taking his own life on that apartment balcony. However, there was one element that was outside of his—or Kitson's—control: the headline.

"It was a bit sensationalist and wasn't really the point of the article at all," Myall argues. The editor opted to use the headline: "Kearnan Myall: 'Several England players I know dread training camp," which Myall believed tried to limit the story to a specific team or, more specifically, nation. "The headline was very much about England. I wasn't happy with it." The more he reflected on the framing of the article, the more some of the aspects of media framing troubled him.

Framing theory, as advanced by Goffman (1974) and explained by Gitlin (1980) pertains to the manner in which "media frames are persistent patterns of cognition, interpretation, and presentation, of selection, emphasis, and exclusion, by which symbol-handlers routinely organized discourse, whether verbal or visual" (p. 7). Such conceptions are a function of a zero-sum game within media content as the elevation of one portion of a narrative involves the diminishment of another portion. Myall's trouble with the headline appeared to be the embodiment of Entman's (1993) articulation of selection frames, namely taking "aspects of a perceived reality and [making] them more salient" (Entman, 1993, p. 52). Because people rely on media to elevate the "most important" issue within a given story (Scheufele, 2000), "the informational content of news reports" becomes less primary than "the interpretive commentary" surrounding it (Gamson, 1989, p. 158).

As a result of the headline, the rest of the narrative read differently than what Kearnan was hoping: "It was still framed that rugby *caused* my depression, which wasn't the case. Rugby *contributed* to it; the environment *contributed* to it, but neither were the *cause* per se." Part of his intention was accomplished, as he was achieved his objective of showing that it was "about more than just about me." The story highlighted how the Rugby Players Association had experienced triple the volume on its Premier players confidential hotline. It also highlighted the degree to which coaching staff was unprepared for handling such concerns: Kearnan's eventual confession to poor sleep and general anxiety was met with a suggestion to "make sure you jerk off before you go to sleep." In that, Myall was able to accomplish his primary goal:

> I definitely didn't want it just to be about *my* story of my struggles because I knew that I'm not the only person that has gone through that. The reason for me speaking was because so many other people *couldn't* and were afraid to speak out.

Nevertheless, the problematic headline lessened the scope of the issues: it was an England problem, not a worldwide concern.

Positive Media Response...with Nuance

If Kearnan were to gauge response to this second, more extensive piece about his mental health, he would place it on the same extreme end of the positive portion of the scale, yet with a much greater magnitude. While response to the *Guardian* article yielded supportive reactions, it was "overwhelming at the time. Hundreds upon hundreds of messages and about 99.9% positive." He reports coaching staff messaging him to apologize for previously being blind or obtuse about the issue. However, it was the widespread embrace of the article from his fellow athletes that resonated the most:

> The most surprising thing was the amount of athletes who I didn't know who reached out. People I played against but didn't know them personally or just athletes from completely different sports, sending me messages saying this is how they felt, too. There were people I had played with who had come closer to killing themselves than I had. I sat and cried several times for messages from ex-teammates, talking to me about what they went through, and knowing it was so similar and yet I had no idea.

The paradox of social media was not lost on Myall as his burgeoning interest in psychiatry had resulted in a keen awareness that "we can't even fathom the effect of our environment we all live in now. Constantly connected to everything. Our brains just are not evolved to deal with that amount of stimulus." Nevertheless, social media proved to be a space for many of those messages of support, as had been found with other athletes making similar disclosures (Parrott, et al., 2020).

His more direct discussion of his night on the wrong side of a balcony caused considerable discussion and emotions among his family, but Kearnan reports being in the right head place to have those dialogues. Everyone wanted to help, with one brief exception: "The only negative one that I saw was somebody tweeting 'Who is this person?.' That didn't bother me, but I do remember it."

Still, one of the most resonating responses came from teammate James Haskell, as reported in an ancillary media story. His response:

> I was shocked by that, I played with him the whole time. I messaged him; I was mortified. Because someone of my character, bravado, quite attacky and everything else, I do have a really compassionate side. I was mortified that he had been going through this stuff and didn't feel that he could've sat down and spoken to somebody about it and he thought about taking his own life (Bridge, 2019, para. 6).

Arguably even more noteworthy was Haskell's call to action in light of his teammates' revelation:

> We do have a massive responsibility, and I think we do have to break stereotypes, just like we're trying to break stereotypes down with homophobia, words that have become common parlance, 'err that's gay', 'this is gay', we've got to cut this stuff out. Same with mental health. Men struggle. We need to be able to open up and speak about it (Bridge, 2019, para. 7).

The Sporting Context

The sometimes toxic cocktail of masculinity and the bawdiness it entails within sport has been chronicled for decades (Messner, 1990), with scholars particularly noting the role media plays within this troubling combination (Duncan & Messner, 1998; Wenner & Jackson, 2008). Still, Haskell's comments regarding the general insensitivity within men's team sports were significant. Myall believes the notion of elite athletes either being immune to mental health issues or somehow having those feelings assuaged by money and status actually leads to larger attempts to mask symptoms.

Part of that, he argues, is because of the performative aspect: "To perform at the highest levels, you have to have a high level of stress tolerance. To be an elite athlete, you need to be comfortable being uncomfortable. I don't think we know what level is acceptable or unacceptable." Such expectations lead to thoughts of invincibility that he finds are not only repeated in the media, but even within a medical world that he believes should be more informed. As an example, he touts a sports medicine journal that published a comparative study of U.S. Olympic athletes, immediately after the Tokyo Games in which gymnast Simone Biles' struggles were a major worldwide story. Still, Myall said he was "bewildered" when reading the headline:

> They worded it something like "elite athletes are not immune to mental health problems." The Tokyo Olympics has just happened and there's still a chance that people think that athletes would be immune because they can run fast and jump high? They will somehow be immune to emotions, depression, or anxiety?

Even beyond the notion of athlete as automaton was the confounding variable of status—both celebrity and economic—that he believes impedes the seeking of help as an athlete rises to higher competitive levels. He reasons:

> The higher up you go, the more reluctant you might be to come out. The athlete who's on top of the world has more of a tangible reason not to speak out. I wasn't necessarily in that position, but I know that I was earning a lot of money, had a really nice house, and driving fancy cars. I had everything that I could materially wish for and so many people would chop their arm off to be in my position. But that actually contributed to my depression because I didn't feel I had the right to be depressed. I was walking past homeless people on the street and yet *I* was the one who didn't want to be alive? That makes it makes it worse.

Team Dynamics: A Complicating Factor

Even if one can resolve the tensions of being a high-profile athlete with all of the access and amenities that affords, team structures were something that Kearnan Myall felt needed to change as most teams, he found, were built under the direct equation that any decision must directly facilitate wins and that "if there's not a performance benefit, many coaches are not going to buy in." He notes one example was when he was an athlete on a highly successful team, with even the potential of fostering and prioritizing mental health as an unneeded path for fear of rocking the (competitively successful) boat. He explains:

The team was doing really well. For several seasons we were great, finishing top four getting into the Premiership final one year. One of our senior players went to the coach and said, I think we need a psychologist—which we hadn't had for six years. Kind of crazy. His response was, 'I'm not paying for somebody so you can talk about your childhood problems.' You have to show coaches that having mentally healthy athletes is going to improve their performance in the long run.

Myall believed team dynamics "run really deep," to the point that you personally feel you're letting the team down. He contrasts that to the very different experience of injury, which fans seem to understand, often with the media providing a standard timeline for recovery, letting the fans know how long an athlete will be unavailable. Such timelines help give athletes the space to rehabilitate a physical injury, but Myall believes physical injuries can still foster team dynamics in other ways:

When an athlete gets physically injured, they're on the sidelines for as long as it takes until they're fixed in a team environment, but the thing that helps is that you *see* that athlete training every day. You *see* them working hard in the gym. You *see* them getting treatment. People are witnessing professional behavior that contributes to the good of the team because they're working to get back as fast as they can.

In contrast, he argues, mental health simply "can't work that way." Instead, treatment is necessarily more private, meaning an athlete is foundationally removed from other elements of the team space: "You *don't see* them talking to a therapist. You *don't see* them trying to get back. So you worry the team will think you're not pulling your weight." The result, he posits, is that one discloses a physical injury often out of necessity—to explain why they cannot perform at the anticipated level—while one hides a mental issue for fear of altering the aforementioned team dynamics. He explains his own reasoning, even when his space on the team was relatively cemented, noting that "because I was in a senior position on the team, I worried that people would lose trust in me, that they would lose faith in my making performance-related decisions that had nothing to do with mental health." Thus, unless an athletes' status on the team is virtually unassailable, there is perceived to be considerable risk in seeking therapy. Myall notes that "unless you're the top dog, you risk of losing your position. If you take time out, that gives three other people an opportunity to take your position in the team."

The Accidental Diagnosis

So how does one get diagnosed with depression when they don't even consider they have a problem, nor do they believe therapy is a viable option for elite athletes? For Kearnan, the answer was that he stumbled upon it when his depression manifest in other destructive ways. "It was a bit strange how it happened," he explains, because "I was seeing a therapist, but I didn't really know what I was talking about with him. When I failed the drug test, I was forced to see a psychiatrist, who gave me the diagnosis." There was a simplicity in the psychiatrist's explanation that was cathartic for Myall: "He was just so casual. It was so helpful. He was just ' yeah, you've got depression. It happens to loads of people.' It all made perfect sense."

At first he thought such a diagnosis was impossible, steadfastly maintaining that "I'm an athlete. I'm not depressed. Athletes can't be depressed." But, by the end of the day, he found himself Googling depression and finding considerable match to what he was feeling. Going into the session, his participation was obligatory: "I was going because I had to, but I didn't care about anything really. I didn't care if I got sacked. Didn't care if the papers wrote that I'd failed drug test." By bedtime, he was experiencing an epiphany: you can't talk about it if you don't understand it.

He sought structures outside the league, because he felt his depression was different than the resources being offered. The league had a confidential helpline, but "it was very much pitched as being for people with drug or gambling problems. [Because that wasn't me], I paid for my own private therapy. I started to understand things a bit better."

However, the need for understanding was not the only revelation for Myall. He also realized that he had the skillset to manage his depression; he had just never applied his sports processes to his private life. The therapist started teaching him, and he absorbed it quickly. "It actually came really easy—not to get rid of the symptoms but to use cognitive processes," he says. "Sports psychology generally is really helpful, but you have to use those elements in all aspects of your life." He articulates these breakthroughs in the context of cognitive therapy:

> With the practical things were what I was taught from mindfulness-based cognitive therapy. All these skills I already had. In the game, I knew how to regulate my emotions. I knew how to control my attention to the point that if I made a mistake I'd just focus on the next thing rather than ruminating about the mistake. I knew it all...but nobody had ever taught me that I could do that in my own life.

> So, away from the game, I'd sit and ruminate. I didn't know that it's unhealthy, so I just carried on doing it.

Just as he was finding elements of sports psychology helpful, the more he learned, the more he was also realizing fissures within the system. The atypical nature of the elite athlete mindset seemed an odd fit with some principles. He explains that:

> Some elements of sports psychology can enhance problematic behaviors by shortcuts. Athletes are often perfectionists; we're never happy with what we're achieving and highly self-critical. When many coaches say to never be happy with what you've done, it's a shortcut to performance enhancement because it's going to increase your motivation. You're going to train harder, but you're treading a very fine line between improving the performance and success. Then, if you still play poorly, you end up with athletes in downward spirals.

Expertise Theory in Action

Much of Myall's treatment fell within the realm of expertise theory (Ericcson, 1996) as he continually sought more understanding of his condition and of the mental states of the people surrounding him. Decades ago, expertise would have been viewed as being derived from someone who possessed the most desirable traits: if one wished to get smarter, they would simply find the smartest person they knew; if one wished to improve mental health, one would seek out a person claiming to not be struggling with mental health issues. Expertise theory changed that equation through the scientific substantiation of expertise built not through traits, but rather via learning and practice.

Popularized in Malcolm Gladwell's massive best-seller *Outliers: The Story of Success* (2008), part of that process involved simply having the opportunity to attain at least 10,000 hours of time learning and practicing. The Beatles were a famous example, playing music at an undesirable club, but doing so for up to eight hours per day for hundreds of nights. The hours added up quickly. Expertise was borne.

Myall's situation is unique in that he possesses over 10,000 hour of being a professional rugby player, all while currently logging consistent hours understanding psychiatry at the highest level. In doing so, he holds the potential to jointly have expertise in two realms rarely combined: the mind of the elite athlete and the elite study of the mind. Myall currently is a student in the Department of Psychiatry at Oxford University, all while also being the human performance lead for GB Snowsports, helping skiers and snowboarders optimize their performance by fusing the physical and the mental. He won't claim expertise, but he will claim to be far more knowledgeable about mental health in sport that he ever has. His coaching has changed, emphasizing how you can "critique your performance without critiquing yourself." He knows the pitfalls of not doing so and can attest to athletes through the perfect lens: he's been there. "When athletes personalize the performance, it becomes critiques of themselves as a human," he explains, noting that when that happens, "their worth is only as good as that performance." Thus, he actively works to reshape athletic thinking to include mental wellness, all while pursuing greater expertise at Oxford. Even then, he has found that the greatest minds in the field still struggle with base definitions and understandings, but also seems to find solace in the admission of the complexity of mental health:

> Oxford is the best medical school in the world, but we still sit in research meetings defining what things are. What constructs are. What depression is. What a treatment entails. We have to still have these discussions because even for the scholars who are most advanced in this area, there's not a consensus of what mental health even is. There's generally a misunderstanding of clinical issues. You can have symptoms of anxiety and depression without having a clinical problem. There are some people who argue that that there is no such thing as mental illness and it's all just a continuum. That we have pathologies and natural emotions and feelings.

2021: A Sports Mental Health Check

"I'd like to think that that has changed slightly even over the last couple of years" says Myall, but talking about it and clarifying the issues seem to be separate goals. He states he is "not trying to pass judgment" on the disclosures of other athletes in 2021, but contends that it's possible the term "mental health" is being misused slightly. For instance, he cites the cases of Naomi Osaka and Simone Biles, noting that:

> A lot of the tensions we're seeing—particularly with athletes withdrawing from competitions—is sort of avoidant behavior that can increase the tension because mental health and performance can be seen as two completely different things.

They don't have to be. You can deliver interventions or programs that will improve performance and mental health as well.

Moreover, while he will concede that for some athletes—particularly in seemingly perpetual year-long sports such as Osaka in tennis—time off is a necessity and facilitates mental wellness. However, he also believes that time off can be the wrong recommendation in cases such as the one he was in during his rugby career, arguing that "if somebody had suggested taking two weeks off and staying at home, that would have been the absolute last thing that I wanted to do. Going to training for an hour took my mind off things. It was helpful."

Moreover, he believes the lack of a timetable for return makes the media stories convoluted, as media often are too quick to claim someone's mental health as resolved, rather than improved. Media narratives become, by definition, incomplete when trying to tell stories about elite athletes and mental health. Notes Myall:

> What we've seen over the last few months is that Simone Biles, Naomi Osaka and other athletes are making a statement. Then the media then writes a story and tries to interpret what that statement might be. But still, realistically, we don't know the details. We don't know any of the medical records. Because they haven't disclosed any of that, the media is going to make that story into something.

Additionally, Myall notes the problem of rebutting a claim that an issue falls within the larger context of mental health. He explains the potential backlash, all while articulating why other factors might be at play:

> Perhaps there's no clinical reason for someone to withdraw from a match. She just got flustered and wasn't performing. As a young athlete, sometimes you have to just say crack on, do terribly, and learn from it. In my opinion, that isn't a mental health issue. But even then, you can't be sure.

Media can be effectively used to reveal stories that previously were stifled or squelched—either by the athlete, a coach, a team, or some combination. Myall believes control is the key to effectiveness in this regard, advancing that "what other athletes have done, including myself, is give the details that they want so they are more in control of the story. I definitely was in control of the story."

Still, the media can also be a beast that must be fed, as athletic calendars and absences shape overall storylines. Because the story is believed to be prescient, media believe it is their job to know why Naomi Osaka isn't playing in a major, or why Simone Biles isn't competing in the Olympic women's all-around final. And, in doing so, stories become incomplete or streamlined:

> To expect someone in the media to be able to accurately report on it is basically impossible. It's an unsolvable problem. You're trying to report on a specific situation, but you can't unless you know their medical records. You'd have to be able to sit down with the psychologist and understand where they're at. Unless you're doing that, you can't really have an opinion on it. Therefore, it's very difficult to report it accurately.

Then, of course, there is the multifaceted world of social media, where all voices, no matter how ridiculous, are offered to the masses. Jonathan Taplin, Director of the University of Southern California Annenberg Innovation Lab, once explained the swamp of social media:

> Plato asked: If we were shielded from the consequences of our actions, how would that change the way we act? We now know the answer…Social media were supposed to be the new public square. Instead, it's a Tower of Babel, with thousands venting anger, and little or no understanding (Taplin, 2015, p. 66).

Kearnan Myall sees the effects of social media in his current academic field, with the ramifications for the elite athlete magnified considerably in recent years. Relating to his own experiences, he offers:

> I'm not that old, but when I started my career, I wasn't even on Facebook. If I had a crap day training or played poorly, I could just go home. There was no way of me getting any feedback on what happened. I just watched TV and have it going around in my own head a little bit. But that was *it*, whereas now—particularly the more high profile athletes—the amount of stimulus, interactions, opinions, and headlines is astounding. I don't think we will understand the effect for another few decades.

Coda: The Benefit of Hindsight

Overall, Kearnan Myall's story is a positive one. Once at the brink of taking his own life, he not only lived to tell the tale, but also is now managing to help others in similar positions to avoid the spirals he knows all too well. He also is generally pleased with how the media rendered his story, but not universally so:

> I don't regret anything at all, but I think I probably would have pushed harder for some things that weren't factually inaccurate, but were slightly misconstrued to make a better story or make a bit of narrative. In the moment, you feel like you're being too specific and persnickety about things, but that's important because years later the article gets referred to, and that's what people's knowledge of the situation is. You want it to be as accurate as possible because those little inaccuracies become bigger over time.

As such, his advice to athletes thinking about disclosing struggles with mental wellness would be to "stay in control of the story, as you can. Give only the information that you're comfortable with and that you feel is appropriate to give." Guarded authenticity seems to be the watchword from Myall, who also cautions people to think through all of the angles of how they want their story rendered, because "details that might not seem that important at the time will become more important over the course of time."

Between his work at Oxford and with GB Snowsports, Kearnan does not find himself with an abundance of free time, yet that does not mean he considers his individual purpose to be cemented, or even clear. "The whole transition out of being an athlete is incredibly personal. You don't know how you feel until you've come out to the other side." Two years post-retirement, he still believes he is "figuring out who I am as a person. It's incredibly challenging."

He also struggles to grapple with the person he is with where his life was even when telling his story in *The Guardian*:

> The focus of that article is so much on rugby, but there were tons of other things from my past and my personal life that also contributed to my depression. I reflect on it and almost feel like it's not true now, even though it's just telling one version of it.

The sport he loves is also a sport he must concede contributed to his anxiety, as well as to his presence on the outside of a 15th-story balcony. "Without a doubt, rugby made it a lot more difficult," he admits, because "you're taught as a rugby player not to show vulnerability. All that is absolutely true. So, rugby truly contributed to the worsening of my symptoms. It stopped me from even understanding what was happening."

He splits his time between his current career at GB Snowsports and preparing for his future career in psychiatry. Both fuse what we know about the physical with what is largely unknown about the mental. Myall claims that the aspects of sports performance that typically are focused on—strength, conditioning, medical, and nutrition—contribute no greater than 50% of an athlete's performance. He understands why: "it's what they can control so tightly." However, he remains mystified and yet also intrigued by the remainder of that performance ledger, which he contends "they're generally leaving completely to chance." He's quick to argue that any notion of "controlling" this other side is mythical, but also steadfastly believes that you can positively influence it rather than merely hoping athletes can handle these anxieties. "Some athletes can manage, and that's amazing," Kearnan says, "but some athletes don't. They're incredibly talented athletes whose performance goes up and down. We act like it's a mystery, but often it's not."

Accepting that his own journey is one without a finish line is something that Myall struggles with, but has gradually accepted. He also needed his partner to accept this stark reality as well, particularly when Myall shared his depression during the COVID-19 pandemic. "I know I'm going to be depressed in the future, but it's about being at peace with that. Understanding that if I feel terrible for a day or a week, that's all right." That also has meant education and constant monitoring with his family who "even now, worry about me quite a lot. If I'm going through a bit of a tough time, they worry that I'm going to kill myself, which I understand why because it's been in the papers."

Suicidal thoughts are still something that he encounters fairly regularly. When that does, he says he "feels more comfortable as they come in different iterations." The key difference appears to be the ability to rationalize a dark moment, differentiating the temporary elements of it rather than fearing their permanency:

> Even the worst moments, the ones where I'm certain that the best thing I can do for everybody is to take my own life are now moments where I can now detach myself from the urge to do something about it. I can seek help. My feelings are not going to stay the same forever.

References

Bridge, B. (2019, Sept. 5). James Haskell ' mortified' by former Wasps teammate Kearnan Myall's mental health struggle admission. *The Coventry Telegraph*. Retrieved at: https://www.coventrytelegraph.net/sport/rugby/kearnan-myall-wasps-james-haskell-16868286

Duncan, M. C., & Messner, M. A. (1998). The media image of sport and gender. In L. A. Wenner (Ed.), *MediaSport* (pp. 170-185). London: Routledge.

Entman, R. (1993). Framing: Toward clarification of a fractured paradigm. *Journal of Communication, 43*(4), 51-58.

Ericsson, K. A. (Ed.). (1996). *The road to excellence: The acquisition of expert performance in the arts and sciences, sports, and games.* Mahwah, NJ: Lawrence Erlbaum Associates.

Gamson, W. A. (1989). News as framing: Comments on Graber. *The American Behavioral Scientist, 33*(2), 157-161.

Gitlin, T. (1980). *The whole world is watching: Mass media in the making and unmaking of the new left.* Berkeley, CA: University of California Press.

Gladwell, M. (2008). *Outliers: The story of success.* New York: Little, Brown and Company.

Goffman, E. (1974). *Frame analysis: An essay on the organization of experience.* New York, NY: Harper & Row.

Kitson, R. (2019, Aug. 19). Kearnan Myall: ' Several England players I know dread training camp.' *The London Guardian.* Retrieved at: https://www.theguardian.com/sport/2019/aug/19/kearnan-myall-england-players-mental-health-training-camp

Messner, M. (1990). When bodies are weapons: Masculinity and violence in sport. *International Review for the Sociology of Sport, 25*(3), 203-218.

Parrott, M. S., Billings, A. C., Hakim, S., & Gentile, P. C. (2020). From #EndtheStigma to #RealMan: Stigma challenging social media responses to NBA players' mental health disclosures. *Communication Reports, 33*(3), 148-160.

Scheufele, D. A. (1999). Framing as a theory of media effects. *Journal of Communication, 49,* 103-122.

Taplin, J. (2015, Sept. 21). Should we let ourselves be anonymous online? *Time,* p. 66.

Wenner, L. A., & Jackson, S. (2008). *Sport, beer, and gender: Promotional culture and contemporary social life.* New York: Peter Lang.

9

Case Study: Brandon Bostick, National Football League

"Instinct just kicked in...and my life changed forever"

For the typical fan, even the most epic of games become somewhat liquid in hindsight. Dramatic hype can focus the mind on an upcoming game, but years later, that same fan might ask a question akin to "I'm trying to remember...who'd we play that year?"

However, for fans of the Green Bay Packers, the 2014 NFC Championship Game against the Seattle Seahawks functions differently. The game was an epic collapse to the point that Wisconsin journalist J.R. Radcliffe (2020) would later claim an exorcism was needed. With 5:04 left in the fourth quarter, Seahawk quarterback Russell Wilson was intercepted for the fourth time, this time by Morgan Burnett. Returning the interception for a touchdown seemed possible, but Burnett's teammate, Julius Peppers, told Burnett to fall to the ground to avoid any error. In Peppers' mind, the game was secured; statistically, it sure seemed right as Pro Football Reference gave the Packers a 99.3% of victory at that point. With three minutes left in regulation and the Packers leading 19-7, the probability of the Packers emerging victorious was 99.9%. It would literally take a one-in-a-thousand scenario for the Packers not to be headed to the Super Bowl.

Of course, as any lottery winner can tell you, long odds come through every so often. As wide receiver Randall Cobb would later put it: "We just fell apart" (Huber, 2020, para. 7). It required a series of blunders and faulty choices, and that's what happened. Defensive lapses and offensive drops made many players culpable in what ultimately became a 28-22 overtime victory for the Seahawks. A failed blitz led to a Wilson to Kearse 35-yard touchdown pass and Packer legend Aaron Rodgers never touched the ball in overtime. After the game, Packer offensive guard Josh Sitton reflected: "Literally one of ten plays you can pick that if we get it, we win the game" (Huber, 2020, para. 6).

But there was one play, in particular, that media and Packer fans seized upon after the game. With the score 19-14, the Packers merely needed to recover an onside kick to salt away the victory. As initially designed, tight end Brandon Bostick would block to ensure that sure-handed wide receiver Jordy Nelson could secure the ball. That was not what happened. As Bostick explained, "Instinct just kicked in. The ball was in front of me and I wanted to grab it. I jumped up, I reached for it … and my life changed forever" (Bostick, 2015). After the game, Bostick remembers a dark, cramped locker room. He sat at his stall for 40 minutes, until it was time to speak with the media. He recalls little of what he said that day. One of the quotes the media did report was: "I just keep replaying that play in my mind over and over" he said, "just trying not to think about it, just trying to get over it. I did my best, but I'll be all right" (Reischel, 2020, para. 15).

Things were not all right for Bostick. As Wood (2018) explained, the aftermath included death threats, racial slurs, and generally being "shredded on social media" (para. 4). His mental health was not foremost on his mind; job security was. The day after the game, Brandon recalls being in head coach Mike McCarthy's office, where he asked two questions. "Will I be back next year?," Bostick asked. The response was yes. "Was I the reason we lost the game?," he continued. The response was no.

Bostick was cut from the team the next month.

The Immediate Aftermath

Fast forwarding seven years, Brandon Bostick finds the days that followed the game simultaneously blurry and yet memorable. Uncertainty was certainly a common theme, as he was unsure if his NFL career was over right when he had assumed it was about to flourish. One thing he knew: he had never been in this type of mental space before. He knew he felt like a failure, but largely could not make sense of his feelings beyond that. "All the different emotions I had never felt before" he offers, admitting that he simply "didn't know what was going on."

His immediate coping response was a combination of partying, alcohol, molly, ecstasy. "I was pretty bad after the NFC Championship. I was using partying and drinking as a band-aid. I needed something to cope with it." Bostick later stated (Christianson, 2020).

Media reports exacerbated the situation. The Seahawks improbable comeback, coupled with the bye week that traditionally precedes the Super Bowl, coincided to create a media maelstrom that often placed Bostick as the subject of unfortunate context for the storytelling. The NFC Championship game had involved a series of dominoes falling just right for the Seahawks and just wrong for the Packers. Whether one concurred with NBC Sports' (2020) later recalling that there were eight dominoes, Josh Sitton's belief that there were ten, or Radcliffe's (2020) assertion that there were 14, that presented a complex and difficult media story to tell. It was simpler to focus on one datapoint and that proved to be Bostick. Suddenly, Brandon was living the life of a public pariah. He recalls:

> Everywhere I went. I go into the bar and "Hey, you're Brandon Bostick." I'm like, fuck. I was at the airport: "Oh, you're Brandon Bostick." I go to dinner: "Oh, you're that guy who fumbled that ball." I was dealing with those things. Every time I went on Instagram and social media, I was like damn, how can I get away from this stuff? (Christianson, 2020).

Exemplification theory (Zillmann, 2000) in the media world focuses on how we tend to prefer single touch points (exemplars) over multiple accumulated cases (frequencies). Media helps an audience decipher information to make judgments, often too simplistically. Humans rely on heuristics to allow a story to be encapsulated and recalled in the mind (Gibson & Zillmann, 1998), even if that creates a story that is too linear; "the war was over X", "the celebrity became famous because of Y." One could have pointed to missed opportunities or needless Packers penalties, but none encapsulated the meltdown visually in the way of the onside kick. Moreover, exemplification occurs most frequently when people believe others find it to be a big deal (via third-person effects, (Scherr, Müller, & Fast, 2013) or when they believe the information is of immediate relevance to a population (Zillmann, 2002). As the most-watched American television program each year, the Super Bowl became the perfect priming mechanism for highlighting Bostick's error. Replays and analysis was focused on how the Super Bowl matchup (Patriots vs. Seahawks) should not logically have ever occurred.

Two weeks of compounding the error weighed heavily on Bostick to the point that he was not sure if he wanted to continue his career, even if teams sought his services. Looking back, Bostick recalls a stock-taking of his career: "I had to figure out what's best for me and why I wanted to continue to play football.

That was my mental health game talking, because I didn't know why I wanted to do *anything*." He kept hearing people say that everyone had sad days, but also was finding that, for him, "every day repeated."

Faced with feelings he "didn't have any access" to, Bostick saw one psychologist, yet ultimately determined he did not require treatment, assuming his feelings (and the media onslaught) "was going to blow over." Instead, Bostick says the goal was to "see if I can get my focus and my love of the game back."

First Things First: Job Security

Based on the structure of the National Football League, finding his desire to play was not merely about football itself—it was about economic realities. Currently, a retired NFL player needs just two credited seasons to qualify for a pension, but when Bostick was facing his situation in 2015, he needed three. He was one year short of qualifying for a modest—yet essential—average pension payment of $43,000 per year (Fitzpatrick, 2020). Bostick explains his mindset:

> I wasn't thinking about my emotions. I was more concerned with finishing my career. I knew my time in the league was coming to an end, but I needed to play one more season because I didn't have my three years to get my benefits. So, it was all about getting one more season.

Because of this economic motivation, Bostick opted to focus strictly on football and finding a way to secure a place on another team's active roster. "I wasn't going to think about anything mental until after I got done playing," he recalls.

That required an adjustment. Before the Seattle game he felt like his career was "just taking off. That [2014-2015 Packers] season, I'd just hit my stride. I was just starting to learn the tight end position, because I had never played it before my rookie year." Now, it was about relearning (and guarding against overthinking) everything he had even known or previously regarded as second nature. He remembers retraining for a hopeful comeback:

> It's about simple things like doubting your hands. Doubting whether you can catch a football. I'd never had to think about that before. Used to be such a natural reaction because I've done it for so long. But, at that point, I had to think about how to do it. Even how to catch it. I just had to learn how to reprogram my mind and reprogram my thoughts just to even play football at that point.

Bostick was formally released from the Packers on February 16, 2015. Two days later, he had secured a place on the full 90-man roster (not the active 53-man roster he needed) with a new NFL franchise. Bostick (2015) told *Sports Illustrated* "My agent called. He said, ' The bad news is, you're staying in the cold. The good news is, you're going to Minnesota.'

He practiced with the Minnesota Vikings and joined them for training camp. Nevertheless, he did not survive the first round of cuts and the Vikings released him on August 30, 2015.

A week later, the Arizona Cardinals signed him to their practice squad, but was never part of the active roster. Before the season concluded, the Cardinals had released him.

A week after his release from Arizona, the New York Jets signed Bostick to their practice squad. The following year, Bostick mustered the strength and focus to make the active roster. He played in all 16 games for the Jets in 2016; for the first time in his career, he started games—seven of them. Bostick had secured his pension and retired the following year.

As former NFL executive Andrew Brandt (2021) asserts, the "vast majority of NFL players don't retire, they are ' retired' by their teams long before they want to leave the game." Bostick generally would agree with that statement, but would also cite exhaustion, both mental and physical, as reasons his career never continued beyond the 2016 season with the Jets. Continued self-medication via constant partying led to a failed drug test that would have suspended him for four games the following season, typically a death knell for any player fighting to make an NFL roster. "My career was over after that," Bostick asserts.

The Silver Lining of COVID: Seeking Therapy

By 2017, Brandon Bostick was a retired NFL football player with mental health concerns that he still could not fully comprehend. Stereotypes surrounding mental health can be negative to the point of hurting one's self-esteem (Link, Struening, Neese- Todd, Asmussen, & Phelan, 2001), but were also increasingly evolving and nuanced to the point that media could be used to diminish stereotypes and portray mental illness as something to be discussed and navigated. As Parrott (2020) synopsizes, media decades ago used to treat mental illness as a plot point to shock or create humor yet, while problematic cases still remain, progress was clearly being made, partly from the advancement of social and user-generated media.

Bostick was seeing these media messages, particularly noticing the increased number of athletes—even active athletes— who were disclosing issues with mental health. Still, for years, therapy was not something he sought out, at least partly because that really was not a consideration given his childhood background in Florence, South Carolina (population 38,000). "Therapists are not a resource for my friends back home," he explains, "They're kind of expensive, so most people can't really afford to go."

Then the pandemic hit in March 2020. Bostick is firm in his belief that sports and mental health would not be remotely as prioritized as they were in the aftermath if not for the pandemic. It was a lightbulb moment for him: "It wasn't until COVID that I realized that it's not normal to feel the way I did." He sought consistent counseling help, discovering that "it was much deeper than just being sad or dropping the ball." Perhaps even more pertinently, Bostick learned he was far from alone. "I remember [Dallas Cowboy starting quarterback] Dak Prescott talking about some of his issues," he recalls, "I started seeing others do it. Those guys started my family. It's a good feeling for sure."

Media had brought on some of his mental health issues, but also—via the stories from other athletes—helped him find his way to therapy. There were other people to speak to before revealing anything to the public, though. For instance, his mother was generally unaware. Bostick states:

> I didn't even tell my mom until 2020. She had no idea. At first, she just kind of brushed over it. But that kind of broke me down. I was feeling too much pressure to be that guy for my family. So then I had the real conversation with my mom and it went well.

Breakthroughs were starting to happen for Bostick, most notably in the fact that, even with treatment, his mental health was likely to fall on an unpredictable continuum, taking solace in the realization that this was the case for everyone. "I had to learn the hard way," Bostick now recollects, "In the NFL, we're big guys and told it's kind of OK to have a big ego and just be tough. But with mental health, it doesn't work like that."

Media's Double-Edged Sword

Getting treatment was one thing. Telling his family was another. But an additional major step for Brandon's mental health journey came on October 9, 2020, when Bostick was a guest of Brice Christianson of the *Unknown Packers Podcast*.

Bostick recalls: "We're just having a good conversation. One thing led to another and before you know it, it just kind of came out. I felt good about it, telling my story for the first time." More specifically, after roughly fifteen minutes of recollections that led, inevitably, to the Seattle game, Brandon Bostick made the impromptu decision to share more of his story with the world. Some excerpts of his interview included:

> [It took] time, slowly, slowly, every day working on myself. I really lost myself and who I was [after that game]…That moment really changed my life, but I don't think I would do it over again if I had a chance. Because it taught me things that I didn't know about myself and it allowed me to grow…I got more from that game than a Super Bowl and all the accolades (Christianson, 2020).

He explained that COVID had been the great motivator to his seeking treatment:

> I was on social media and everyone was saying if you don't come out of COVID with something positive, then you were wasting your time. I took that to heart and went to a recovery center for anxiety and depression, which I didn't know I had. COVID has been a blessing for me…During COVID, I got my college degree…while I was in a rehab center. I got a therapist now (Christianson, 2020).

He further revealed that the journey had been long but that it also was very necessary. "I had been partying to get over that shit since 2015…Now, each day, I'm learning about myself. Learning about my emotions." Brandon ultimately advanced his new goal: "I'm slowly just trying to build myself up and go back to the top again".

The revelation was so inspiring that even the host decided to disclose his own mental health issues, telling the audience about the reasons he had quit drinking alcohol as the result of a night where he attempted suicide, but couldn't even remember doing so.

The next day, Brandon decided to take ownership of the issue, even more by posting on Twitter:

> In honor of #WorldMentalHealthDay, thank you to @unknownpackers for having me share my story. I would also like to thank @kevinlove, @DeMar_DeRozan, @dak, and @haydenrhurst for their courage addressing the stigma of mental health. #MentalHealth #NFL

Responses from the public were nearly uniformly positive, echoing the experiences of most of the athletes he mentioned, most specifically Kevin Love and DeMar DeRozan (Parrott, et al., 2021). "I mostly got good reactions," he summarizes, noting they were better reactions than when he was explaining himself before by saying "hey I messed up. I made mistakes but I think I've owned up to it."

Social media also functioned as a connector to others to build networks of support, including many former players. "All these guys have been more open," claims Bostic, "there's more people being vulnerable now." The fact that media, specifically social media, ultimately became a source of strength for him was an interesting twist on his relationship with his online presence. He remembered when he was younger and "I grew up on Instagram. I wanted to be verified. I wanted to be famous." But the Seattle game changed that feeling ("Once that play happened, everyone's on my social media stuff. Everyone.") and then therapy, combined with public disclosure, had changed that relationship again. Reminiscing about what therapy taught him, Bostick says:

> I had to learn how to control my emotions because I knew they were going to bring it up again the next time the Packers play the Seahawks. Therapy helps you focus on what can control and how you react to things, but I didn't have that back then.

Peace in Uncertainty

In hindsight, Brandon Bostick finds himself living a much healthier life. He can embrace his past that might have led to his hiding his mental health concerns, noting that Florence, South Carolina is not a place where mental health is a topic of discussion. He also still acknowledges the realities that impeded his getting help for many years, even admitting that the circumstances of an NFL career still likely mean that players struggling to make the team will mask symptoms and struggles for fear of their standing with the team. He summarily explains that:

> I think there's definitely a stigma. I mean, everything I've encountered has been good, but I definitely wouldn't disclose my issues when was I was playing. I wasn't a superstar. I was on the edge, so I think that would I felt like that would have hurt my chances.

His stance seemingly is one of knowledgeable realism, simultaneously applauding the Detroit Lions for hiring a full-time therapist while noting that there are still limitations—both in time and power structures—that make such resources of limited impact for an NFL player. "Full-time, on-site therapists can work," he argues, "but in that moment, is a player thinking: am I going to spend an hour talking to a therapist? Probably not. I'm going to be thinking about my performance on the field."

Still, he has advice to impart to others experiencing mental health issues, words that he believes are applicable to someone whether an elite athlete or not. "My advice would be to stand up for yourself," he states, and "know who you are. Stay true to who you are at the core. Make sure you got the people around you that support you even when things are bad." He also think familial disclosures are key, saying it is crucial to "tell your parents, even if you think they're going to judge you. It helps."

His days now find him coaching youth football alongside a Packers teammate, James Jones. Jones' presence is an added benefit because "he was there with me in Seattle when the whole thing went down." However, his lessons and revelations about mental health have permeated his coaching style in ways he would not have anticipated years ago. He explains:

> When I'm coaching football now, I don't coach that way I would have before, because I know the damage and where it can lead. So, when I coach these kids now, I'm saying you don't have to be tough. It's OK if you make a mistake. It's OK if you want to cry.

His mental health is noticeably improved, mostly because of his support system that he believes is significantly better than the one he had when he was in the NFL. "When I was playing I didn't have a support system outside of the game. It was only people who supported me during football and some random people," he explains. "Now, I'm looking for people that can support Brandon."

As for the fateful onside kick in the NFC Championship game, Bostick admits he still has flashbacks, but is now equipped to handle them better. If his mistake is the exemplification of a game in which many others were made, he has learned to live with it. He believes he's "at peace with it. I think it's been good for me now that I'm opening up about my struggles. I think people can relate to that." His mental health is also unpredictable, but he is better able to cope and compartmentalize: "Everyone has those dark moments of dark day. I think people are really starting to understand what is going on with me now." His status, as a sports injury report might say, is day-to-day. But, as sports anchor Dan Patrick once memorably opined when hosting ESPN's SportsCenter: "He's day-to-day, but then again, aren't we all?" (Bernreuter, 2009).

Bostick finds himself at peace with the play, at peace with life, and ready to tackle new challenges. "Every day is different," he believes, "and every day is not going to be the same. And that's OK. So, I just started taking one day at a time."

References

Bernreuter, H. (2009, Aug. 6). Top ten ESPN SportsCenter anchors. MLive. Retrieved at: https://www.mlive.com/sports/saginaw/2009/08/top_ten_espn_sportscenter_anch.html

Bostick, B. (2020, Feb. 26). ' I jumped up, reached for the ball...and my life changed forever. *Sports Illustrated*. Retrieved at: https://www.si.com/nfl/2015/02/26/brandon-bostick-nfc-championship-game-onside-kick#gid=ci0255850c90052580&pid=from-slightly-different-angles-two-si-photographers-captured-the-moment-and-the-mishap-that-forever-changed-brandon-bosticks-life-john-w-mcdonoughsports-illustratedthe-mmqb

Brandt, A. (2021, Aug. 3). Retrieved from: https://twitter.com/AndrewBrandt/status/1422528596183339008

Christianson, B. (2020, Oct. 9). Brandon Bostick: On Tap. *Unknown Packers Podcast*. Retrieved at: https://anchor.fm/the-unknown-packers-podca/episodes/S3E53_Brandon-Bostick-On-Tap-ekq77g

Fitzpatrick, T. (2020, July 1). Did you know NFL players earn a pension? *National Public Pension Coalition*. Retrieved at: https://protectpensions.org/2020/07/01/know-nfl- players-earn-pension/

Gibson, R., & Zillmann, D. (1998). Effects of citation in exemplifying testimony on issue perception. *Journalism & Mass Communication Quarterly, 75*(1), 167–176.

Huber, B. (2020, Jan. 5). Packers-Seahawks history lessons are mostly bitter. *Sports Illustrated*. Retrieved at: https://www.si.com/nfl/packers/news/packers-seahawks-history-lessons

Link, B. G., Struening, E. L., Neese-Todd, S., Asmussen, S., & Phelan, J. C. (2001). Stigma as a barrier to recovery: The consequences of stigma for the self-esteem of people with mental illnesses. *Psychiatric Services, 52*(12), 1621–1626.

McKeever, R. (2015). Vicarious experience: Experimentally testing the effects of empathy for media characters with severe depression and the intervening role of perceived similarity. *Health Communication, 30*(11), 1122–1134.

NBC Sports Northwest (2020, Jan. 11). Remembering the 2015 NFC Championship game. Retrieved at: https://www.nbcsports.com/northwest/seattle-seahawks/remembering-2015-nfc-championship-game-seahawks-vs-packers

Parrott, S. (2020). Media stereotypes of mental illness: Nurturing and mitigating stigma. In A. C. Billings & S. Parrott, (Eds.), *Media stereotypes: From ageism to xenophobia* (pp. 239-256). New York: Peter Lang.

Parrott, M. S., Billings, A. C., Buzzelli, N. R., & Towery, N. A. (2021). ' We all go through it': Media depictions of mental illness disclosures from star athletes DeMar DeRozan and Kevin Love. *Communication & Sport, 9*(1), 33-54.

Radcliffe, J. R. (2020, Jan. 8). Things you forgot from that 2014 Packers postseason loss—and why Brandon Bostick isn't the only one to blame. *Milwaukee Journal-Sentinel.* Retrieved at: https://www.jsonline.com/story/sports/nfl/packers/2020/01/08/what-you-remember-2014-green-bay-packers-debacle-and-what-you-forgot/2845283001/

Reischel, R. (2020, Jan. 9). A look back at the 2014 NFC Championship Game—and the Green Bay Packers' historic collapse. *Forbes.* Retrieved at: https://www.forbes.com/sites/robreischel/2020/01/09/a-look-back-at-the-2014-nfc-championship-game---and-the-green-bay-packers-historic-collapse/?sh=3c7e594c49b7

Scherr, S., Müller, P., & Fast, V. (2013). Do third-person perceptions amplify exemplification effects? *International Journal of Communication, 7,* 1603–1621.

Wood, R. (2018, Nov. 13). How Brandon Bostick found peace after botched onside kick cost Packers shot at Super Bowl. *PackersNews.com.* Retrieved at: https://www.packersnews.com/story/sports/nfl/packers/2018/11/13/former-packers-te-brandon-bostick-finds-peace-after-botched-onside-kick/1988979002/

Zillmann, D. (2000). Mood management in the context of selective exposure theory. *Communication Yearbook, 23,* 103–123.

Zillmann, D. (2002). Exemplification theory of media influence. In J. Bryant & D. Zillmann (Eds.), *Media effects: Advances in theory and research* (pp. 19–41). Mahwah, NJ: Lawrence Erlbaum Associates.

10

Case Study: Gracie Gold, Olympic Figure Skater

"I was shocked that the skating world was shocked"

There's no spotlight quite like women's figure skating. The personalities within it contrast widely. Add costumes, music, and a person's fate being determined in a few minutes on the ice and the media product can become downright combustible. The two nights of Tonya Harding and Nancy Kerrigan's 1994 Olympic competition join eight other Super Bowls in the top 10 television ratings in American history. From a 2002 judging scandal to the most recent 2022 Olympics in which Kamila Valieva was permitted to compete on a probationary level even after a positive drug test, the sport—particularly women's figure skating—yields big drama that equates to big ratings. Almost always, an American skater figures to be in the medals equation.

In the mid-2010s, Story A in U.S. women's figure skating was Gracie Gold.

As Christine Brennan offers in Chapter 5, Gold was "the skater of her generation." Finishing just outside of the medal podium (fourth place) at the age of 18 in the 2014 Sochi Winter Olympics, Gold's Olympic window remained open. If mapped precisely, the next four years would outline her path to another run at the medals in PyeongChang at the 2018 Winter Olympics.

By the beginning of 2017, that map was unrecognizable. "I was aware that I wasn't thriving, but I thought that it was just a failure on my part," Gold recalls. She thought it was just a matter of desire and a sign of weakness. She made all sorts of assumptions, each placing the blame for her struggles squarely on one set of shoulders: her own. "I figured I just wasn't trying hard enough. I just wasn't working hard enough. I just didn't want it enough." She felt confident that it was not a mental health issue. That involved a formal diagnosis. Certainly, she thought, that didn't include her situation. She explains:

> In my mind, there had always been a kind of a checklist that you have to cover for society to feel like it's acceptable for you to have the diagnosis. If somebody close to you dies, or you lose your job, it's acceptable. If you're a soldier with PTSD, it's acceptable. But it was just hard for me to fit my own situation into that checklist. It didn't seem to fit.

In hindsight, Gold did fit into that checklist. She just needed to expand her definition.

From Denial to Recognition

Part of the reason Gracie Gold was not cognizant of her own mental health concerns was the confluence of stressors within other aspects of her life. "My mental health crisis coincided with the implosion of my family," she recollects. As a result, "they knew something was up with me, but I did feel a bit ostracized." She rationalizes this as understandable given the circumstances: "They had their own things. I wasn't the only person who needed help. We were all aware of our own crises, but you can't pour from a cup that's empty."

Still, the signs were appearing in 2016 and, as noted in Chapter 5, others could notice. The concerns that Gracie Gold ultimately realized she had pertained to depression, suicidal ideation, and disordered eating. It was the latter concern that started to bleed into the media sphere. Gold was taken aback that her speaking about figure skating being a lean sport seemed worthy of the moniker of breaking news:

> Christine Brennan wrote a big article in *USA Today* about how I'd talked about body types. I was surprised that she and others were surprised. It's semi-common knowledge that certain sports require certain body types. When you are lifting your body several feet in the air, being super lean helps. It's also true in ballet, gymnastics, beach volleyball, and other lean sports. Everyone knows that. Why didn't they put it together that this means the potential for disordered eating is incredibly high?

Having now received treatment and better knowledge on the condition, Gold can speak more freely and honestly about the role the desire for leanness plays in the desire to be a champion. "Your weight and the calories that you've eaten that day are not figured into your score," she admits, "but somehow it feels like they are." She had seemingly accepted this belief as not just her reality but any elite skater's reality:

> It's always been so strange to me that body types are taboo to speak about. I didn't really train a lot that summer, so I had put on some weight and lost some of my physical shape. I had just been on vacation for too long and that affected my endurance and strength. So, I tried to explain that my body wasn't where it needed to be for this sport. I was shocked that the skating world was shocked. Haven't you noticed that there aren't any super tall or plus-sized figure skaters?

For Gold, the slightest difference in weight was a potential domino effect, because "a change in your body means a change in quickness, which usually affects your timing." As a result, she would "use food, training, and nutrition as a form of control. An athlete wants to control as much as possible. We can't control the judges' scores, but we can control how many calories we can eat." She separates out skating from the need to be lean in a noteworthy manner, contending that: "I can't say most of my disordered eating came from a little bit of the pressure of skating, but a little bit comes from trying to maintain a leaner figure." Thus, for Gold it "became a coping mechanism. If I could train on 200 or 400 calories a day, somehow it made me feel better."

Of course, few knew of these thoughts and behaviors. Faced with a self-concept that even she admitted she did not like, she sought to "make a different version of myself." That involved moving to Detroit, where depression magnified in ways she had not anticipated:

> I made new friends, but they didn't know what it was like to train with me every day. They didn't know that some of the things they were seeing that were red flags. They just thought this was how I was. They figured I wasn't the go-getter they thought. I didn't leave my house for days, but they didn't know how weird that was for me. Now, looking back, they've said they're sorry. They didn't have the tools to help. They didn't know if it was appropriate to step in.

As she later told Crouse (2019), a good day was one where she brushed her teeth and hair. There were days where that was too much to handle. She recalled covering every mirror in her new-found suburban Detroit home, just so she would not have to look at herself. Her lack of deep understanding of how mental health unfolds was not uncommon for someone her age, or really any age at the time. Yet, absent the tools to understand what she was experiencing, she assumed she was to blame. There was a flaw in her personality, drive, or work ethic. She rationalizes that "if I'd known that wasn't it, I would have spoken out sooner and gotten help sooner." Nevertheless, as is the case for many athletes, it took some time for her to realize that simply redoubling her effort levels would not produce a meaningful remedy. "I had to figure out that I wasn't lazy. It wasn't that I didn't have the drive anymore. I had a chemical imbalance within my brain. Most people don't immediately jump to that conclusion."

Eventually, she was aware of her own struggles enough to seek treatment. It was there that she realized just how much she had attempted to conceal not only from her friends and family, but even from herself:

> Hiding anything is rarely good. If you are hiding something, it's for a reason. I didn't feel like I was hiding something, though. I just didn't know what was going on with me. I thought a lot of mental health conditions were textbook: You're really sad, so you cry. To me, that was depression. I didn't know depression can manifest in a variety of ways. I didn't know it might not occur *because* of you. You can just be anxious for no reason.

Upon leaving formal treatment, Gold was not only confident in how to navigate her own wellness, but also in the ability and willingness to speak about it in public when the topic inevitably arose. "Once I learned about what was really going on, there was no shame in speaking out about it," Gold says, arguing that "if someone was going to make fun of me for being clinically depressed or put me down for having an eating disorder, that should be their shame and ignorance, not mine."

Explaining an Absence: Gold Opts for Honesty

Gracie Gold felt that her prolonged (and, to this point, unexplained) absence from the sport meant she would require explanation when she did reenter the figure skating community. She quickly dismissed any option other than being as transparent as possible, conceding that "of course, there were moments when I thought we should just say I'm injured or something more palatable for the general public. But I knew if I did that, I was part of the problem." The lack of spin to her situation left only one remaining path: being as candid and open as possible. "I just decided to be honest but I didn't know what else I could say. Might as well go with the truth," she recalls. She informed the media that she was getting treatment for depression, disordered eating, and suicidal ideation. "It never seriously crossed my mind to be anything but honest. It seemed like bad karma."

Even if Gold knew the truth was going to be her path forward, that did not mean she felt the entire process was voluntary. The mechanics of the skating schedule and her role within it required an explanation to quell what appeared to be an array of rumors about her future as a competitor. She elucidates:

> When I first started talking about mental health, I wasn't intentionally talking about it. I had been in an inpatient treatment facility and had fallen off the face of the earth. For quite some time after, it was an oddly quiet summer. I hadn't really done any big events. So, I return in Arizona and people had some questions. They were all ones I would have expected: ' we haven't heard from you…are you semi-retired?, why are you coaching in Arizona now?' Training was far behind and I had to release a press statement because I was withdrawing from my Grand Prix events.

What gave her the confidence to speak about her mental health in considerable detail was the knowledge she had gained. This did not merely bolster her expertise on the subject; it emboldened her confidence in speaking without guilt or hesitation: "At that point, I knew what depression and suicidal ideation was, so I didn't feel any shame around it. I was happy to inform people what was going on." That process of transparency quickly made her realize that these types of subjects were not commonplace in the world of elite sports. She remembers that after she initially revealed her treatment, "I realized that nobody not a lot of people had done so before. When they did, they whispered it or there was a lot of shame around it." She also remembered that the issues she was grappling with were generally not on the palate of the hypothesized options media advanced to explain her absence. "They felt it *had* to be an injury or it *had* to be that I wasn't performing well," she explains. "Obviously, I wasn't physically injured. Still, there was such a stigma about mental health. This was all before Simone Biles and everyone else. No one talked about it."

Now she was curious to find out how the media reported the story, not to mention how her family, friends, and fans would react.

Multi-Dimensionality and Authenticity: Many Fans "See" Gracie Gold for the First Time

If there were two words that encompassed how people responded to Gold's revelations, those would be "warm" and "welcoming." While her family and friends generally felt they were piecing together a larger puzzle that had unfolded in the preceding years, figure skating fans were responding in a different manner. The previous media iteration of Gracie Gold has been generally positive, but also limiting and static. This new version of Gold was much more accessible. "It humanized me," Gold believes. "The media had previously painted me in a very All-American, upper-middle class type of way. It was a really nice story, but it also felt like I was living in a kids sports movie." Gold admits that "there was not a lot that was relatable about how the media portrayed me unless you were from the Midwest, or a talented figure skater," conceding that her previously-guarded media personae ultimately meant that "I didn't check any other boxes."

Now, she found that fans were responding to her on a much more personal level. "My story resonated with so many others in so many ways. People could connect with me in a way I know some felt they couldn't before." Rather than feeling that fans were knowing too much about her private life, Gold embraced the added intimacy that talking about mental health provided. "They could see I'm a real person, not just kind of ice skating Barbie doll."

Meanwhile, Gold discovered that her honesty was reaping more personal rewards as well. As one example:

> I'd always been thick as thieves with my twin sister, Carly, but this was happening during the only six to eight months where we weren't really that close. That added to my own mental health crisis. But then once I spoke openly about it to the public, my family was great. It made sense to people. It explained things.

She does recall that while the response was overwhelmingly positive, it was not universally so. "The only negative feedback I got in the media was the timing, because I revealed it a few months before the 2018 Olympics." This appeared curious to a handful of sportswriters and fans:

> Some people were saying I didn't want to compete against the Russians and that this was me making excuses in advance. That wasn't the case at all: I had beaten the Russian skaters before. I wasn't afraid of them. If I thought I was going to do so poorly, I could have just quit skating.

Even with that line of criticism, Gold felt she could easily navigate any of this rockier part of her narrative because she knew that her battles with depression, suicidal ideation, and disordered eating were not personal faults. She felt informed about her own health to the point that she could contrast that knowledge with what she could dismiss as less educated positions about her diagnosis, and of mental health in general. She countered any criticism with:

> I was literally dying. What would some of these people know? What do they know about my situation or my life? If they are so ignorant that they would think that I would use clinical depression and suicidal ideation to avoid competitive ice skating, how am I supposed to respond to that?

On the Desire to Place Blame

In the coming years, many tropes would be applied to Gold (and other athletes with similar revelations), each trying to ascribe blame for suboptimal mental health on a variety of sources. For instance, some had argued a corporation like Nike was placing additional strain on athletes to be photogenic and lean; Gold dismissed that notion outright. Others believed the skating world was toxic and facilitated unhealthy attitudes and behaviors. Gold believes that "mental health has such a big impact, especially in the skating community" and even will go as far as to label it "the elephant in the room, particularly disordered eating not only in skating, but in many other sports where size matters." However, she says it is important to uncouple the skating (which she loves) from the external elements of the sport (in which she argues there are considerable problems). "If I weren't a figure skater, I likely wouldn't have had these same specific mental health problems, but I'm sure I would have encountered something," explains Gold, arguing that "you just have to figure out the culture." She uses a non-skating analogy to advance her point:

> Let's say you're a dancer. You can be a dancer and just love it. Be totally normal about it. But then we have what *Dance Moms* showed us, which was this weird, toxic culture that can emerge within the dance. I'm sure those kids really liked the dancing part of it even if they hated other parts. Skating is the same way—there's a toxic side, but I never wanted kids to think I'm saying they shouldn't skate. All the bad parts of competitive skating are preventable if you put the right tools in place.

The one element of her chosen sport that she finds is the most difficult to navigate pertains to weight, where she believes there are some realities that cannot be ignored. "Size inclusivity has increased a lot over the last few years, but I'm not sure that applies to Olympic athletes," she contends. "We have handicapable and plus size models, and Rihanna's body inclusive and all that is good. But it doesn't change that if you want to succeed in Olympic skating, you better be lean."

> To argue against the leanness argument is to deny reality and physics, she claims, explaining that: It's a tricky balance. It is a lighter weight body sport compared to others. You have four minutes and 10 seconds on the ice and you have to leave the ground 12 times. It's a lot easier to lift yourself if you are on the leaner side. But then if you get too lean, you're losing strength. You're losing some power. That makes it harder to maintain energy at the end of a program.

Because of this narrow window one seeks between power and energy, she believes that "most skaters will struggle with some sort of disordered eating at one time or another," but that these struggles will vary: "It could for a short amount of time; it could be a long time. For some, it will become a really big issue and something they struggle with their whole life."

Still, she remains an advocate for both her sport and the Olympic movement. Gracie Gold is not an athlete wishing she could have carved out an entirely different life path that did not include skating in the Olympics. She simply believes there needs to be greater cognizance and knowledge about the side effects, which took her considerable time to grapple with herself. She believes the aforementioned HBO documentary, *The Weight of Gold,* should not be reduced to being viewed as just about mental health. Instead, she contends:

> The HBO documentary was about so much more than that. It was each of us asking the question: what would we do if we could go back in time? Because we would all still do the Olympics over again. We just would have done it differently. We would have been aware. It's like when you take a prescription drug, they have to tell you the side effects. That documentary was about making people aware of the side effects of being an Olympian.

Home on the Ice: Gold Redefines Success and Wellness

As much as advocating for mental health conversations became a passion for Gracie Gold, it still is not her first love. That remains skating. She recalls being at a crossroads after the 2018 Olympics. At first, she was "pretty adamant that I wasn't going to skate again." She admitted that she was out of shape. Her desire to become more physically fit evolved from a desire to be healthy for the rest of her life, not because she aspired to be at the top of the medal podium. "Getting back out there felt like climbing Mount Everest. But I still wanted to do shows," she recalls.

But there was one factor that helped prod her on her journey back: "I still really liked skating. I always have." Part of her comeback involved setting realistic expectations: "I decided we can meet in the middle. I had to get comfortable saying I'm no longer an elite athlete, but I could still skate. I didn't have to do triple triples again." Slowly yet surely, Gold began to round into form. As she did, she realized "there was still something there." She became comfortable with amending those expectations again—in a more ambitious direction. "I had goals I wanted to hit, but once I hit them, I created new ones." With enthusiasm, she rediscovered herself as well as her abilities on the ice. "I just kept going," she eagerly recalls. "It was like when I was a kid. Once a week became twice a week, which then became three times a week. It snowballed. Suddenly, I was jumping just as well as I did when I was younger competing."

After being absent for the 2018 and 2019 U.S. nationals, Gold qualified in 2020…and 2021…and even 2022. At 26 years old, the hopes of making the Olympic team were not realistic. Yet she still had goals. She excelled with a surprisingly competitive short program, scoring higher than she had in the event in six years and making the final group of six skaters for the free skate. "This nationals for me is the cherry on top of what I consider a pretty successful comeback," she said after the strong short program (Hersh, 2022, para. 2).

Dropping to tenth after the free skate did little to damper her enthusiasm and confidence about both skating and her more broadly-defined life. Continuing to speak about mental health appears to be a cornerstone of that process. Her mindset is now one of controlling a conversation for the good: "Talking about things like depression and eating disorders can be difficult, but I started to realize: you can make it weird, or you can choose to have a normal conversation. That's a choice we have the power to make."

She can identify other people and groups that could have been more helpful in her greatest times of need, but sees little point in doing so, believing that "sometimes I didn't help myself and sometimes others were at least partly to blame." She understands the desire to blame, but sees little utility in doing so, acknowledging that "it's a normal reaction for people want to point fingers, because if something can just spontaneously happen, that's more frightening."

Advocacy for discussing, diagnosing, and understanding mental health now appears to be part of her DNA, stressing that "We just have to normalize this. Athletes can get injured physically, and athletes can get injured mentally. Nobody expects you to skate with a broken ankle, so why should you skate if you're injured mentally?" She emphasizes the need to seek out specialists, which she discovered was imminently helpful when navigating her own path. However, the conversation can happen anywhere, and Gold wants to see it percolate into any part of life where someone feels comfortable to do so: "People debate whether they should discuss it or not. I don't even consider it a debate now. You should. With whom? Anybody that you trust with that information. You don't have to have a psychologist in order to start."

References

Crouse, K. (2019, Jan. 25). Gracie Gold's battle for Olympic glory ended in a fight to save herself. *The New York Times*. Retrieved at: https://www.nytimes.com/2019/01/25/sports/gracie-gold-figure-skating-.html

Hersh, P. (2022, Jan. 6). Gracie Gold's comeback yields its most fruitful success in nationals short program. *NBC Sports*. Retrieved at: https://olympics.nbcsports.com/2022/01/07/gracie-gold-us-figure-skating-championships-comeback/

11

Case Study: Trey Moses, College and Professional Basketball

"The sadness belittled me, suffocating me like a python."

In her viral graduation column, *Chicago Tribune* columnist Mary Schmich (1997) offers many insights to the college-aged, including that "the real troubles in your life are apt to be things that never crossed your worried mind, the kind that blindside you at 4 p.m. on some idle Tuesday" (para. 6).

For college basketball player Trey Moses, that turned out to be 9 a.m. on an idle Thursday.

It was then, on August 17, 2017, that Moses woke to find a series of missed calls and voicemails after 4 a.m. from his best friend and teammate on the Ball State basketball team, Zach Hollywood. Hollywood and Moses had grown close, forming what likely seemed an odd couple to some: Hollywood "long, lanky white kid" and Moses a "big, tattooed African-American" (Dauster, 2019, para. 40). Both had personal struggles they were seeking to overcome together. It was Moses who had attempted suicide three months earlier; Hollywood later said he was hurt that Moses had not confided in him on his darkest feelings.

Now Moses feared the inverse may have happened. None of the signals pointed to that, though, as Hollywood had seemed genuinely happy the night before. However, when Moses finally opened the door to Hollywood's apartment, his worst fears were realized.

Zach Hollywood had taken his own life.

In the months and years that followed, Moses worked to make his friend's death a clarion call—first to enact his own mental wellness, and then to help others. By 2019, Moses was ready to share his story with the world. Unlike the other stories in this book, this seemed to be a two-step process. The first was told in April through NBC Sports college basketball beat writer Rob Dauster (2019); the second was a first-person account Moses advanced two months later in the *Indianapolis Star* (Moses, 2019). Whether he was talking about it in traditional media, social media, or just amongst his family, friends, and acquaintances, one premise held true: the more he talked about it, the better he felt.

Fostering Self-Awareness and Self-Monitoring

It was not always that way. Moses remembers first experiencing depression in junior high. As he explained in his *Indianapolis Star* account of his history:

> Seventh grade was the first time I experienced sadness. This was not just normal sadness. I was a 12-year old boy, not sad about losing basketball games, not sad about getting bad grades or even losing friends. This sadness was unexplainable. This sadness was scary. This sadness took control of a once happy boy and completely destroyed him. The sadness belittled me, suffocating me like a python, completely taking my voice, my breath and my feeling away day by day (Moses, 2019, para. 4).

The thoughts were overwhelming, so he confided in a friend. She did not know what to do with such information, which led to her telling a guidance counselor, which led to a meeting with a guidance counselor, which led to his lying and saying he was just joking about those dark thoughts. His lesson from the experience: "never tell anyone ever again" (Moses, 2019, para. 8).

Feelings and actions escalated from there. High school led to Moses's increasing desire to self-harm, doing so via cutting and burning himself. Even being a stand-out basketball player and receiving a scholarship to Ball State University offered little resistance to what he was experiencing. "A change of scenery meant nothing," he later explained (Moses, 2019, para. 10).

By the end of his sophomore year, Moses decided to end his life. Taking a large number of pills, he waited for the pain to go away. Instead, he got scared. He called a friend and she took him to the hospital. He stayed two days. He told few people about the attempt, but one was Zach Hollywood. They spent the summer bonding and talking about their depressions and anxieties. But in August,

Hollywood was experiencing his darkest moment and Moses, understandably asleep, was left with the voicemails.

Finding a Storyteller

Using the media to tell his story was, quite predictably, a later stage in the evolution of Moses's mental health narrative. Early on—after his own suicide attempt and even more so after losing his friend—Moses relied on his parents and close friends to help him navigate where he should go to alleviate his darker moments. "My family has been a very important part of my mental health journey," he explains, and "my mom has been my best friend forever". Moses's father responded somewhat differently, but ultimately no less productively in helping him traverse difficult times:

> At first, with my dad, it was a tough enough kind of thing. He didn't understand the details of what I was going through. But after we had some talks, his love is overwhelming. I feel so much support from him. At this point, whenever I do interviews or share my story to someone, he's the first one to watch, the first one to listen, the first to say he loves me, and the first to tell me how proud he is.

Formal therapy was also a key component of Moses's future path, and he embraced it. He had already been diagnosed with severe depression since his freshman year in college. However, it was a sports psychologist named Dr. Chris Carr who helped guide him and then find his own counselor. Carr had a long history of working with professional sports teams in a variety of league contexts, counting the Indiana Pacers, Kansas City Royals, Green Bay Packers, Columbus Crew, and Indiana Fever among his clients. Moses found the sessions exceedingly helpful, particularly when "we got past that point of just talking and more into the sport side of things, and how to handle different situations."

A year and a half later, Moses was ready for the conversation he'd ultimately have with Rob Dauster:

> By the time I got to Rob, I was in a good space and I was ready to talk. I've always been a person that—no matter what—I always put everyone else first no matter what I do. I've always had the bad feeling that there's so many people that know I can help. So many people die just needing a feeling of someone, not just feeling alone. I almost *had* to talk to Rob.

One mantra Moses now lives by is that "everyone needs to know just a few good people". As he can likely also attest, it helps if one of those good people is a sportswriter you can trust. For Moses, Dauster was someone he knew and trusted. They had chatted via social media and exchanged numbers. When Moses was at the 2019 Final Four to speak with college coaches about mental health, they re-established their connection and saw an opportunity to tell a story in hopes of helping others. "I wanted so badly to just help everyone else with what I was going through," Moses explains, and "going with a trusted journalist is very important."

When the story broke, some of his friends and family were surprised, but many were not as "even before, I kind of spoke about on social media. I hadn't really told my story yet, but was just trying to be a voice for those who do struggle." He describes responses to the initial story as almost universally positive, albeit coupled with people who indicated to him that he should have shared his story with them earlier. Social media was a revelation for him, functioning largely as a positive force and way to exchange short messages with people who indicated their support of him and, quite often, needed his support in their own mental health journeys.

The Ultimate Storyteller: Himself

"After that," explains Moses, "it was just kind of like a no brainer for me to put my story out there myself." The ability to fill in more of the details and use the first person voice seemed to be a power that Moses was eager to utilize. He does not believe he would have done so without the ability of Rob Dauster to frame and articulate the issues he dealt with (and is dealing with). Moreover, Dauster helped to synthesize his thoughts in useful ways. As Moses details:

> Rob gave me the confidence to write my own story. Without Rob, I don't know that I would have ever truly put something out there. I do a lot of journaling, in general, and I truly enjoyed writing out my emotions.
>
> Still, I don't know that I would have ever had the confidence to like to put it out there myself if Rob had not shown me how to do so.

The other factor motivating Moses to reframe his story in the first person was a nagging sense that he could even make a greater impact for a larger number of people—both in sports and beyond. Moses explains his rationale:

The response to Rob's story is what pushed me to tell my story, because it was the first time that my story was really put out there, and impacted so many people. In my head, I kept thinking: could you imagine how many more people could impact if I wrote it in my own words? People could really feel what I went through. What I was trying to say. What message I was trying to get out there. Rob did so well with that, and I just wanted to make try to make it even more—and I felt like I was in a good enough place at that point to do it.

Claiming he just "needed to touch as many people as I could," first sought out *The Players' Tribune* as a venue to tell his story, but for a variety of circumstances, the local newspaper, the *Indianapolis Star*, seemed like the best way to reach the most people. In terms of the actual content, he did not seek to do anything differently from Dauster's initial story as the content was accurate and fair. The objective therefore became a shift in tone: "I wanted to be as emotional as I could. There was nothing that I wanted to hide." He also claims to have had zero interest in how he came across personally, with authenticity being prioritized in such an equation. Moses explains that "a lot of times, people put out their own stories and hide certain things. They're worried. They are writing from a place of fear. Worried that they will come off too strong or that others would judge." In contrast, Moses vehemently recalls, "I didn'' want to do any of that." Raw emotion was at a premium, with nothing too dark to write about.

Again, the story was overwhelmingly received in a positive light. Particularly on social media, Moses felt as if his story "went a little more fire on Twitter. I think it was just the power of being from my own words." Honesty, he claims, paid off in resonance for his audience. He could tell in the types of responses he had sparked:

> A lot of people were kind of excited, ready to hear it come from me and not someone else. I loved it. I kept thinking: if I can affect one person, and they're saying, 'Oh wow, look how much Trey opened up' or they're thinking 'look how much you know an athlete is going through' then maybe they'll know they are not alone. Maybe they would buy what I was preaching and know that it's OK not to be OK.

Moses kept thinking of exponential abilities that telling his story in media afforded. Chain reactions seemed to be happening, at least based anecdotally on the responses he had received to the pair of articles: "It's just a trickling effect, slowly changing the world. Changing the stigma around mental health."

Basketball: Help or Hindrance?

The visibility that Moses was granted as an college athlete was not lost on him. Not everyone experiencing mental health struggles has a professional writer to tell their story, or a flagship newspaper willing to write a person's first-person account. However, being involved in collegiate sports created its own anxieties and correlates. He understands the double-edged sword of sports in his own personal story:

> Basketball has always been a way for me to get out of it. To be able to be comfortable again and know I was going to be OK. But at the same time, your job is on the line every single day. So you, you have to add that pressure back in. And when I struggled on the court, I struggled off the court, too. It took on even more added pressure because I found myself thinking: Oh man, I've got to perform. The pressure of performing is very real. It creates this anxiety inside of you every single day, which only hinders athletic performance and mental health.

Moses also realizes that access to resources, including Dr. Carr and other therapy, are not as readily available to all and that sport opened those possibilities for him. In the end, he developed a coping mechanism that he thinks "sounds bad" but ultimately was liberating:

> I just tried not to take it seriously. You know, it's just basketball. Basketball is nothing more than a game. I love the game and I love everything that it has done for me. But at the end of the day, the relationships I've built matter more. All the friends that I've made mattered more. The people impacted by my story mattered more. Basketball helped me tell my story, but there are so many things that matter more.

Moving Himself—and Others— Forward

Moses has embraced that his mental health is a life-long journey, but he believes his mental health advocacy is a life-long commitment as well. He admits that "every time I talk with someone it hurts a little to go back there, but I do it because it almost always makes an impact." While he sometimes wishes his basketball prowess could have led to even more people hearing his story ("Could you imagine the microphones some of these athletes have? Think of Simone Biles and how many people see her social media posts or whatever she puts out!") he still believes consistency of message is just as crucial for societal change. Moses believes America is having a mental health "moment" particularly in sports, but also argues that "we have to continue to just speak on it. Even little conversations and press tweets, social media posts, whatever. It's all important because there's so many people you can reach."

His advice is not just to talk to people, but also to tell them if they are part of your inner circle. Having an inner circle of close, trusted, family and/or friends creates the support system necessary to survive and, quite often, thrive, but Moses says others might not know you have elevated them to that lofty status. He expands:

> Yes, everyone needs to know a few good people but here's the thing: they may not even know they are one of the few good people when you open up. Sometimes it's good to tell them so they know you're not sharing this with everyone.

Being selective in who you tell is key, Moses says, but too often he feels people view this as an all-or-nothing proposition, which is problematic for people who feel comfortable talking, but only with select individuals as opposed to the wider world. He extrapolates:

> A lot of times we get caught up in either telling everyone or telling no one. At the end of the day, telling everyone isn't a bad idea, but you really need to make sure that your people are ones that you feel comfortable telling—not just now, but years later. When you're really going through it, both sides have to have an understanding of what's really going on in your life.

Moses is glad he used media to tell his story, but also understands that broadcasting one's feelings to mass populations is not always advised. Still, another piece of advice he lives by is a weekly practice that incorporates social media accounts in a much more private, person-to-person manner:

> I still do a lot on social media. I do a Monday mental health check. That's me simply trying to see how people are doing. I personally message every single person and it matters. So yes, it's still kind of tough to talk about, but at the same time I know I'm doing what I'm supposed to be doing. This is not going away for me. This is something I plan to do in the future.

Navigating an Uncertain Basketball Future

After graduating from Ball State University in 2019, Moses occupies a hybrid career that seems somewhat odd even by today's standards: international professional basketball player/pre-school teacher. He has played in Bulgaria and Australia and plans to return to Australia for another season once the circumstances of the COVID-19 pandemic deem it possible. He is still haunted by the day he found Zach Hollywood's body, but it also helps to show others just how much a person can navigate and find a way to manage: "It's definitely the hardest thing I've ever been through, so I do know the struggle."

His willingness and ability to convey the message with so much emotion has been highly resonant. People leave a conversation with Moses feeling differently than when they began it. Moses believes his mission is somewhat simple when one reduces it to its core. "I'm just using my stories and try to touch other people," he says. "These people know lots of people who are taking their own lives. I have to do everything I can to stop it."

One of the most prestigious awards the National Collegiate Athletic Association (NCAA) gives out each year is the Inspiration Award. It is an honor bestowed upon the coach or player "who used perseverance, dedication and determination to overcome life-altering situations, and most importantly, are role models giving hope and inspiration to others." In 2020, Moses was the NCAA Inspiration Award recipient.

His mission is undeterred and he reports wanting to embrace every opportunity to speak about mental health, whether in a sports context or not:

> I'm happy to continue to use my voice. No matter what happens with the trolls on social media, no matter what anyone says, I just know 100 percent that this conversation has to continue. We have to be open and honest when we do speak about it because it's not easy. At the end of the day, mental health is probably even more important than physical health, because if your mind is not right then you're not going to be able to perform as well.

Moses says he still struggles and, given the circumstances with Zach Hollywood, does not believe his life is ever going to get easier. Coping and managing have instead become his watchwords. Moses notes that "they always say, 'time heals all wounds' and just I don't agree. I just think over time you learn how to cope and manage on your own."

His voice is how he believes he can best cope and manage, as he believes there is a higher calling to his advocacy:

> God has put me here to make a difference. To tell my story. I don't want to be selfish and keep it in inside. I could have kept my story for myself and dealt with it internally. My goal for so long has been to impact the world. I really think I am.

He does not prescribe this heavy advocacy path for everyone and understands "that other athletes won't want to share as much as I have." Still, he knows what works for him and will readily secure the microphone for as long as it is presented to him. "I can't speak for everyone," he offers, "but for me I would rather always speak on it and deal with the repercussions of maybe feeling soft or whatever people throw at you. That's still better than keeping it inside."

References

Dauster, R. (2019, Apr. 8). It's OK not to be OK: Moses' battle for mental wellness. *NBC Sports*. https://collegebasketball.nbcsports.com/2019/04/08/its-ok-to-not-be-ok--moses-battle-for-mental-wellness/

Moses, T. (2019, June 8). 'I saw the body of a brother and a best friend': How Moses deals with depression and loss of a teammate. *Indianapolis Star*. https://www.indystar.com/story/sports/college/2019/06/18/ball-states-moses-lost-friend-teammate-zach-hollywood-suicide/1171967001/

Schmich, M. (1997, June 1). Advice, like youth, probably wasted on the young. *Chicago Tribune*. https://www.chicagotribune.com/columns/chi-schmich-sunscreen-column-column.html

12

Case Study: Amanda Beard, Olympic Swimmer

"It's your life. It's your truth."

When Amanda Beard thought about the swimming pool early in her career, she saw more than water, lanes, and platforms. Beard, who would become a seven-time Olympic medalist, saw escape. Since her youth in Irvine, California, Beard turned to the pool as a place to avoid emotional turmoil. When you are under water, arms and legs pumping, you can rarely hear voices and sounds from above the surface, she says. Pain courses through your muscles, negating the anxieties of regular life. Indeed, when Beard competed against other swimmers as a teen, quickly ascending the ranks from amateur to Olympian, she experienced "the purest mental break" (Beard, 2012, p. 22).

Her perception of the pool—and her athletic ability—transformed as she quickly transitioned from simply learning a proper breaststroke to becoming one of the world's best at it. Fourteen years after her first Summer Games, Beard told a reporter for *The New York Times* that "I'd go to swim practice, put my face in the water, and I didn't have to talk to anybody. Swimming was like my escape, but it was also like this huge prison because I felt like I had to swim up to people's standards" (Crouse, para. 18).

A prison. An escape. When Beard describes her life in interviews with journalists, she often describes dualities. She experienced ambivalence toward her first Olympic Games in 1996, where—as a mere 14-year old—she won gold and two silver medals, yet felt both isolated and bored. She was a teenager competing against adults, carrying a teddy bear named Harold to competition and even the medals stand. As she grew older, Beard's beauty and celebrity helped propel her into a modeling career, but internally she questioned her own physical appearance.

There was also her public image, one in which she appeared an enthusiastic, dedicated, and competitive athlete who could do no wrong. The real Beard, she later admitted, feared becoming a role model because of the potential public backlash she envisioned once people discovered her reality.

The Reality and the Image

Beard grew up in Irvine as one of three daughters whose father and mother were educators. A self-described tomboy, she loved sports, including hockey, gymnastics, and swimming. She was good at swimming, excelling in competition on a local team before upping the ante and joining a highly competitive team where the swimmers were faster and older. A good coach helped Beard perfect her breaststroke, and it transformed her life: by the time she graduated junior high school, she was competing for Team USA in the 1996 Olympic Summer Games in Atlanta.

It was during her youth that her mother and father divorced, an experience Beard described as a source of emotional turmoil although her parents treated one another with respect and never fought in front of the children (Beard, 2012). Beard spent hours each day training before, during, and after school. She actively avoided problems ranging from her parent's divorce, typical teen angst, or the academic challenges brought on by dyslexia by staying busy.

She won three medals, including an individual silver, during the 1996 Games. Still, she felt as though she did not belong among the other Olympians, all of whom were older and seemed to have no fun swimming. Returning home a celebrity provided little respite. She felt out of place in high school, and people who previously ignored her wanted to be her friend, which led her to question the authenticity of virtually all the relationships in her life.

Beard returned to the 2000 Olympics, competing in Sydney, Australia, and bringing home a bronze medal for the 200-meter breaststroke. She attended the University of Arizona, where she helped the Wildcats swim team win a national championship. In 2004, she broke the world record for the 200-meter breaststroke and won three medals—including an individual gold—at the Summer Olympics in Athens, Greece. Again, the success masked personal turmoil. Beard began purposely cutting herself during college, saying it helped relieve tension.

Such an act served as the introduction to her autobiography, published by Simon & Shuster in 2012 and titled *In the Water They Can't See You Cry*. The book, co-authored with Rebecca Paley, begins with a graphic scene in which Beard harms herself with a razor in the bathroom.

All of this was private, though, relegated to the backstage of the public persona she cultivated through an athletic and modeling career in which Beard appeared in four Olympic Games and the cover of *Playboy* and *Maxim* magazine. As with other aspects of her life, her relationship with the mass media presented a duality: she did not enjoy being in the glare of the spotlight, but she also missed the attention when it disappeared. She disliked the squeaky clean persona of her early competitive years, yet she also helped nurture it. When she fell short of expectations in the 2008 Beijing Olympics, she feared being bombarded with questions from the news reporters standing between the pool and exit—but then, when no one paid her mind, she felt badly that she was viewed as outside of the public's attention.

Such conflict illustrates the dilemmas elite athletes experience with the mass media. News stories, magazine covers, and other mass attention can propel careers. However, attention and expectations can nurture doubt in one's identity and abilities. In her memoir, Beard describes the anxiety-inducing comments she received from photographers, hairdressers, make-up artists, and other about her physical appearance. In her *Maxim* photo shoot, she experienced an epiphany: "All I had to do was follow direction," she wrote (2012, p. 152). "Like a mannequin, I was created purely through another person's vision of how I should look."

Again, Beard's relationship with the media has been defined by dualities. It is fitting, then, that a journalist working for the so-called "newspaper of record" in the United States helped Beard shed the persona and publicly embrace her identity.

"It's very emotional and raw, but ... it's also empowering."

As chronicled in the comments from Karen Crouse in Chapter 5, it was not without considerable hesitation that Beard first publicly shared her experiences with depression in an article for *The New York Times* on July 31, 2010. It was fourteen years after she first appeared in the international media spotlight and two years after her final Olympics, during which she served as a co-captain of the women's swimming team during the 2008 Beijing Summer Games. For more than a decade, she had adopted the role of the ultimate athlete, winning medals, and breaking world records in the pool. Crouse, who wrote the *Times* profile, described the image "as airbrushed as her photographs in magazines" but then relayed what most readers would have perceived to be a considerable curveball: "Her toothy smile and surfer girl insouciance hid deep emotional pain" (2010, para. 9).

Beard, then 28 and an Olympian for half her life, shed the public image and revealed her struggles. Throughout the winning years, she told Crouse, she was "never really, really happy" (para. 8). The *Times* piece dedicated few words to Beard's career highlights, instead detailing how isolating her life of elite competition felt. In the story, Beard recounted her experiences with depression, obsessive tendencies, body dysmorphia, and self-harm, including her path toward recovery through the assistance of therapy, medication, and the support of family, including her boyfriend (now husband) Sacha Brown.

Before the *Times* piece, the only people who knew about Beard's experiences were family, close friends, and her partner. Nonetheless, the article revealed "new bits and pieces," she said, that even they did not know. The story details how her parents' divorce left her sad and angry. It also publicly revealed for the first time the fact Beard experienced problems with alcohol, recreational drug use, and self-harm. "I was extremely nervous and hesitant," she says in an interview for this book, describing the countdown toward the story's release and how friends and family would receive it. "It's very emotional and raw, but then, you know, it's also empowering."

Beard recalls that the article helped her reveal her true self to the public. She might project confidence while standing on the block or diving into the pool, she says, but in reality she was lacking confidence in herself in other aspects of life. "How you seem on the outside, or how you present yourself to the world can be very misleading," she says.

Indeed, in the *Times* piece, Beard's father described her as particularly adept at seeming gregarious while experiencing anger and sadness inside. In her memoir, Beard describes difficult romantic relationships with other star athletes and how public appearances did not line up with private life. For example, in the run-up to the 2000 Sydney Olympics, *Vanity Fair* was under the impression she was still dating her fellow swimmer Ryk Neethling. In reality, they had broken up after a tumultuous relationship, according to her memoir, but she agreed to the photo shoot because it would be good for her career. Beard began cutting herself in secret, she says. She also developed unhealthy habits such as purging—forcing herself to vomit after meals—and avoiding meals to lose weight.

In 2010, as she prepared for national competition, Beard shared these experiences with Crouse, who informed Beard that her story could be inspiring for other women who had gone through similar struggles. In her memoir, Beard recalls saying she would think about it, writing that: "I was a lot better at communicating than I used to be, but airing my innermost secrets in the paper of record was a lot of sharing" (2012, p. 237). She further explains that she "worried about opening myself up for criticism on issues about which I'd only received support. I also didn't want people to pity me, treat me differently, or think I was making a pathetic ploy for attention."

Later, in an interview for this book, Beard described herself as nervous coming forward with "my little inner demons that I was fighting." Still, she was in a process of self-revelation as well: "I found that the more that I talked about it and shared it, the more I became really connected with people on a much more emotional level," she says. "All the friendships and relationships I had in my life—it made me think 'Why did I not do this earlier?'" She even added that "it's hard, but I wish that I would have spoken up and really reached out for help and been OK with admitting that I have some issues I need to deal with. I could have shared what they are."

In the *Times* story, Beard describes two events as catalysts that led her to reconsider her outlook on life. Beard's family and friends rallied around her after she finished 18th (missing the semifinals) in the Beijing Games, making her realize that she did not need to win to be loved. The second event was the birth of her son, Blaise Ray Brown, on September 15, 2009, which shifted the focus of her life from competition to motherhood. In the *Times* article, she questioned how she could feel down when her infant son found everything hilarious. Beard later had a daughter, Doone Isla Brown, on June 19, 2013. Crouse described Beard's new perspective as "liberating because it helped her shed the wrinkle-free persona that had become such a constricting second skin" (para. 11).

"People easily forget that athletes are human."

Beard's interviews with the *Times* were what ultimately inspired her to write her memoir, because Crouse said her story might help younger athletes navigate difficult times. Beard says she wanted to present readers a real picture of her life and the life of elite athletes, instead of "250 pages of just swimming." Focusing just on athletics and medals was problematic to Beard, as she felt it "didn't feel like that's reality." Instead, she wanted to widen the framing of her life for the audience to truly understand, for all of the people wondering "what is happening in between all those moments. You know, those moments when you close the bathroom door and cry your eyes out."

In her memoir, Beard describes her ambivalent experience with the 1996 Olympic Games when she was 14. There were perks; she could eat at TGI Fridays three meals a day, devouring broccoli and cheese soup each night. But she often felt bored and alone. She was shocked when older athletes invited her out one night. She was equally shocked when they ultimately entered a bar, finding that the bartender didn't kick her out, and shared a pitcher of beer with her fellow Olympian teammates. She hardly sipped the beer, she says, but it did foreshadow events to come. She describes caving in to peer pressure related to alcohol and drugs several times during her competitive years.

The aftermath of the 1996 Summer Games were equally ambivalent. On one hand, Beard enjoyed the perks that came along with the medals, including a limo ride to the *Tonight Show with Jay Leno*. On the other, she struggled with the thought of being treated differently in her private life. She returned to her swim team and high school a celebrity; the school sent an antique Bentley and driver to pick her up for class, where she was greeted by 200 people, including a school administrator who had never spoken to her but made sure to do so from then on. Ninety swimmers joined her high school swim team after the Olympics, 200 percent more than the year before. Their parents wanted autographs and advice. Everyone wanted a nascent position to greatness.

Mass media were a frequent presence, as reporters called the Beard home for interviews and celebrities such as Oprah Winfrey and Katie Couric tried to book Beard for their shows. In doing so, she believes an illusion was being created by the mass media. Her sisters dared her to take a teddy bear named Harold to competition, and she accepted the dare. An icon was accidentally born, she recalls. "The image perfectly captured what people wanted to see: as my sisters put it, an innocent and her bear. The fantasy was one of some mythical girl who could win the Olympics while still remaining pure and sweet" (2012, p. 59).

Later, in an interview for this book, Beard described her experiencing navigating the pressure of being a teenage Olympian:

> You know, you're kind of pushed out into this world and you tell yourself: 'OK, I have got to figure it out along the way.' Well, along the way, there are a lot of bumps and a whole lot of just falling on our face. As an athlete, when I fell on my face, I blamed myself when the truth was we weren't equipped to handle it all.

Among her personal bumps in the coming years was that Beard experienced puberty and its accompanying growth spurts after the 1996 Olympics. The changes threw off her swimming routine and also made her question her appearance, as many teenagers do. She recalls internalizing comments she overheard boys making about girls' bodies at school. All the while, people held onto the perception of Beard as the great Olympian, which became even more problematic as Beard found swimming different and more difficult with her bodily changes. Once, at a competition, another girl introduced herself as a big fan, saying Beard would blow them all away in the pool. Beard finished 4th instead, and the girl would not make eye contact. It would not be the last time she experienced such treatment, though it would be one of the first times she hated swimming.

The mass media reared its head again, too. Beard recalls finding her father's stash of newspaper clippings, except this time sportswriters were calling her "fat, washed up, and finished" (p. 73). She was 15.

Beard was all-too familiar with the funhouse mirror media coverage can present: "We're used to hearing their marriage is perfect and their parenting is perfect. The media is now finally willing to show that's such a façade. We're finally seeing athletes and their personalities more honestly. People gravitate towards that." Describing one of her own experiences with the media, Beard wrote that (2012, p. 119), "People easily forget that athletes are human and not a public commodity to be tossed aside when the dividends on everyone's emotional investment are disappointing." Athletes are perfectionists, she says, meaning that she'd naturally question every flaw of her life, both in the pool and beyond: "I'd constantly ask: why wasn't I good enough? Why wasn't I perfect? And then I stuffed it down inside and I wouldn't talk about it. I wouldn't work through those feelings, or everything I was going through."

Beard says the experience of a young Olympian is like a teenager starting a career, being put into a corporate office and told to just "go for it." "That's honestly when your support team around you becomes so incredibly important," she says. "Your coaches, your friends, your family—they're going to keep you on the straight and narrow and help guide you."

"Do what's right for you."

Beard's interview with the *New York Times* was published in 2010, her autobiography in 2012. Social media remained in its infancy, meaning she lacked the direct engagement between athlete and fan that is common today. Therefore,

Beard says she did not need to navigate the additional pressure of her disclosure becoming fodder for Twitter and Facebook conversations. Still, she describes the response from family and friends as "amazing." "They stepped up to be really supportive and loving and caring," she says. Their response was to relay that "this is so great. Good job," Beard recalls. "Some people could have looked at the things I said and really ripped me apart. 'Why would you include me?' You know, I talked about my own family and our own issues. But instead, my parents were terrific, saying, 'that was very brave. We're so proud of you.'" Beard encountered a similar response from the public, including fellow athletes and coaches. In her memoir (2012, p. 238), she writes, "When I arrived at Nationals, so many people pulled me aside to divulge their issues. Top-level swim coaches, fellow athletes, men and women - they all had stories, either their own or of someone very close to them, that mirrored mine." She was not alone.

Online reviews of her memoir follow two themes: readers expressing disappointment that Beard spent less time providing behind-the-scenes accounts of the Olympics, combined with other readers applauding the book for the same reason, saying she provided inspiration to anyone who experienced depression or body dysmorphia. *Swimming World Magazine* featured "A Teen's Review" of the book, in which a reviewer wrote that "hearing that an Olympic legend has struggled with the same challenges we have inspires us to persevere and fight to become the best version of ourselves (Smarjesse, 2016, para. 9)."

Beard expects any personal disclosure will elicit mixed responses, including people who "want to connect" and people who "don't want to hear it." No matter what, she says, "I think we're moving in the right direction as people understanding mental health a little bit better and being more aware of it."

She recommends people who want to discuss mental health should "do what's right for you and bounce ideas off the people that are *truly* close to you in your own tight little inner circle. That's what truly matters." People will appreciate elite athletes as humans the more they encounter honest stories in which athletes share their real personalities, Beard says, including the highs and lows they experience. "You know, we always watch movies. We read these wonderful stories about movie stars and athletes living in beautiful homes, driving crazy cars, but they're human," she says. "We like to see that human side of them because then we feel like we can actually relate. We can see them on a more human level than putting them up on a pedestal, which I think is fantastic."

Conclusion

Like other athletes, Beard adopted the guise of an unfazed exterior but cloaked a maelstrom of emotions underneath. "How was I supposed to know? I wasn't an expert in that part of the world," Beard recalls. Thus, she had to find her own path—with the guidance of family, friends, and coaches. "I had to educate myself by reaching out to people who could help guide me and give me the tools to be able to figure it out," she explains. Looking back, she says she found her voice and hopes others can find the confidence to speak up sooner rather than later. "Don't put it off until tomorrow," she says. Communication is incredibly important in mental health, including prevention, maintenance, and treatment. People adopt different strategies for sharing their mental health experiences with others. Based on her experiences, Beard recommends anyone who experiences mental health issues to share their experiences with someone. "You can just do it within your close circle around you, whatever you feel comfortable with," she says. She believes that "I think if you want to do it, do it as more of a therapeutic thing. Make it about letting go of information. Whether or not it gets picked up [by anyone in media], who cares?"

She further clarifies that:

> You don't have to make it this big, 'I'm going to put this out on social media for everyone to know.' That might not be the right route for everybody. It may be more like, 'Hey, I have these five people in my life that I admire and trust, and I want to have this conversation.'

For athletes (and others) with public forums, Beard recommends focusing on oneself rather than public reaction, because "if you speak up and you talk about things and it never gets published, why should that matter? Think of it like washing yourself of information."

"It's your life," she adds. "It's your truth."

Beard indicates she plans to continue to speak her truth for as long as people are willing to have the conversation, doing so because she believes you have to "take advantage of the moments that you do have that you're presented with and have no regrets." She also believes there is a finite amount of time that her stories will retain their relevancy:

> At some point, someone is not going to want to sit down and talk to me about my experience. They're not going to write an article about me or include me in a

book forever, so I'm going to try to talk to as many people as I possibly can while I can. That makes sense for me.

Instead, she seems the practical embodiment of the concept that slow and steady can win the race. "Every single day is a time to continue to figure it out, navigate and become stronger. You learn how to be better. You grow. You learn," she says. "You can't be perfect and that's OK. You're going to continue to fall down once in a while. Hopefully, each time you fall down you're getting stronger and learning how to stand up more quickly."

References

Beard, A., & Paley, R. (2012). *In the water they can't see you cry*. New York: Simon & Shuster.

Crouse, K. (2010). For champion Olympic swimmer, a simpler time. *The New York Times*. https://www.nytimes.com/2010/08/01/sports/01swimmer.html

Smarjesse, K. (2016). A teen's review of 'In the water they can't see you cry'. *Swimming World Magazine*. https://www.swimmingworldmagazine.com/news/a-teens-review-of-amanda-beards-in-the-water-they-cant-see-you-cry/

13

Case Study: Corey Hirsch, NHL Goaltender

"I was 15 seconds away from being a statistic, and nobody knew."

Call it serendipity.

Corey Hirsch spent more than a decade in professional hockey, tending goal for the New York Rangers, Vancouver Canucks, and other teams while personally navigating life-threatening challenges from obsessive compulsive disorder (OCD). At a book launch after his retirement, Hirsch met Dr. Diane McIntosh, a renowned Canadian psychiatrist and author of *This is Depression: A Comprehensive, Compassionate Guide for Anyone Who Wants to Understand Depression*. They shared a passion for wanting to improve public understanding of mental health, but approached the subject from different perspectives: Hirsch, an elite athlete, struggled for years with unwanted and - at times - suicidal thoughts; McIntosh had insight about such issues from her professional training and experience.

Months after the encounter, the former goaltender received a message from the psychiatrist pitching an idea for a podcast about mental health in the sports world. The idea crystallized during the COVID-19 pandemic when millions of Canadians and people around the world navigated social isolation, anxiety, and depression. *Blindsided* was soon born, a podcast in which Hirsch and McIntosh interview elite athletes about their experiences with mental health in sport. The podcast is produced by *The Players' Tribune*, an industry publication that has become a central platform in the discussion of mental health in sport.

At the time of writing, the podcast produced 10 episodes featuring interviews with athletes such as professional golfer Bubba Watson, NFL quarterback Kurt

Warner, and tennis star Taylor Townsend. *Blindsided* lets listeners "hear moments when mental health became the athlete's most important focus," (Hirsch et al., 2022, para. 5) coupled with discussion of mental health conditions. "It gets clinical," the podcast says, permitting listeners "to leave with a deeper understanding of mental health conditions that all people face. It then shows how athletes, in particular, face them down" (Hirsch et al., 2022, para. 6).

The podcast has been well-received, garnering a 5-star rating on Apple and earning a 2022 Webby nomination for best sports podcast. "Corey is such a warrior on his quest to help others with mental health issues," one reviewer wrote. "Diane is such a great complement to him with her medical knowledge…real life stories of vulnerability and success."

In an interview for this book, Hirsch describes a common thread coursing through the stories. Elite athletes who experience depression, anxiety, or other common conditions often remain silent because they fear the responses of teammates, coaches, front offices, and fans. Behavior can be misconstrued as anti-social when, in reality, it is the byproduct of mental illness. Late arrivals to practice. Poor performances on the ice, court, or pitch.

"It's absolutely unbelievable," Hirsch says. "It's all so similar, so *very* similar."

Hirsch describes interviewing Kevin Love, an NBA All Star who experienced severe anxiety, and Bubba Watson, the two-time Masters winner who experiences severe social anxiety. Like Hirsch, the professional athletes encountered public criticism from fans (and even teammates) for their behavior without understanding the factors involved. Hirsch does not assign blame; such responses can be expected when you remain silent about the struggles you are experiencing. That's one reason he has embraced a post-hockey identity as mental health advocate.

"What do me and Bubba Watson have in common?" Hirsch initially asks. As it turned out, the answer was: quite a lot:

> It was the same thing—the upbringing, the desire to be the best, other people not liking you because you seem standoffish, but you're really just trying to get out of bed, get through the day, and continue to plow forward. It really is incredible the things in common we have as human beings.

"I Didn't Have a Choice"

The athletes featured on *Blindsided* also share in common public disclosures about mental health, a recognition that their stories could nurture positive outcomes because of the stature afforded to elite athletes. Hirsch first used *The Players' Tribune* to share a personal story of mental illness. In February 2017, Hirsch co-wrote an essay headlined "Dark, dark, dark, dark, dark, dark, dark, dark" (Hirsch, 2017) in which he recounted his experiences navigating professional hockey while struggling with obsessive compulsive disorder and suicidal ideations generated by the mental and physical exhaustion accompanying OCD. People who experience OCD ruminate on intrusive thoughts related to death, religion, sex, and accidentally harming others. Intrusive means the thoughts are unwanted, and the desire to avoid the thoughts can create a boomerang effect where the thoughts keep coming—"dark, dark, dark, dark, dark," as Hirsch put it. The illness affects 2.2 million adults in the United States (ADAA, 2022) and more than 380,000 people in Canada (CPA, 2021).

The best way Hirsch can describe it, he says, is to picture driving down the road and wondering, "What if I jerked the wheel to the right? We've all had that silly thought, right?" he asks. However, then he explains how it was different for him than most others:

> Someone without an OCD brain would just go, 'That was a stupid thought,' and they would go on with their day and not even think about it. [Meanwhile}, someone like me would go, 'Why did I have that thought? Does that mean I want to crash my car into somebody? Does that mean I want to kill myself? Does that mean I want to kill another person?' I would go home and it would be 24 hours a day, 7 days a week, trying to figure that out.

Hirsch says most people experiencing OCD can recall an exact moment when the problems begin. Intrusive thoughts smothered his mind one night while he was out with teammates from the New York Rangers during a playoff run. "Something just broke," he says. "I started getting these really negative, catastrophic thoughts in my head that wouldn't go away."

He went back to the hotel and went to bed, hoping the thoughts would disappear by morning. They did not. Instead, they lingered, bothering Hirsch to the extent he still does not publicly share them. Over time he experienced severe anxiety and panic attacks, reaching the point where he felt he could hardly function or hold a conversation. He worried his NHL career would be done.

"At one point, I called my mom to help me so I could get to practice," Hirsch recalls. "We go out and I'm showing her the sites, but I'm not really there, you know. I'm in my own head." From there, his thoughts turned darker:

She'd never been in New York City. We go to the top of the Empire State Building, and I look over the edge, and I say: 'I wish I could jump.' My mom started bawling. She didn't know what to do, nobody knew what to do. I just knew I wasn't going to tell anybody else. I begged her not to tell anybody.

To calm his mother down, Hirsch promised he would not "do anything stupid," and he would "get through it." He later told an ESPN reporter that before the playoffs, sitting in his hotel room, he bashed his hand in an attempt to break it, hide the injury until practice the next day, and then pretend a puck caused the harm so he could go home. It didn't work. He played, and the Rangers ultimately won the Stanley Cup.

For a hockey player, a rare Stanley Cup victory is meant to be a pinnacle moment where self-actualization feels realized, if only for a moment in time. Not that night. "I drank out of the Cup, a smile on my face, but really I'm just dying inside," Hirsch says.

He skipped the parade and headed home, hoping he could dodge the anxious thoughts. He got a reputation for not being a team player, for being a "bad guy." People assumed he was upset because he did not get enough playing time. Hirsch met with a therapist, but the experience did not go well because she did not diagnose OCD. Hirsch says he worried the thoughts would remain forever and decided he did not want to live. He drove his Plymouth Laser to the mountains in Kamloops, British Columbia, to "see how fast this car can go. And my plan was just to drive it off the end of the road, right off the mountain."

As he sped toward the cliff, reaching 140 miles per hour (Burnside, 2017), Hirsch says another thought entered his mind. "I don't know why, but it stopped me. I hammered on the brake. I was 15 seconds away from being a statistic, and nobody knew."

Instead of relief, Hirsch felt shame. "I was like, 'Well, I can't even kill myself. What kind of loser am I?'"

Hirsch decided he had two options: live and figure it out, or die. He could try one. If that failed, he would choose the other. So he returned to New York, where the team sent him to the minor league because he was the last one on the ice in the morning and the first one off the ice at the end of the day. Hirsch was traded to the Vancouver Canucks, where the clash between professional success and mental anguish simmered. He won awards for his goaltending—but he also lost 30 pounds. "I didn't want to be around anybody, I didn't want anybody to see me like this, and then really again, I'm back down on my knees again, like the way I was in New York," he recalls. "It just started to hit me harder and harder and harder again."

On the road in New York while playing for the Canucks, Hirsch finally could take no more. He approached a trainer during morning skate and asked for help. He still started the game that night, punching Islanders winger Andrei Vaislyev as the team lost 5-0.

The next day, while preparing to face the New Jersey Devils, Hirsch's mental health plummeted. "I remember that I couldn't even see pucks. I'm standing in the net and having an out-of-body experience," he remembers. "I'm like, 'I can't do this anymore. I can't do this. I can't do this to my teammates because if I play tonight, we're going to lose.'"

Hirsch approached his coach and told him he could not play. At that point, he says, "everyone sees something's wrong." The coach called an emergency meeting and informed the team. If asked by the media, the coach said, Hirsch was missing the game because of the flu. But everyone involved knew it was not the flu. "My head is in my hands. Everybody's looking at me and no one's talking to me," Hirsch says. "It was the most embarrassing, shameful, and awful moment of my life." From there, it was about survival:

> I shower up, and get on the bus like I'm really sick at this point, I'm 145 pounds and skin and bones. I sat at the front of the bus, and I remember my teammates just walking by, one by one, just not even looking at me, not even acknowledging me.

Some teammates were supportive, including veteran Dave Babych, who ensured Hirsch had company at dinner when the team was on the road (Burnside, 2017). Babych once found Hirsch curled in the fetal position in the locker room. "It wasn't that the players didn't care," Babych told ESPN (Burnside, 2017, para. 43). "It was just that nobody understood what it was or how to deal with it. You're just a human, and you're concerned. And it was a little scary, to be honest with you."

Another teammate, Trevor Linden, described the NHL as "a tough place to be" when struggling with mental health (Canucks, 2017). "It's an unforgiving place." Hirsch describes trying to talk to Linden, but being unable to communicate the gravity of what he was experiencing (Canucks, 2017). "I feel bad today that I didn't know, that I didn't have more insight into what was actually going on," Linden said (Canucks, 2017). "But none of us did and that was just a sign of the times I think." Hirsch acknowledges that "Some guys were great...but most guys didn't understand."

Personally, Hirsch felt that, "I just threw my career away. But I didn't have a choice."

To a certain extent, the culture of the NHL and its perspective on mental health has changed over time. Time has also provided Hirsh hindsight.

"I look back today, and I saved my life. I *saved* my life."

"I Have to Use My Platform"

Hirsch ultimately found help when a therapist visited his house, "because heaven forbid you got seen as an NHL player walking into a therapist's office." Hirsch decided he would share everything - including the intrusive thoughts - and "if he tells me I'm flipping nuts, well, I'm just going to kill myself."

Instead, after 20 or 30 minutes, the therapist looked at Hirsch and said, "You have obsessive compulsive disorder. It's not curable, but we're going to get you going on the right track. I just started bawling right there," Hirsch recalls.

The diagnosis surprised Hirsch, because he always heard OCD involved constant hand-washing, fear of germs, and repetitive behaviors. Still, the diagnosis helped Hirsch identify the reason for his troubling thoughts, and therapy helped provide a path toward recovery. The experience underscores the importance of mental health literacy, or knowledge concerning symptoms, diagnoses, treatments, and other information relevant to mental health. Hirsch now advocates for mental health literacy among athletes and the general public, especially youth.

Years later, Hirsch admits that a diagnosis is "only 50% of the battle," but that he still felt better. He remained silent about his diagnosis with colleagues in the NHL, and his reputation as a "bad guy" lingered throughout the league. After years of struggling, he finally met an OCD specialist who helped him. He also attributes his recovery to medication.

Over time, Hirsch says he encountered other people who experienced OCD—and also realized people can die by suicide after suffering it. He recalls one athlete in particular. While living in Arizona, Hirsch met a current player who was in rehab during the middle of the season for substance abuse issues. The men went for coffee and Hirsch shared his own struggles. "He's like, 'That's *exactly* what I have and what I'm going through," Hirsch says, describing how the man almost died twice from overdoses. "I didn't really realize how deadly it is," Hirsch says. "Untreated depression, OCD, bipolar—they can be deadly."

Hirsch decided that given his platform as an elite athlete, he had to help. "I have to tell my story," he concluded. "If one more person out there kills themselves because of OCD, it would be shame on me if I didn't use my platform."

A Platform—and an Apology

Hirsch stepped atop that platform in 2017, when he published "Dark, dark, dark, dark..." in *The Players' Tribune*, recounting his experience with OCD while playing professional hockey. He also granted interviews with the news media and began speaking at public functions such as the book release for McIntosh. "After (*The Players' Tribune* piece) came out, you know it just changed my life," Hirsch says. "It made me want to be able to help people. It led me into a new passion."

Elite athletes often adopt a selfish mentality, he says, which makes sense because the outcomes of games can be dependent on your performance. A quarterback throws a touchdown and wins a game; a quarterback throws an interception and loses. A goalie gives up a point and it could doom the team - plus a career.

That changed for Hirsch, who once helped the Canadian hockey team to a silver medal in the Olympics. He explains his new mindset:

> I think the meaning of life is about helping people. I've gotten way more out of helping people and meeting people than I ever did any win in the National Hockey League or Olympic final. I guess I've found my life purpose, my life passion. I think guys struggle outside of the game to find another passion. I think that's why athletes struggle, and man I'm lucky that I found it.

Hirsch admits that the disclosure represented a step outside his comfort zone. He felt scared before the *Tribune* piece appeared. Then, he says, "It blew up."

During this same period, the Canucks profiled Hirsch's story of "living the NHL dream until mental health issues nearly cost him his life" (Canucks, 2017). Hirsch says friends called and cried over the phone. "When you struggle with mental health issues, communication is of the utmost importance," he says, because:

> When people don't know things, they will make up their own conclusions as to what is going on. 'Why is he missing practice? Well, you know he's been hanging out with his new girl, she's got to be the problem.' They'll make it up. They'll come to their own conclusions.

Hirsch says he had teammates apologize, saying they would have done anything to help had they known. He says the reverse is true. They should not apologize because he never said anything. "That article was also an apology to my teammates," he says. "It was to help people, and it was an apology to the guys that didn't know what was going on with me."

Hirsch now openly shares what was going on, hoping to inspire others to pursue help instead of waiting years as he did. As he told ESPN in 2017, "By hiding it, you're just digging a hole. And the more time passes, the deeper the hole gets. That's why early awareness and early diagnosis is so important" (Burnside, 2017, para. 21).

Hirsch hopes the *Blindsided* podcast can help spread awareness. He says the partnership with McIntosh works well because he can interview elite athletes about the world of sport while McIntosh provides insight into medical conditions and treatment:

> I can talk to Kevin Love about being an athlete and mental health, but I can't talk to him about the clinical side. It's not just about diagnosing them—Diane tries to help people understand what it is, what people are going through. So when you put the two together, I think it's just unbelievable.

In April 2022, the podcast was nominated for "Best Sports podcast" by The Webby Awards, the "leading international award honoring excellence on the Internet" (Webby, 2022).

Challenging Traditional Notions

The decision to disclose mental health issues can be difficult for anyone, including athletes. Hirsch offers advice for athletes, teams, and organizations to help navigate the consequences of coming out. His key advice for players: get help. "You'll be a better player. People think if they get help, it's going to take something away from them," he says. That mindset is completely misguided. "It will make you a better player."

In the *Tribune* (2020), Hirsch cites the example of Robin Lehner, who in 2018 shared his experience with mental illness and alcoholism while goaltending for the Buffalo Sabres. The season after his disclosure, Lehner won the Masterton Trophy for perseverance and dedication to hockey, and ranked among the finalists for the Vezina Trophy for top goalie. Lehner "was so courageous in stepping up and talking about his battles with addiction and bipolar disorder," Hirsch told the *Tribune* (2020, para. 8). "And what happened? On the ice, he was stronger for it. I'm sure he felt free."

In addition to communicating, Hirsch recommends people remove the stigma attached to medication and conversations about suicide. There is a misconception that asking a loved one about suicidal thoughts might spark self-harm; Hirsch challenges the notion. "People think medication's going to change their game. If you need medication, you need medication. It's going to make you a better player because you can *function*."

Hirsch recommends that teams invest in the mental health of athletes because it could also reap financial rewards. "There's a humanity side and a business side," he says. "I'm OK with both." He explains his rationale, noting that teams might spend $3 million paying an elite athlete and mental illness could jeopardize the investment, because an athlete who cannot compete will not contribute to the success of the team. Hirsch also points toward statistics concerning the prevalence of mental illness in the adult population. One in five U.S. adults will experience mental illness, meaning that team of 50 players would translate into and average of 10 having mental illness, Hirsch says.

Finally, Hirsch challenges traditional attitudes concerning strength and masculinity in sport. Competition can nurture a misguided notion that strength means pushing through pain. Being tough means showing no weakness, and being a man means remaining tight-lipped about emotion. "It's not about hiding your stuff and going it alone," Hirsch says. "A man deals with the stuff." He advances the following reframing:

"We're taught to suck it up. If I killed myself, even if I was successful, do you think guys would come to my funeral and say 'Yeah, what a man! He sucked it up! He went out like a man! He didn't talk to anybody!'"

No, Hirsch argues, mourners would instead wonder: "Why didn't you come talk to me? Why didn't he tell me?"

Thus, people have to open up about such issues.

"Talk to your buddies," Hirsch says. "If they don't understand, they're not your people. You'll always find a friend that will understand and try to help you."

This final recommendation also extends to talking about mental health with youth. In the United States, teenagers are experiencing depression and anxiety at levels previously not seen. The COVID-19 pandemic exacerbated depression and anxiety among youth, who experienced social isolation, disruptions in routine, and increased stress at home because of parental unemployment, illnesses and other negative factors (Stephenson, 2021). "Talk about mental health in your homes," he says. "Talk to your kids in the home, because that's where it starts."

Hirsch is also advocating for mental health education in schools. Youth should feel comfortable talking about mental health and seeking help when they need it, he says, and education about depression, anxiety, OCD and other conditions can help shed the stigma. Hirsch says he has "a bit of a chip on his shoulder" about the lack of mental health education for children because he could have avoided the crisis he experienced later in life had he known about the symptoms and treatments for his condition.

In 2020, Hirsch followed up his original essay with an interview in *The Players' Tribune* headlined: "I'm not brave at all," in which he describes the biggest lesson he learned after sharing his story. "It was literally staggering to me how many current and former athletes - and just regular people - have reached out to me and said, 'Hey, I need help' (Hirsch, 2020, para. 4).

He also learned a second big lesson. "You have to set boundaries on social media. Even if 99.9% of your interactions are positive, if you struggle with your mental health all it takes is one or two cruel comments to ruin your day. I have 47 years of life experience as my armor, and it can still put me into a bad place. Think of all the kids out there who experience this kind of toxicity" (para. 5).

Although more athletes are disclosing personal experience with mental health, Hirsch says more active players could do so at the professional level (Hirsch, 2020). "Don't get me wrong, I get it," Hirsch told the *Tribune* (para. 6). "People tell me all the time, 'Man you're so brave for telling your story,' and I always tell them the same thing: 'I'm not brave at all. It took me 20 years to do it, and even then I was scared of how people would view me."

Beyond the podcast and media interviews, Hirsch is using his platform to reach out to youth to challenge stigma. He feels "blessed" to have a platform to talk about mental health, but he also acknowledges that not everyone feels the same way about openly sharing their own experiences with depression, anxiety, or another concern.

"The only thing I do say is, don't hide it. Don't hide it in shame, don't sweep it under the carpet. There's nothing to be ashamed about."

References

Anxiety and Depression Association of America. (2022). Understanding anxiety and depression. https://adaa.org/understanding-anxiety/facts-statistics

Burnside, S. (2017). After opening up about his struggle with anxiety, Corey Hirsch now helping other players cope. *ESPN*. https://www.espn.com/nhl/story/_/id/18691270/nhl-open

ing-struggle-ocd-anxiety-former-new-york-rangers-vancouver-canucks-goalie-corey-hirsch-helping-other-players-find-support

Canadian Psychological Association. (2021). "Psychology works" fact sheet: Obsessive Compulsive Disorder. https://cpa.ca/psychology-works-fact-sheet-obsessive-compulsive-disorder/

Canucks. (2017). Corey Hirsch's story of struggle and recovery. YouTube. https://www.youtube.com/watch?v=0D8URDg0lKI

Hirsch, C. (2017). Dark, dark, dark, dark, dark, dark, dark, dark. *The Players' Tribune.* https://www.theplayerstribune.com/articles/corey-hirsch-dark-dark-dark

Hirsch, C. (2020). I'm not brave at all. *The Players' Tribune.* https://www.theplayerstribune.com/articles/corey-hirsch-nhl-hockey-mental-health

Hirsch, C., McIntosh, D., & Warner, K. (2022). About Blindsided. Episode 8: Kurt Warner. *The Players' Tribune.* https://www.theplayerstribune.com/posts/kurt-warner-nfl-st-louis-rams-undrafted-free-agent-blindsided-podcast-mental-health

Stephenson, J. (2021). Children and teens struggling with mental health during COVID-19 pandemic. *JAMA Health Forum, 2*(6). https://jamanetwork.com/journals/jama-health-forum/fullarticle/2780778

The Webby Awards. (2022). People's choice. https://vote.webbyawards.com/PublicVoting#/2022/podcasts/general-series/sports

14

Case Study: Katie Uhlaender, Olympic Skeleton

"You have to allow yourself the space to be all of what's inside of you."

Four-time U.S. Olympian Katie Uhlaender once worked for a functional neurology clinic, where people sought help after experiencing post-traumatic stress disorder (PTSD) or other trauma-induced mental health issues. At times, she questioned whether PTSD was real. It would seem, she pondered, that you should be able to say, "it happened," and then move on. But in 2017, her perception of trauma—and her life—changed. Her friend and fellow Olympian, Steven Holcomb, died after ingesting a combination of alcohol and sleeping medication.

Uhlaender was the person who found him in his room at the U.S. Olympic Training Center in Lake Placid, New York.

They knew each other 14 years and became best of friends, each excelling in their Winter Olympic sports. As another athlete told reporters, "Whenever you saw Steve, you better believe that Katie is somewhere nearby" (Kamrani, 2017, para. 4). Holcomb offered her encouragement when she became bedridden in a Colorado Springs hospital because of an auto-immune response. His advice was simple: "You need to be you," he told her.

In addition to losing her friend, the experience made Uhlaender question the path of her own life and the "win at all costs" attitude of elite competition. Uhlaender, a five-time Olympian and multi-sport athlete, competes for the United States in skeleton, a sport in which individual athletes ride down a frozen track head-first, reaching speeds faster than 80 miles an hour. In the Beijing games of 2022, she became the only U.S. woman to compete in five Olympics in a sliding sport (Costantini, 2022). What would be a taut, stressful, death-defying act for the average person was a typical day for Uhlaender. Thrive in such an environment and an athlete may feel as if no barriers should be problematic. That, of course, would be wrong.

Uhlaender discovered the sport after high school and learned she could win. Indeed, she has twice won the world championship in skeleton and finished fourth in the 2014 Olympics behind a Russian competitor who was accused of doping. The sport requires dedication, to say the least, because training and travel can interfere with Olympians' abilities to hold down full-time jobs; competing requires a substantial amount of money; and training and competing can take a toll on one's body.

After the death of her friend, Uhlaender began to question the mental health-related costs. Holcomb was a three-time Olympic medalist described as the best bobsledder of his generation and the most famous bobsledder for the United States (Bull, 2018). That did not keep him from ending his life in a very dark place, whether that death was intentional or not.

"I would be looking at my life and wonder why an Olympic champion would take such huge risks," Uhlaender recalled. "I don't think he intentionally killed himself, but no one could argue his actions caused him to pass away. He's an Olympic champion, an Olympic medalist who had tons of things going for him. It made me question all the choices I had made."

Her reconsideration of her priorities seems founded. Website Olympedia features a page solely dedicated to Olympic athletes who have taken their own life. At the time of this writing, that number stood at 167. And those are just the cases that could be substantiated.

Uhlaender wondered whether she and others could have done more to help. She describes fighting for rights from the U.S. Olympic Committee because:

> They were in a better position than any of us to say something about it, and to get him to stop. Sport was his life and if they had said 'Hey, if you don't stop, you can't compete,' I guarantee you he would have straightened up. It was like the more leeway he got, the less he felt anyone cared.

Uhlaender says the life-changing event was a "huge wake-up call in terms of what it means to identify mental health struggles and how to handle it."

It also represented an epiphany for her own mental health, as she continues to experience flashbacks every now and then of finding her friend, knowing that any help that could have been provided was now futile. Not only does she know trauma exists, she has become an advocate for helping athletes nurture their own mental health and the health of other elite competitors. As she wrote in a recent opinion column for *Global Athlete*, an international advocacy organization (2020): "Sport mirrors life and teaches us our values within a society from an early age. Only by coming together can sport or society tackle the issues that challenge both."

Coming Together

It was a coming together event in which Uhlaender first publicly discussed mental health.

Uhlaender recalled her friendship with Holcomb and her own experiences trying to cope in the aftermath of his death in the HBO Documentary "*The Weight of Gold*." She, Michael Phelps, Lolo Jones, and other Olympians described how the intense international competition can nurture anxiety, depression, and even suicidal ideations. Since the documentary, Uhlaender has spoken about her experiences in media interviews, symposium panels, and social media, advocating for greater mental health resources for athletes.

When she thinks about her first time speaking out about mental health, she recalls "The Road Not Taken" by American poet Robert Frost, which concludes "Two roads diverged in a wood, and I—I took the one less traveled by, And that has made all the difference." "Everybody thinks it's a poem about individuality," Uhlaender explains. "In one layer, it is. But in another layer, it's about confronting regret and realizing that no matter what road you take, you're going to think back and wonder about the other one." Thus, she concludes, the only thing you can do is "take the path that is not influenced by other people's decisions."

The prospect can be difficult, given the myriad external influences on athletes' lives, including the expectations of coaches, teammates, sponsors, teams, and even family and friends. Athletes can spend so much time focused on competing (and the goal of winning) that they neglect other parts of their lives while also navigating intense pressure. Olympic athletes often go into financial debt training and competing. Shortly after discussing her experiences for this book, Uhlaender launched a GoFundMe to raise $36,000 for the U.S. World Skeleton Team so basic life expenses could be provided.

Reaching the level of Olympic athlete also requires a narrow focus on life, which can lead athletes to experience "post-Olympic blues" as competition gives way to retirement and questions concerning the meaning of life when one's identity has been forged often exclusively from what they can accomplish in the sporting arena. Olympians can become celebrities, win accolades and medals, and then return home to waning fanfare and mundane activities such as cooking, cleaning, working, and grocery shopping. As sports columnist Christine Brennan once observed, the interest of Olympic fans is both fleeting and fickle, as "you go from an ember to a wildfire in a very short amount of time. And then often you cool back down to that ember status and move on" (Billings, Moscowitz, & Yang, 2016, p. 49). The Olympics require years of work toward a singular goal and then the competition ends. What is the meaning?

It is a question Uhlaender herself pondered as she approached her final Olympics following a nearly 20-year competitive career. The Robert Frost poem is not the only literature Uhlaender cites when discussing life, her perceptions of the world, and mental health. She quotes Aristotle and the Swiss psychiatrist Carl Jung, Joseph Campbell, and French philosopher Michel Foucault as she discusses the human experience. She is exceedingly well-read. She is also, seemingly, continually searching for insight.

While the HBO documentary focuses on US athletes, they are by no means alone in their experiences. British competitors have described experiencing post-competition depression (Howells & Lucassen, 2018), and Australian researchers have developed recommendations to help prepare athletes for post-Olympic life (Bennie et al., 2019). Interviews suggest Olympians better navigate depression when they have interpersonal support structures and can find meaning outside elite competition.

Coupled with her personal experiences, Uhlaender's studies have led her to believe people should avoid being confined "to one box." Although elite competition requires sacrifice, dedication, and toughness, athletes should ensure they have space to grow. "You can't just be whatever you do," she says. "You have to allow yourself the space to be all of what's inside of you."

While Uhlaender prepared for the Beijing Olympics, she avoided being confined to a single box by expanding her ambitions: She would like to earn a bachelor's degree, perhaps in political science. She also loves photography, and works as a camera assistant for the long-running CBS hit series, *Survivor*. It was there—even more than the Olympics—that she discovered a true family feeling.

Athletes are often told to ignore emotion, which can be unhealthy because repressed emotions will ultimately rise to the surface, she says. Uhlaender believes athletes can temporarily suppress emotion while competing, but she underscores the importance of addressing the emotions once a competition concludes. For Uhlaender, that step comes when she writes and draws in her journal each night, reflecting on her thoughts and emotions from the day. She has kept the journal since her 20s, and among the folded pages is a drawing by her friend Holcomb.

The Response

Uhlaender describes the response to her discussion of mental health as positive. Sport reflects society, she says, and public attitudes toward mental health have been progressing quickly in concert with movements related to race, social equality, and other subjects. Attitudes are different today than in 2009, a period in which Uhlaender thinks she would have been told to "suck it up" if she mentioned mental health after her father passed away. She now chronicles that time period of another time in her life where mental wellness and roads not taken.

Katie's father, Ted Uhlaender, played and coached professional baseball, helping the 1972 Cincinnati Reds win the National League Championship. Their bond was strong, but often needed to be from a geographic distance, as she frequently was far from her father's Atwood, Kansas home for training and competition. When she heard her father had suffered a heart attack, she felt the immediate need to travel home to be with him. However, pressures—both self-induced and from her team and various sports stakeholders—kept her in Park City, Utah for the FIBT World Championships. Katie spoke with her father before she competed. After earning a silver medal, she spoke from the awards podium to say she raced to give her family an emotional lift. She was unaware at the time that her father had already died ("Former Major League outfielder Ted Uhlaender dead at 69", 2009).

Six weeks later, she shattered her kneecap.

Shortly before the 2010 Vancouver Olympic games, she shattered it again.

The combination of familial and athletic trauma made life for Uhlaender exceedingly difficult. "My spirit was broken, and although there were good times sprinkled in with the bad, I spent much of the next few years picking up the pieces and putting them back together," she later wrote.

In 2013, during her first week of sliding on ice in training, she hit her head and got a concussion. She began treatment at a concussion clinic in Dallas, feeling both "confused and defeated." It was there she met a group of people who embodied her father's lessons concerning heart, integrity, and tenacity: U.S. combat veterans receiving treatment for traumatic brain injury. "The veterans being treated with me were examples of never giving up, and I was able to go to Sochi with a renewed sense of courage."

As she competed in Sochi, Uhlaender wore her father's championship ring around her neck. She turned in her best Olympic performance to date, placing fourth, missing the medal stand by .04 of a second, a fraction she notes is "quicker than you can blink."

"Even though he was no longer here, I still looked to my father for support after the Games," she later wrote. "During his playing days, he went to two World Series without winning a title, but he still gets fan mail decades later because ultimately his legacy is about much more than winning or losing. I guess sometimes your willingness to fight is enough to inspire people."

Mental health, she says, is beginning to be understood in society. Times have changed since 2009, and she expects she would no longer be told to "suck it up" if she needed time to process such a life-changing moment. By speaking out, Uhlaender and other athletes hope they can challenge the stigma attached to mental illness and encourage people to seek therapy or other forms of support.

The goal aligns with recent recommendations from an international think tank of mental health professionals and athletes from Denmark, Canada, Brazil, and the United States, including representatives from the National Basketball Association and US Olympic and Paralympic Committee (Henriksen, 2020). The think tank described an athletic environment that, at times, could be best described as hostile toward mental health. Mental health may be stigmatized. Paths toward treatment may be blurred, unclear (Henriksen, 2020). Funding for mental health remains limited. Cultures of abuse and collusion continue to exist, the representatives wrote (Henriksen, 2020).

Uhlaender sees a need for sporting organizations such as the U.S. Olympic Committee to invest greater time, attention, and resources toward the mental and physical well-being of athletes—recommendations comparable to the ones advanced by the international think tank. The call is also one echoed by competitors such as Michael Phelps and Simone Biles, the Olympic gymnast who withdrew from the Tokyo Olympics. Rather than one entity, she says, the Olympics should have different organizations to promote, regulate, and ensure the well-being of athletes, which includes mental health. Uhlaender says she and other athletes question whether organizations such as the Olympic Committee will step up, so they are increasingly advocating on their own behalf.

Toward that end, Uhlaender pinned the trailer for *The Weight of Gold* on her Twitter account, where fans described her story as "eye opening" and praised her strength for sharing. "Your dad must have been very proud," one person responded. "Don't forget that. People needed to hear your story. Thank you so much for telling it."

Finding Your Tribe: Uhlaender's Advice

Uhlaender recommends that both athletes and non-athletes much find a "tribe," a supportive community that will permit you to explore and "be yourself without fear of being yourself." It can be difficult to do so among elite athletes, she says, since each individual might consider other athletes competition for positions or resources. Meanwhile, finding a tribe of people outside the sports world is also challenging, as Olympic realities can appear unrelatable to those of the typical citizen. Consequently, Uhlaender argues that the world of sport can be isolating at times, recalling an experience in which a famous Olympian told her she needed to "create my own team" because other athletes, the Olympic Committee, and the team itself could not be relied upon for emotional support.

Uhlaender ultimately found her tribe in the Mamanuca Islands of Fiji while working as a camera assistant on *Survivor*—an Emmy Award-winning television show in which strangers must work together to find food, fire, and shelter before one-by-one voting each other off the island. She recalls one day, about three months into the job, when she summoned the strength to talk about Holcomb. Anxiety creeped in, she says, and then she broke into tears. "I was so embarrassed," she says, "but I had a group of women come over, and they just all gave me a big hug. They're like, 'It's OK. We all have our moments, tell us what's going through your head.'"

She recalls the words emerged rapidly, released in stream-of-conscious blurts, along with a flood of emotion. Still, Uhlaender says she never felt uncomfortable or as though she was being judged. "I let myself go through those emotions," she says. "It didn't feel so heavy. I was so used to judging myself for having feelings. I was an athlete, and you want to be stoic, right, you're like 'I have emotions but they're back here - I'm busy.'"

Now that has changed for her.

"I found my tribe. They're resilient, they're competitive. We're competitive. But the difference is, when I have a bad day and I'm crying, or I'm off, they ask if I'm OK," she says, arguing that athletics should give themselves space to be who they are as individuals. "You can allow yourself to be weak or to cry or to feel emotion, and it's not going to take away your ability to kick some ass," she says. In addition, Uhlaender contends that people should stand by one another. In times of crisis, a person might ask to be left alone. She recommends saying: "Well, I'm just going to be right here. I'm not going to leave your side, I'm here for you. Most times we don't need to say anything...Just show you care and you are there for them."

References

Bennie, A., Walton, C. C., O'Connor, D., Fitzsimons, L., & Hammond, T. (2019). The post-Olympic Games experience: A qualitative investigation of Australian Rio Olympians. *Frontiers in Psychology, 12*, 1-13.

Billings, A. C., Moscowitz, L. M., & Yang, Y. (2016). Frames of the Olympic host: Media coverage of Russia's anti-gay legislation. In R. Lind (Ed.), *Race and gender in electronic media: Challenges and opportunities* (pp. 38–54). New York: Routledge.

Bull, A. (2018, February 6). The life and death of Steve Holcomb, forever seeking that perfect line. *The Guardian*. https://www.theguardian.com/sport/2018/feb/06/steve-holcomb-blind-bobsled-winter-olympics

Costantini, L. (2022). U.S. skeleton team wraps up winter games with sixth place finish from Katie Uhlaender. *Team USA*. https://www.teamusa.org/News/2022/February/12/US-Skeleton-Team-Wraps-Up-Winter-Games-With-Sixth-Place-Finish-From-Katie-Uhlaender

"Former Major League outfielder Ted Uhlaender dead at 69". (2009, Feb. 14). *The Associated Press*. Retrieved at: https://usatoday30.usatoday.com/sports/baseball/2009-02-14-ted-uhlaender-obit_N.htm

Henriksen, K., Schinke, R., McCann, S., Durand-Bush, N., Moesch, K., Parham, W. D.,... & Hunziker, J. (2020). Athlete mental health in the Olympic/Paralympic quadrennium: A multi-societal consensus statement. *International Journal of Sport and Exercise Psychology, 18*(3), 391–408.

Howells, K., & Lucassen, M. (2018). 'Post-Olympic blues'–The diminution of celebrity in Olympic athletes. *Psychology of Sport and Exercise, 37*, 67–78.

Kamrani, C. (2017, September 26). Skeleton slider, Olympic veteran Katie Uhlaender opens up after losing her best friend, Steve Holcomb. *The Salt Lake Tribune*. https://www.sltrib.com/sports/2017/09/26/skeleton-slider-olympic-veteran-katie-uhlaender-opens-up-after-losing-her-best-friend-steve-holcomb/

St. Clair, S. (2013, October 1). Katie Uhlaender rediscovering herself after father's death. *Los Angeles Times*. https://www.latimes.com/sports/la-xpm-2013-oct-01-la-sp-sn-katie-uhlaender-20131001-story.html

Uhlaender, K. (2020). An opinion piece by Katie Uhlaender. *Global Athlete*. https://globalathlete.org/our-word/an-opinion-piece-by-katie-uhlaender

15

Disclosing Mental Illness: Strategies & Considerations

> "Tell me what I can do now to help...Talk to me, I'm listening...You are not alone in this, I'm here for you."
>
> —Campus MindWorks

In August 2020, professional basketball players found themselves in the so-called "bubble," competing away from family, friends, and fans in Disney World, Florida. Paul George, the All Star forward for the Los Angeles Clippers, struggled early in the playoffs, shooting 10/47 in three games. When asked about it, George told reporters, "I underestimated mental health, honestly. I had anxiety, a little bit of depression. Just being locked in here. I just wasn't there. I checked out" (TMZ, 2020, para. 9). George said he spoke to a team psychiatrist and "my energy, my spirit was changed. That's all I needed" (para. 12).

The admission elicited swift response. Teammates and coaches rallied around the superstar, playing video games with him, knocking on his door at the NBA compound, and having long talks about things unrelated to basketball (Youngmisuk, 2020). On social media, fans apologized for criticizing his play and praised him for speaking up. Journalists began highlighting the challenges faced by players as they spent two months separated from their communities, including ongoing protests against police brutality across the United States. One headline read: "Maintaining mental health a daily challenge for those inside the NBA bubble" (Wong, 2020).

Not everyone understood the challenge, or appreciated George's disclosure that he had been in what he called a "dark place." Critics claimed the athletes' experiences paled in comparison to the unemployment, illness, and death being witnessed in communities outside the bubble. Charles Barkley, the Hall of Fame NBA player and commentator, criticized George by arguing that "I don't think guys making millions of dollars should be worried just because they're stuck in a place where they can go fishing, play golf, and play basketball to make millions of dollars. That's not a 'dark place'" (Beer, 2020, para. 9). Raja Bell, another retired player, told *The Ringer NBA Show* "keep that shit to yourself, nobody wants to hear that" (para. 9).

George's experience illustrates a portion of the positive and negative consequences athletes (and others) face when disclosing personal experience with mental illness. On one hand, disclosure can elicit support and even empower an individual affected by depression, anxiety, or another condition. On the other hand, people who disclose stand a very real chance of encountering stereotypes, prejudice, and discrimination. There's a reason why some of the common refrains within this book could be encapsulated with "I didn't speak because someone would ask what do I have to complain about?" or "I didn't speak because I knew someone else was in a worse situation." Those counterarguments are, unfortunately, very real and must be factored into the equations when determining the degree to which one wishes to speak about mental health.

Given the consequences, it behooves athletes, coaches, and others in the world of sport to keep in mind several considerations before disclosing mental illness. In this chapter, we review those considerations based on research and experiences of athletes. We highlight considerations and offer recommendations on disclosing mental illness while also buoying one's mental health.

The Pros and Cons of Disclosure

As the preceding chapters illustrate, the United States is witnessing a growing mental health movement in sport. Athletes from different racial, economic, gender, and competitive backgrounds are sharing experience with mental illness through social media, personal essays, and news interviews. As Michael Phelps articulates in Chapter 7, the pandemic also hastened this reckoning as "we've had to get in our own shit" to face mental health aspects of our own personal lives.

The disclosures are especially important because of the heightened role of the celebrity athlete in modern culture. Elite athletes work years to reach the pinnacle of competition, and they often enjoy fruits from the effort such as prestige, endorsement deals, and million-dollar paychecks. They work hard to reach peak physical conditioning, demonstrating strength, and their professional success and failures appear on full display for the world to see and offer comment. People respect elite athletes for this grit and determination. When an athlete also demonstrates vulnerability, sharing stories about sadness, fear, or ruminating thoughts, the message can be incredibly influential because it is coming from someone who bucks stereotypes and commands respect. Charles Barkley, who criticized Paul George's admission, once famously declared, "I am not a role model." Sir Charles was wrong then, too—athletes are role models, and their stories can challenge stereotypes, prejudice, and discrimination related to mental illness.

When people talk about stigma, they often focus on ***public*** beliefs, prejudices, and discrimination. Equally important is ***self***-stigma, which occurs when people buy into negative stereotypes about themselves and mental illness. One can see self-stigma in the comments of athletes who question their personal strength because they experience depression, anxiety, or another illness. Psychologists have proposed that people who remain "in the closet" about mental health challenges stand a greater chance of experiencing reduced self-esteem and self-efficacy, or a person's belief they can be successful.

Conversely, people who disclose mental illness can experience empowerment. One can see this outcome in the experiences of Phelps, whose spur-of-the-moment "fuck it" attitude about disclosure elicited a shift in his identity from Olympic Great to Mental Health Advocate. One can also see empowerment in the comments of Kevin Love as he described how therapy helped him feel comfortable in his own skin for the first time. In addition, psychologists suggest that disclosure can help people avoid the stress of being secretive (Corrigan & Rao, 2012). When a basketball player remains "in the closet" about their depression, they might also worry about being found out by coaches, fellow players, friends, and family. A player like Brandon Bostick, struggling to prolong an NFL career, likely felt such a disclosure could tip the scales enough to end his chances of securing a much-coveted pension. Overall, then, disclosing mental illness can bring about positive changes for both society and the individual who shares. Still, disclosure does carry risk. An athlete might encounter prejudice and discrimination. Relapses might be more widely noticed than before. Therefore, athletes, coaches, and anyone else affected by mental illness should contemplate the decision to disclose (when possible). When they do, they should consider their personal comfort, the messages they wish to convey, and the audience they intend on addressing.

Personal Considerations

It is incredibly important that athletes take into account their personal comfort levels when determining the extent to which they want to share personal experience with mental illness. When possible, the decision should be one based upon a consideration of the benefits and consequences of disclosure. Such deliberation may not be possible at times. For example, teams have outed players who otherwise might not have shared their mental illness with the public. At other times, a moment may present itself in which the individual feels compelled to speak—as demonstrated by Phelps, the 23-time gold medal winner whose split-section decision to open up offered relief and empowerment.

People who experience depression, anxiety, and other illnesses are not alone, as the chapters in this book testify. There is no need to navigate mental illness in isolation. However, mental illness is a personal journey. Symptoms may be shared, treatment approaches common, but people navigate life with mental illness in individual ways. So, too, should the disclosure of mental health be considered personal. One athlete may feel compelled to openly broadcast his/her mental illness, while another may be more inclined to share with close family and friends. Still another athlete may share troubling thoughts with a therapist, but otherwise wish to remain private about their experience. Each approach is perfectly acceptable and respectable. One should just ensure that being quiet - or even being open - does not interfere with one's mental health.

Psychologists have identified five types of strategies for disclosing mental illness (Corrigan & Rao, 2012). *Social avoidance* occurs when an individual stays alone to avoid stigma. When an individual adopts the method of *secrecy*, they venture out into the world, working, studying, or socializing while keeping their experience with mental illness to themselves. With *selective disclosure*, an individual chooses one group with whom to be open (e.g., family) but another group to keep in the dark (e.g., co-workers). Researchers in California (Pahwa et al., 2017) interviewed 60 people with severe mental illness to gain insight into the decision-making process behind disclosure. Many of the respondents selectively disclosed their mental illness, choosing to tell one group while not telling others based on a variety of factors.

Indiscriminant disclosure involves being completely open about mental health, sharing personal experience with friends, family, social media followers, or others. The final strategy - *broadcasting* - resembles indiscriminate disclosure, except people who broadcast demonstrate pride in being labeled "a person with mental illness."

The National Alliance on Mental Illness, an advocacy organization in the United States, has numerous resources for people who are interested in disclosing (NAMI, 2022). Among other tips, the organization recommends people disclose when they are ready, feeling well, and when disclosure serves a purpose. The organization also acknowledges the risks inherent in disclosing. Friends might feel uncomfortable and even end relationships. Disclosures might create problems at work. It might help to develop lists of pros and cons, and NAMI recommends planning out the conversation in advance. Below, several considerations are described in relation to the message, and audience. Additional resources are available through NAMI, the Here to Help Foundation in Canada, and other mental health advocacy organizations.

Message Considerations

Athletes convey myriad types of information when discussing their personal experience with mental illness. When it comes to the message, athletes should consider the type of information they want to share and the message they wish to convey. An athlete might simply want to shed the figurative weight of keeping mum about mental illness. Should they share symptoms? If so, how much detail should they go into?

An athlete wishing to advocate for mental health might consider three common approaches from the communication field: education, protest, and contact. An athlete can educate the public about mental health by discussing the prevalence of depression among the U.S. population, or the potential for treatment to be effective in reducing anxiety. Education seeks to help others become more literate in relation to mental health, understanding causes, symptoms, treatments, and other important information. By equipping people with information, an athlete can challenge stigma by lessening misunderstanding. For example, the Indianapolis Colts launched a "Kick the Stigma" campaign to educate fans about mental health and provide financial support for mental health organizations in the Indianapolis community. The campaign featured testimonials from current and former players, including Hall of Fame quarterback Peyton Manning.

Advocating for mental health "doesn't mean that people have to go public with their issues," Manning told viewers in one campaign video (Indianapolis Colts, 2021). "It just means it's OK to go and ask for help. Everybody's dealing with something out there, and there are people out there that want to help you. But you got to kind of make that first step to go and say 'I need help.'" An athlete might feel compelled to advocate for mental health, but question whether they are able to educate the general public about the subject. In these cases, an athlete might point fans and followers toward experts in the field or educational resources. For example, Canadian mental health organizations partnered on the Here to Help Foundation, which provides a clearinghouse of information about mental health through its website (Here to Help Foundation, 2022).

A second approach to challenging stigma—protest—involves the direct confrontation of stigmatizing policies, attitudes, and beliefs. For example, sports commentator Skip Bayless criticized Dak Prescott as showing weakness after the Cowboys quarterback opened up about being depressed in the pandemic and the wake of his brother's death. The comment elicited protests against Bayless on social media in the form of straightforward comments like "fuck you" and "you're an idiot." However, Bayless retained his $5 million salary and survived the onslaught, perhaps even buoyed by the ability to be relevant in another news cycle.

A more effective approach would be to point out the problem with the commentator's statements—they are false and nurture stigma—while providing evidence contradicting the statement. Still another approach would be to ignore the commentator and focus on praising Prescott for the strength it required to come forward. Mina Kimes, an NFL analyst at ESPN, wrote that "Dak Prescott's honesty about battling depression after his brother's death will not only help countless people; it makes him a stronger leader, because of his authenticity and vulnerability" (Beer, 2020, para. 11). As for Prescott, when asked about the comments, he said, "I think being a leader is about being genuine and being real...I think it's important to be vulnerable, to be genuine, to be transparent. I think that goes a long way when you're a leader and when your voice is being heard by so many, and you can inspire" (Beer, 2020, para. 7).

A third approach to mitigating stigma, and perhaps the most influential, is contact. Contact occurs when a member of one group (e.g., someone affected by depression) meets a member of another group (e.g., someone who stigmatizes mental illness) in a supportive and educational setting. Research suggests contact can be effective in challenging prejudice, even in mediated environments (Banas et al., 2020). When we meet someone from a stigmatized group, and our get-together goes well, we can walk away with less stereotypical beliefs and better attitudes about the person and group they represent. Contact can also tap into our emotions, eliciting empathy toward people who are suffering prejudice, discrimination, or other ordeals.

As illustrated by the preceding chapters, contact may occur through the mass media. Audience members can "meet" and "know" a celebrity, professional athlete, or other media personality. Most readers do not personally know Michael Phelps or Katie Uhlaender, Brandon Bostick or Simone Biles. Still, they might feel as though they do. When athletes disclose personal experience with mental illness, fans might consider the revelation as affecting a friend. The more athletes disclose, the more "contact" fans experience with people who have experienced depression, anxiety, suicidal thoughts, and other tribulations. The more athletes disclose, the more normalized conversations about mental health become. The more those conversations become normalized, the more dialogue replaces the silent stigma of mental illness.

Audience Considerations

Finally, people who are disclosing mental illness should bear in mind the audience they are potentially reaching. Illustrating the strategy of selective disclosure, an athlete might want to openly share thoughts, feelings, and fears with family and close friends. However, the same athlete might want to simply acknowledge personal experience with depression when speaking to sports writers, fans, and social media followers. Researchers have studied employee's motivations for disclosing mental illness in the workplace, which in the case of professional athletes could include trainers, coaches, owners, and other supervisors. Jones (2011) reviewed research concerning mental illness disclosures in the workplace, finding that people often shared information with supervisors but not fellow employees. In terms of outcomes, the research suggested that the quality of a person's social network could be incredibly important. When personal relationships are strong, disclosure can elicit support from coworkers. However, disclosures might strain tenuous relationships. Such an outcome was evidenced in Kevin Love's disclosure experience on the Cleveland Cavaliers. While the head coach knew about Love's experience with anxiety, teammates did not. They only learned when they demanded an explanation for Love's absence from a game and practice, accusing the star of feigning illness.

Beyond disclosure, an athlete who wants to *advocate* for mental health should recognize the different needs of different audiences. Experts stress the importance of three factors in persuasion: the communicator, message, and recipient. An activist athlete's message will probably change based on the target recipient. To illustrate, a retired basketball player might react differently to Paul George's comments about feeling anxiety and depression inside the bubble than, say, a teen who feels isolated in the world but idolizes the NBA star. What audience, if any, are you as an athlete attempting to reach with your message? Who are you trying to persuade, and what barriers might they raise that would prevent your message from connecting? Bearing the audience in mind, is there a different focus you should adopt when discussing mental health? Are there different lessons to convey? To illustrate, both Michael Phelps and Kevin Love have developed eponymous non-profits to equip children with tools for mental health. The websites for the Michael Phelps Foundation and Kevin Love Fund each provide educators and other adults information to share with children about identifying and regulating emotions. While applicable for anyone, the tools are designed with the target audience of adolescents in mind. The website for the Phelps Foundation breaks down lesson plans by school grade, providing teachers lesson plans, assignments, handouts, and even exams tailored for preschool through high school. For example, the kindergarten lesson plan features a "Good Feelings Journal" exercise in which children draw a picture of something that makes them feel good and then describe the picture in a sentence. An emotional exercise for high schoolers, meanwhile, asks students to practice empathy by imagining themselves in another person's shoes.

Such a targeted approach can also be used for disclosures. Love, for example, first publicly disclosed his mental health struggles in *The Players' Tribune*, a publication primarily catering to athletes. The essay discussed experiences that other athletes would find relevant - such as the misguided mentality of "toughing it out"—but also dove into experiences people outside the world of sport would share, such as mourning the loss of a grandmother. By appreciating the audience, Love conveyed to athletes that they are not alone and should speak up while also illustrating for typical readers that athletes are human.

And that, Love says, is one of the major payoffs of his disclosure and therapy. He feels comfortable in his own skin.

Considerations for Family, Friends

When Paul George opened up about his mental health during the NBA Playoffs, he described the response from teammates and coaches as one of the things he appreciated most. "Everybody reached out, whether it was in person, through a text," he said. "All of my guys showed up for me. They helped me. They were there when I needed them" (Esnaashari, 2020, para. 6). The comment illustrates one important way in which family, friends, and teammates can support an athlete who discloses experience with mental illness: being there. In the case of George, teammates knocked on his door, played video games with him, texted, and reached out in other ways to illustrate he was not alone. Katie Uhlaender, the 5-time Olympian profiled in Chapter 14, echoes the sentiment. She recommends friends and family respond to disclosures by saying: "Well, I'm just going to be right here. I'm not going to leave your side, I'm here for you. Most times we don't need to say anything...Just show you care and you are there for them."

The Here to Help Foundation acknowledges that "supporting someone you care about can be stressful or confusing" (para. 1). The organization's website offers personal stories, questions and answers, and opportunities to reach out for referrals via email. Comparable information is available through mental health advocacy organizations in the United States, such as the National Alliance on Mental Illness. NAMI suggests that people with mental illness share suggestions on how loved ones might help, in addition to disclosing experience with a disorder.

CampusMindWorks at the University of Michigan recommends several methods for lending support: listening, offering to be available for support, asking what you can do to help, and reassuring a person that you care (CampusMindWorks, 2022). Question phrasing is important. For example, statements such as "Tell me what I can do now to help," "Talk to me, I'm listening, or "You are not alone in this, I'm here for you" can be helpful.

Considerations for Journalists

Throughout this book, athletes have highlighted the important role of the mass media—journalists, social media—in discussing mental health. Journalists balance a fine line while covering athletes' mental health disclosures. On one hand, journalists are not public relations practitioners; therefore, one should not expect sports reporters, editors, and commentators to advocate an athlete's message or simply serve as conduits for athletes to reach the general public. On the other hand, the journalism profession demands the cultivation of sources. Put simply, treating sources (including athletes) with respect builds rapport and trust, leading to exclusive interviews and increased access. More important, professional journalists follow ethical guidelines that recommend seeking truth, acting independently, minimizing harm, and being accountable to the public (Society for Professional Journalists, 2022).

Toward this end, journalists should follow professional guidelines related to word use when covering mental health. The Associated Press Stylebook, nicknamed the Bible of Journalism, added an entry concerning mental illness in 2013. The Stylebook recommends journalists interview people who are affected by mental illness to discuss their own diagnoses (rather than doctors, families, etc.). Journalists should avoid using mental health terms as slang, such as describing an athletic performance as schizophrenic (NAMI, 2013), or sensationalizing an athlete's experiences to generate audience engagement.

The SPJ Code of Ethics describes the pursuit of news as "not a license for arrogance or undue intrusiveness," (para. 2), which suggests sports reporters should avoid pressing athletes for disclosures related to mental health. The ethical code also recommends reporters "show compassion for those who may be affected by news coverage," and to "weigh the consequences of publishing or broadcasting personal information" (para. 3). Professional athletes should be media savvy, given the frequency of their interactions with the press, but the same might not be said for up-and-coming athletes, high school phenoms, teenage Olympians, and others. An ethical journalist would ensure vulnerable sources understand the potential implications of public disclosures. Again, journalists balance a fine line—they should practice ethical reporting, but not feel inclined to be an athlete's PR person or agent.

Conclusion

Be true to yourself.

If we were forced to condense the 14 chapters of this book into one piece of advice for athletes (and others), this would be the statement. Michael Phelps credited an epiphany for his realization that he should be himself, no apologies, rather than subscribing to the image of a Golden Child 28-time Olympic medalist everyone *thinks* they know. For Katie Uhlaender, the realization came during a tear-filled conversation with new non-athlete friends on the beaches of Fiji where she was helping film the new season of Survivor. Kevin Love, in his essays for the *Players' Tribune*, describes feeling joy after walking into a room as the real Kevin Love, rather than the All-Star basketball player.

The recommendation appears straightforward, but unpack it, and it is good advice for athletes who are trying to decide whether they should talk about mental health. Talk when you want, to whom you want, sharing what you want. But be sure to talk to someone - even a licensed professional if you wish to maintain privacy - because keeping strong emotions bottled up or following the stale advice of "sucking it up" rarely works.

As the athletes iterate throughout this book, mental health has no beginning or end. Mental health courses throughout life, featuring ups and downs, highs and lows. Rarely does it follow the script of *Rocky* or *Hoosiers* or the myriad other Hollywood sports films in which the protagonist encounters adversity, struggles, overcomes, and moves on. It's a journey. And it's important to know you're not alone.

Resources

Free resources are available for people who experience mental illness, as well as family members, friends, educators and others who are interested in learning more about mental health. Several resources are listed below. However, the list is by no means exhaustive. Resources are often available in local communities. In addition, the resources listed below are based in the United States.

The Substance Abuse and Mental Health Services Administration (SAMHSA) provides a free, confidential, 24/7 treatment referral and information service in English and Spanish, plus resources including an online treatment locator. Visit https://www.samhsa.gov/

The **National Suicide Prevention Lifeline** provides a free, confidential crisis service that is also available around-the-clock. The telephone number is 1-800-273-TALK (8255). The number is also offered *en español* at 1-888-628-9454.

The **National Institute of Mental Health** lists resources for finding primary care providers, government resources, crisis help, and other services. It also provides information concerning mental health, including symptoms, treatment, diagnoses and other helpful information. Its website is https://www.nimh.nih.gov/health/find-help

The **National Alliance on Mental Illness** is an advocacy group with chapters in communities across the United States. Its website provides information about mental health and opportunities to connect with people who are navigating comparable events in life. https://www.nami.org/Home

The Michael Phelps Foundation offers resources for teachers, parents, and others who are interested in teaching children about mental health and wellbeing. Its website includes lesson plans for different age groups. https://michaelphelpsfoundation.org/

References

Banas, J. A., Bessarabova, E., & Massey, Z. B. (2020). Meta-analysis on mediated contact and prejudice. *Human Communication Research, 46*(2–3), 120–160.

Beer, T. (2020). Skip Bayless says 'I don't have sympathy for Cowboys' Dak Prescott discussing depression. *Forbes.* https://www.forbes.com/sites/tommybeer/2020/09/10/skip-bayless-says-i-dont-have-sympathy-for-cowboys-qb-dak-prescott-discussing-depression/?sh=3eb21ff3505e

Corrigan, P. W., & Rao, D. (2012). On the self-stigma of mental illness: Stages, disclosure, and strategies for change. *The Canadian Journal of Psychiatry, 57*(8), 464–469.

Esnaashari, F. (2020). Paul George reveals he was dealing with depression in NBA Bubble. Sports Illustrated. https://www.si.com/nba/clippers/news/paul-george-reveals-depression-and-anxiety-issues

Here to Help Foundation. (2022). https://www.heretohelpfoundation.org/activek/home

Indianapolis Colts. (2021). Peyton Manning, kicking the stigma. *YouTube.* https://www.youtube.com/watch?v=ItG_PRnwY0M

Jones, A. M. (2011). Disclosure of mental illness in the workplace: A literature review. *American Journal of Psychiatric Rehabilitation, 14*(3), 212–229.

NAMI. (2013). Entry on mental illness added to AP Stylebook. https://www.nami.org/About-NAMI/NAMI-News/2013/Entry-on-Mental-Illness-Added-to-AP-Stylebook

NAMI. (2022). Your journey. Reasons to talk to others. https://www.nami.org/Your-Journey/Individuals-with-Mental-Illness/Disclosing-to-Others

Pahwa, R., Fulginiti, A., Brekke, J. S., & Rice, E. (2017). Mental illness disclosure decision making. *American Journal of Orthopsychiatry, 87*(5), 575–584.

Society for Professional Journalists. (2022). Code of ethics. https://www.spj.org/pdf/spj-code-of-ethics.pdf

TMZ. (2020). Charles Barkley blasts PG13 for bubble depression – stop complaining! *TMZ.* https://www.tmz.com/2020/08/26/paul-george-opens-up-about-anxiety-depression-in-nba-bubble-after-slump/

Wong, A. (2020). Maintaining mental health a daily challenge for those inside the NBA bubble. *Yahoo Sports.* https://www.yahoo.com/now/maintaining-mental-health-a-daily-challenge-for-those-inside-the-nba-bubble-163615581.html

Youngmisuk, O. (2020). Clippers' Paul George says he dealt with anxiety, depression inside NBA bubble. *ESPN*. https://www.espn.com/nba/story/_/id/29743235/clippers-paul-george-says-dealt-anxiety-depression-bubble

Notes on Authors

Andrew C. Billings is the Ronald Reagan Chair of Broadcasting and Executive Director of the Alabama Program in Sports Communication in the Department of Journalism & Creative Media at the University of Alabama. He is the author of many journal articles and book projects. Recent works include *Mascot Nation: The Controversy over Native American Representations in Sports* (with Jason Edward Black, University of Illinois Press, 2018), *Media and the Coming Out of Gay Male Athletes in American Team Sports* (with Leigh Moscowitz, Peter Lang, 2018), and *The Rise and Fall of Mass Communication* (with William Benoit, Peter Lang, 2020). His work has been cited over 8,000 times and he has been interviewed by media outlets over 600 times, including ESPN's *Outside the Lines* and *The New York Times*.

Scott Parrott is an Associate Professor in the Department of Journalism & Creative Media at the University of Alabama. He researches media and mental health. He co-edited the book *Media Stereotypes: From Ageism to Xenophobia* (with Andrew C. Billings, Peter Lang, 2020). He also wrote the book *Media & Mental Health: Using Mass Media to Reduce the Stigma of Mental Illness*, scheduled for release by Peter Lang in 2023.

Index

A

ADHD, Phelps diagnosis of, 13
advocacy: of Biles, 54–56; for BLM, 38; of Gold, 138; of Love, 31–32; narrative dimension of, 14–15; of Phelps, 12–15, 96–98; public, 12–14
Affordable Care Act, 15
Ai, Muhammad, 47
Akers, Michelle, 47
anxiety, 3–4; Myall on, 114–115; social anxiety disorder, 25; social media and, 27
Arizona Cardinals, 121
Armour, Nancy, 54
Associated Press, 15
Associated Press Storybook, 188
Athletic (magazine), 20
Atkinson, M., 6
Atlanta Falcons, 83
Atlanta Hawks, 23–24

Atlanta Olympic Summer Games, 150
audience, disclosure considerations and, 185–186
Auerbach, Nicole, 20
Australian Open, 41
authenticity, Gold on, 134–135

B

Babbit, Luke, 23
Babych, Dave, 163
Back on the Record with Bob Costas (television), 62
Ball State University, 140, 146
Barkley, Charles, 7, 180, 181
Barty, Ashleigh, 57
basketball: Love on, as escape, 28–29; Moses on, 144, 146–147. *see also specific topics*
Bayless, Skip, 184

Beard, Amanda, 66; celebrity of, 154; Crouse and, 151–152; on cutting, 151; early career of, 150–151; on media, 151, 154–155; memoir of, 153–155; on mental health, 156–158; *New York Times* article of, 151–153; on pressure, 154–155; public image of, 150; public mental health disclosure of, 151–153; on social media, 156–157; on swimming, 149–150

Beatles, the, 110–111

Beijing Summer Games, 2008, 152, 153, 174

Belcher, Jovan, 67

Bell, Raja, 180

Bieber, Justin, 54

Biles, Simone, 8, 39, 41, 71–72, 96–97, 107, 185; advocacy of, 54–56; Brennan on, 74–75; career arc of, 47–48; Costas on, 74; greatest gymnast status of, 47; media narratives on, 48–50, 52–53; on mental health, 48, 54–56; Moses on, 145; Myall on, 111–113; Osaka, N., compared with, 42–43; patriotism of, 55–56; Phelps and, 19–21; support for, 53–54; on Tokyo Summer Games, 18–21, 30, 48–50, 65

Billings, A. C., 14

blackface, 43

Black Lives Matter, 37; Osaka, N., advocacy for, 38

Bledsoe, Drew, 25

Blindsided (podcast), 159–160; athletes featured on, 161; Hirsch on, 166

Blitzer, Wolf, 51

blues, post-Olympic, 28, 174

body image, Gold on, 130–131

Bostick, Brandon, 181, 185; on COVID-19, 121–124; on job security, 118, 120–121; on media response, 118–119, 123–124; on mental health, 124–126; on NFC Championship, 125–126; on relearning, 120–121; on retirement, 121; on social media, 123–124; on therapy, 121–122

Boston Celtics, 3

Boudia, David, 94

boundary setting, on social media, 168

Bowman, Bob, 90–91

Boys and Girls Clubs of America, 18–19

brain trauma, depression and, 67

Brennan, Christine, 8, 49, 56, 129; on Biles, 74–75; on Gold, 68–69, 129–130; on journalism, 75; on Olympic fandom, 174; on Phelps, 69

broadcasting, as disclosure strategy, 182

Brown, Blaise Ray, 153

Brown, Doone Isla, 153

bubble, COVID-19, 85, 179

Buffalo Sabres, 166–167

Burnett, Morgan, 117

Business Insider, 56

C

Campus MindWorks, 179; on support methods, 187

Carayol, Tumaini, 43

care deserts, 15

Carr, Chris, 141, 144

Catlin, Kelly, 71

celebrity status: of Beard, 154; of Olympians, 97; of Osaka, N., 37; of Phelps, 97

Child Mind Institute, 13

Chiles, Jordan, 52

Cincinnati Inquirer, 41

Cincinnati Reds, 175
Cleveland Cavaliers, 4, 23, 26, 28, 31, 185
Cobb, Randall, 117–118
Code of Ethics, SPJ, 188
cognitive therapy, 109–110
Coles, Laveranues, 71
Columbus Crew, 141
communication, in mental health, 157
community: mental health and involvement of, 81–83; Phelps on, 17–18; Uhlaender, K., on, 177–178
contact, for stigma reduction, 184
Costas, Bob, 8, 61, 62, 63; on Biles, 74; on media narratives, 75–77; on mental health, 64–65, 67; on Phelps, 11–12
Couric, Katie, 154
COVID-19, 15, 18, 32, 51, 83; Bostick on, 121–124; bubble, 85; media narratives during, 71–75; NBA during, 85; Phelps on, 98–99, 180; Rawlins on, 87
Crouse, Karen, 8, 62; Beard and, 151–152; on demystification, 63; Gold and, 131–132; on media narratives, 71; on mental health challenges, 63–64, 66; on Phelps, 69–70
cutting, Beard on, 151

D

Dallas Mavericks, 25
"Dark, dark, dark, dark..." (Hirsch), 161, 165
dark places, 179–180
Dauster, Rob, 140; Moses and, 141–142
Davies, Charlie, 101
Davis, Viola, 44
Deggans, Eric, 44

depression, 3–4, 28–29, 32; brain trauma and, 67; Gold on, 137–138; MDD, 102; Moses on, 140; Myall on, 101–102, 109–110; of Olympians, 174; Osaka, N., on, 40; Phelps on, 93
DeRozan, DeMar, 5, 26–28, 31, 42, 71, 80–81; Love and, 32
Detroit, Gold in, 131–132
Detroit Lions, 125
disclosure, mental health, 3; audience considerations, 185–186; of Beard, 151–153; broadcasting, 182; empowerment from, 181; family considerations, 186–187; indiscriminate, 182; journalist-related considerations, 187–188; message considerations, 183–185; of Myall, 102–103; national, 104–105; personal consideration about, 182–183; of Phelps, 89; pros and cons of, 180–181; selective, 182; stigma and, 181; strategies for, 182
Duregger, G., 55

E

eating disorders, 131
education: mental health, 168; for stigma reduction, 183–184
emotions, Phelps on, 98–99
empathy, 184
empowerment, from disclosure, 181
Entman, R., 104
ESPN, 9; on mental illness, 87; Rawlins on, 86–87
"Everyone is Going Through Something" (Love), 27
exemplification theory, 119
expertise theory, Myall and, 110–111

F

family considerations, 186–187
Favre, Brett, 3
Felix, Allyson, 76
FIBT World Championships, 175
Fiji, 177
Finn, C., 19
Flair, Ric, 30
Floyd, George, trauma from death of, 87
framing theory, 104
French Open, 42
Frost, Robert, 173

G

games, defining, 2
Gates, Kevin, 26–27
Gauff, Coco, 43–44
GB Snowsports, 103, 111, 114, 115
gender stereotypes, Osaka, N., facing, 43
George, Paul, 185–187; on mental health, 179–180
Gibson, K., 6–7
Gitlin, T., 104
Gladwell, Malcolm, 110
Gleeson, S., 55
Global Athlete, 173
Goffman, E., 104
GofFundMe, 173
Gold, Gracie, 16; advocacy of, 138; on authenticity, 134–135; on blame, 135–136; on body types, 130–131; Brennan on, 68–69, 129–130; Crouse and, 131–132; on depression, 137–138; in Detroit, 131–132; on honesty, 132–133; on mental health, 130–132; multi-dimensionality of, 134–135; on shame, 132–133; on success and wellness, 137–138; on suicide, 133; on *Weight of Gold*, 136–137
Golden Child myth, 90, 91
Gorczynski, P., 6–7
Grand Slam, 35–36, 38
Graves, W., 54
Green Bay Packers, 3, 117, 119, 121, 141
Gregory, Sean, 8, 30, 48, 62, 71; on media narratives, 75–76; on mental health, 64; on Twitter, 76
Greinke, Zack, 3, 25
Guardian, The (newspaper), 104–105
Gunter, Kensa, 83, 87; on mental health, 84

H

Haiti, Osaka, N., on, 42
Hamm, Mia, 47
Handler, Chelsea, 54
Hanson, Tommy, 5
Harding, Tonya, 129
Harry (Prince), 42, 57, 95
Haskell, James, on mental health, 106
Hawley, N., 1
Here to Help Foundation, 183, 184; goals of, 187
Hill, Jamele, 53
Hirsch, Corey, 79; on *Blindsided*, 166; interviews with, 168; Love and, 160; on masculinity, 167–168; on mental illness, 80; on OCD, 161–163; OCD diagnosis, 164; in *Players' Tribune*, 166–168; on shame, 162–163, 168; on social media, 168; on stigma surrounding conversation about suicide and medication, 167; on Watson, 160–161
Hoch, Scott, 1–2
Holcomb, Steven, 175; death of, 171–172

Hollywood, Zach, 139, 146
honesty, Gold on, 132–133
Hoosiers (film), 1
Horford, Al, 3
Houston Rockets, 25
Hurst, Hayden, 83

I

Indiana Fever, 141
Indiana Pacers, 141
Indianapolis Colts, 9, 79; Kicking the Stigma initiative, 81–83, 183
Indianapolis Star (newspaper), 140; Moses on, 143
Indiana University, 81
indiscriminate disclosure, 182
Instagram, 8, 40, 72
International Olympic Committee (IOC), 16; Phelps on, 20
In the Water They Can't See You Cry (Beard), 151
introversion, Osaka, N., on, 40–41
IOC. *see* International Olympic Committee
Isray, Jim, 82

J

Jackson, Kalen, 82
James, LeBron, 26, 30, 47
Japan, 42–43
Jewett, R., 6
job security, Bostick on, 118, 120–121
Jones, A. M., 185
Jones, James, 125
Jones, Lolo, 16, 94
Jordan, Michael, 47
journaling, 175

journalism: Brennan on, 75; disclosure considerations and, 187–188; social media and, 53

K

Kansas City Chiefs, 67
Kansas City Royals, 3, 141
Kelly, Megyn, 43
Kerrigan, Nancy, 129
Kevin Love Fund, 31–32, 186
Kicking the Stigma initiative, 81–83, 173
Kilgallen, Michaela, 43
Kimes, Mina, 184
Kirk, Charlie, 52
Kitson, Robert, 104

L

Larson, C. H., 6
Las Vegas Raiders, 83
Lauer, Matt, Phelps interview by, 92
Layden, Tim, 12; Phelps and, 89
leadership, 184
Le Clos, Chad, 90
Lee, Sunisa, 57
Leeds Academy, 101
Lehner, Robin, 166–167
Leonard, Darius, 82–83
Leonhardt, D., 13–14
Lin, Jeremy, 30
Linden, Trevor, 163–164
Lindstrom, S., 51
London-Daily Mail (newspaper), 94–95
Los Angeles Clippers, 179
Los Angeles Rams, 81
Love, Kevin, 21, 42, 49, 57, 71, 80–81, 188; advocacy work of, 31–32; on basketball as escape, 28–29;

202 | Index

DeRozan and, 32; on happiness, 44; Hirsch and, 160; non-profits of, 186; panic attacks of, 4, 8, 23–26; on social media, 27; support for, 30–31; Wade and, 30–31

Lue, Tyronn, 24, 31, 79

M

major depression disorder (MDD), 102
Mamanuca Islands, 177
Manning, Peyton, 82, 183
Markle, Meghan, 42, 57, 95
Marshall, Brandon, 25–26
masculinity: Hirsch on, 167–168; mental health and, 106–107
mass media. *see* media
McCarthy, Mike, 118
McDonald, C., 55
McEnroe, John, 66
McIntosh, Diane, 159, 165
MDD. *see* major depression disorder
media: Beard on, 151, 154–155; Bostick on response of, 118–119, 123–124; Costas on narratives in, 75–77; COVID-19 and narratives in, 71–75; Crouse on narratives in, 71; current narratives in, 75–77; Gregory on narratives in, 75–76; language on suicide, 87; mental health narratives, 86–88; mental illness and, 6–7, 121–122; Myall on local, 103–104; Myall on narratives in, 112–115; narratives on Biles, 48–50; Osaka, N., and, 38, 41; Phelps on, 94–96; post-Phelps era in, 69–71; pre-Phelps landscape in, 65–69; value of, 56–57. *see also* social media
Medicaid, 15

mental health: Beard on, 156–158; Beard public disclosure of, 151–153; Biles on, 48, 54–56; Bostick on, 124–126; communication in, 157; community involvement with, 81–83; Costas on, 64–65, 67; Crouse on challenges of, 63–64, 66; education, 168; George on, 179–180; Gold on, 130–132; Gregory on, 64; Gunter on, 84; Haskell on, 106; masculinity and, 106–107; media narratives on, 86–88; Moses on, 144–146; Myall disclosure of, 102–103; Myall on, 108–109; NBA resources for, 80–81, 83–84; Phelps as advocate for, 96–98; Phelps on disclosure of, 89; physical health and, 61–62; proactive approaches to, 83–86; of professional athletes, 2, 107; sociology of, 5–7; stereotypes surrounding, 121–122; stigma of disclosure of, 181; timelines for prognosis of, 50–52; in United States, 15–18
Mental Health Awareness Month, 87
Mental Health Month, 93
mental illness: disclosure of, 3; ESPN on, 87; Hirsch on, 80; media and, 6–7, 121–122; Osaka, N., on, 39–40; prevalence of, 2; resources, 189; stigma of, 25, 80; treatment for, 3
Michael Phelps Foundation, 12, 15, 186, 189; goals of, 97–98
Microsoft, 98
Miller, Bode, 16, 94
Miller, Lauryn, 32
Mind Health initiative, 80–81, 83, 86
Minnesota Timberwolves, 28
Minnesota Vikings, 121
MIT Sloan Sports Analytics Conference, 83

moments, capturing, delicacy of, 62–65
Montana, Joe, 1–2
Morgan, Piers, 52
Moses, Trey, 139; on basketball, 144, 146–147; on Biles, 145; Dauster and, 141–142; on depression, 140; on *Indianapolis Star*, 143; on mental health, 144–146; on NCAA Inspiration Award, 146–147; on self-awareness and self-monitoring, 140–141; on social media, 143–146; on storytelling, 141–144; on therapy, 141–142, 144
Myall, Kearnan: on anxiety, 114–115; on Biles and Osaka, N., 111–113; on control, 115; on depression, 101–102, 109–110; on diagnosis, 109–110; expertise theory and, 110–111; on local media, 103–104; on media narratives, 112–115; on mental health, 108–109; mental health disclosure of, 102–103; national disclosure of, 104–105; at Oxford University, 111; retirement of, 102; on social media, 106; on stress, 107; on suicide, 115; on team dynamics, 107–109; on therapy, 109–110; on time off, 112

N

NAMI. *see* National Alliance on Mental Illness
Naomi Osaka (documentary), 38, 44
Nash, Steve, 66
Nassar, Larry, 52
National Alliance on Mental Illness (NAMI), 183, 189; goals of, 187
National Basketball Association (NBA), 8–9, 27, 80, 176; during COVID-19, 85; mental health resources of, 80–81, 83–84
National Collegiate Athletic Association (NCAA), Moses receiving Inspiration Award, 146–147
National Hockey League (NHL), 80, 161
National Institute of Mental Health, 189
National Suicide Prevention Lifeline, 189
Navratilova, Martina, 44
NBA. *see* National Basketball Association
NCAA. *see* National Collegiate Athletic Association
Neethling, Ryk, 152–153
Nelson, Jordy, 118
New Jersey Devils, 163
New York Rangers, 161
New York Times (newspaper), 63; Beard article in, 151–153
NFC Championship, 117–119; Bostick on, 125–126
NHL. *see* National Hockey League
non-profits, 186

O

Obama, Michele, 54
obsessive compulsive disorder (OCD), 159; Hirsch diagnosis with, 164; Hirsch on, 161–163; suicide and, 164–165
Ohno, Apolo, 16
Olympedia, 172
Olympians, Phelps on struggles of, 94
Orris, Andrea, 52
Osaka, Mari, 38
Osaka, Naomi, 4–5, 8, 21, 57, 61, 71, 72–73; Biles compared with, 42–43; Black Lives Matter advocacy of, 38; celebrity of, 37; on depression, 40; gender stereotypes faced by, 43; on

Haiti, 42; on introversion, 40–41; media and, 38, 41; on mental illness, 39–40; Myall on, 111–113; Phelps on, 97; on press conferences, 35–36, 38–42; public response to, 42–44; sponsorship deals of, 36; support for, 43–44

Outliers (Gladwell), 110

Oxford University, 111

P

Paley, Rebecca, 151
pandemic. *see* COVID-19
panic attacks, of Love, 4, 8, 23–26
parasocial relationships, 29
Park, A., 48
Parrott, M. S., 29, 121–122
Patrick, Dan, 126
patriotism, of Biles, 55–56
Peppers, Julius, 117
personal considerations, disclosure, 182–183
Phelps, Michael, 7, 42, 53, 57, 75, 79; ADHD diagnosis of, 13; Biles and, 19–21; Brennan on, 69; celebrity of, 97; on community, 17–18; Costas on, 11–12; on COVID-19, 98–99, 180; Crouse on, 69–70; on depression, 93; dominance of, 11–12; drunk driving arrests of, 12; DUI arrests, 90, 92; on emotions, 98–99; on empowerment, 16–17; events leading to revelation of, 90–91; as father, 98; interviews with, 93–94; on IOC, 20; Lauer interviewing, 92; Layden and, 89; on media, 94–96; media landscape following, 69–71; media landscape prior to, 65–69; as mental health advocate, 12–15, 96–98; on mental health disclosure, 89; narrative dimension of advocacy of, 14–15; non-profits of, 186; on Olympian struggles, 94; on Osaka, N., 97; public advocacy, 12–14; public embrace of, 92–94; public image of, 44, 188; on red flag events, 18; in rehabilitation, 90–91; rumors about, 94–95; on shame, 91; on social media, 94–95; sponsorships of, 97; in *Sports Illustrated*, 89–90, 92; on suicide, 14–15, 90; on swimming as calming mechanism, 18; TalkSpace partnership with, 93; temporary retirement of, 12; at Tokyo Summer Games, 18–21; on Twitter, 92; on vulnerability, 17; on YouTube, 93

physical health, mental health and, 61–62

physical injuries, team dynamics and, 108

Pink, 44

Players' Tribune, The, 4, 27, 31, 32, 61; Hirsch in, 166–168

post-Olympic blues, 28, 174

post-traumatic stress disorder (PTSD), 171

Powell, Ashley, 79, 81

Prescott, Dak, 184

press conferences, Osaka, N., on, 35–36, 38–42

professional athletes, mental health of, 2, 107

Pro Football Reference, 117

PTSD. *see* post-traumatic stress disorder

Q

question phrasing, 187

R

Radcliffe, J. R., 117
Rawlins, Melissa: on COVID-19, 87; on ESPN, 86–87
red flag events, Phelps on, 18
rehabilitation, 70; Phelps in, 90–91
relapses, 181
resources, mental illness, 189
retirement: Bostick on, 121; of Myall, 102
Richards, DiDi, 25–26
Rihanna, 136
Ringer NBA Show, 180
Rio Olympics, 89, 96
"Road Not Taken, The" (Frost), 173
Robach, A., 52
Rodgers, Aaron, 118
Roland-Garros, 4–5, 35–36
role models, 181
Rothschild, N., 57
Rousey, Ronda, 5
Rugby Players Association, 105

S

SAMHSA. *see* Substance Abuse and Mental Health Services Administration
San Diego Padres, 3
schizophrenia, 188
Schmich, Mary, 139
Scutti, S., 14
Seau, Junior, 5
selective disclosure, 182
self-awareness, Moses on, 140–141
self-monitoring, Moses on, 140–141
self-stigma, 181
shame: Gold on, 132–133; help and, 51; Hirsch on, 162–163, 168; Phelps on, 91
Show, Eric, 5
Silver, Adam, 83
Siniakova, Katerina, 35–36
Sitton, Josh, 118, 119
skeleton, Uhlaender, K., on, 171–172
Smith, Kellie, 47
Sochi Winter Olympics, 129, 176
social anxiety disorder, 25
social avoidance, 182
social learning theory, 93
social media, 30; anxiety and, 27; Beard on, 156–157; Bostick on, 123–124; boundary setting on, 168; Hirsch on, 168; journalism and, 53; Love on, 27; Moses on, 143–146; Myall on, 106; Phelps on, 94–95
sociology, of mental health, 5–7
Souter, G., 6
Speak Up for Kids campaign, 13–14
SPJ Code of Ethics, 188
Sports Illustrated (magazine), 43; Phelps in, 89–90, 92
sports psychology, 110
Stanley Cup, 162
stereotypes: of elite athletes, 99; about mental health, 121–122
stigma: contact for reduction of, 184; education for reduction of, 183–184; Hirsch on, 167; mental health disclosure and, 181; of mental illness, 25, 80; protest as management strategy, 184; self-stigma, 181
storytelling, Moses on, 141–144
Strug, Kerri, 56
Substance Abuse and Mental Health Services Administration (SAMHSA), 189

suicide: Gold on, 133; Hirsch on stigma surrounding conversation about, 167; media language on, 87; Myall on, 115; OCD and, 164–165; Phelps on, 14–15, 90
Summer Hard Court Swing, 41
support methods, 187
Survivor (television), 174, 177
swimming: Beard on, 149–150; Phelps on, as calming mechanism, 18
Sydney Olympics, 2000, 150–151, 152–153

T

TalkSpace, 14–51; Phelps partnership with, 93
Taplin, Jonathan, 113
team dynamics: Myall on, 107–109; physical injuries and, 108
Teen Vogue, 40
therapy, 108; Bostick on, 121–122; cognitive, 109; Moses on, 141–142, 144; Myall on, 109–110
This is Depression (McIntosh), 159
Thompson, K., 48
time off, Myall on, 112
Tirico, Mike, 20, 97
Tokyo Summer Games, 76, 97, 176; Biles on, 18–21, 30, 48–50, 65; Phelps at, 18–21
Toronto Raptors, 26–27
Townsend, Taylor, 160
trauma: Floyd death and, 87; Uhlaender, K., on, 171. *see also* post-traumatic stress disorder
tribes, Uhlaender on, 177–178
Trumpism, 72
twisties, 8, 19, 48, 51

Twitter, 53, 123–124, 143–144; Gregory on, 76; Phelps on, 92

U

Uhlaender, Katie, 79, 94, 185, 188; as camera assistant, 174, 177; on community, 177–178; concussion of, 175–176; on Frost, 173; on journaling, 175; on mental health, 173–175; on PTSD, 171; relationship with father, 175; on *Survivor*, 174, 177; on trauma, 171; on tribes, 177–178; U.S. Olympic Committee and, 172–173, 176; on *Weight of Gold*, 176–177
Uhlaender, Ted, 175
United States, mental health in, 15–18
University of Michigan, 187
University of Southern California, Annenberg Innovation Lab, 113
USA Gymnastics, 19
US Olympic and Paralympic Committee, 176
U.S. Olympic Committee, 79, 97; Uhlaender, K., and, 172–173, 176
Us Weekly, 63
U.S. World Skeleton Team, 173

V

Vaislyev, Andrei, 163
Valieva, Kamila, 129
Vancouver Canucks, 159, 162–163, 165
Vancouver Olympics 2010, 175
Vieira de Silva, Marta, 47
vulnerability, Phelps on, 17

W

Wade, Dwyane, 23; Love and, 30–31
Waller, Daren, 83
Wambach, Abby, 47
Warner, Kurt, 160
Wasps RFC, 101, 102, 103
Watson, Bubba, Hirsch on, 160–161
Weight of Gold, The (documentary), 16, 94, 96–97; Gold on, 136–137; Uhlaender, K., on, 176–177
wellness, Gold on, 137–138
White, Royce, 25, 31, 80
White, Shaun, 94
Whitlock, Jason, 67
WHO. *see* World Health Organization
Wilder, Charlotte, 29
Williams, Serena, 5
Wilson, Russell, 117
Winfrey, Oprah, 154
Wood, R., 118
Woods, Tiger, 68
World Championship Trials, 91–92
World Health Organization (WHO), 87

Y

Young, Cy, 4–5
YouTube, 27–28; Phelps on, 93

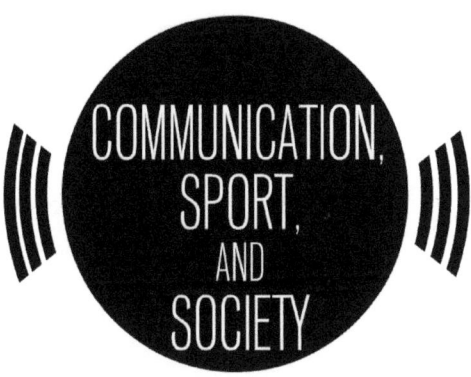

Lawrence A. Wenner, Andrew C. Billings, and Marie C. Hardin
General Editors

Books in the Communication, Sport, and Society series explore evolving themes and emerging issues in the study of communication, media, and sport, broadly defined. The series provides a venue for key concepts and theories across communication and media studies to be explored in relation to sport. The series features works building on burgeoning media studies engagement with sport, as well as works focusing on interpersonal, group, organizational, rhetorical, and other dynamics in the communication of sport. The series welcomes diverse theoretical standpoints and methodological tactics seen across the social sciences and humanities. While some works may examine the dynamics of institutions and producers, representations and content, reception and fandom, or entertain questions such as those about identities and/or commodification in the contexts of mediated sport, works that consider how communication about sport functions in diverse rhetorical and interpersonal settings, how groups, families, and teams use, adapt, and are affected by the communication of sport, and how the style, nature, and power relations in communication are wielded in sport and media organizations are particularly encouraged. Works examining the communication of sport in international and/or comparative contexts or new, digital, and/or social forms of sport communication are also welcome.

For additional information about this series or for the submission of manuscripts, please contact the series editors:

Lawrence A. Wenner | Andrew C. Billings | Marie C. Hardin
lwenner@lmu.edu | acbillings@ua.edu | mch208@psu.edu

To order other books in this series, please contact our Customer Service Department:
peterlang@presswarehouse.com (within the U.S.)
orders@peterlang.com (outside the U.S.)

Or browse online by series:
www.peterlang.com

www.ingramcontent.com/pod-product-compliance
Ingram Content Group UK Ltd.
Pitfield, Milton Keynes, MK11 3LW, UK
UKHW021327180426
11947UKWH00017B/1480